T0355535

# Ethnic Conflict and Protest in Tibet and Xinjiang

Studies of the Weatherhead East Asian Institute, Columbia University

**Studies of the Weatherhead East Asian Institute,
Columbia University**

The Studies of the Weatherhead East Asian Institute of Columbia University were inaugurated in 1962 to bring to a wider public the results of significant new research on modern and contemporary East Asia.

For a list of titles in this series, see page 269

# Ethnic Conflict and Protest in Tibet and Xinjiang

## Unrest in China's West

EDITED BY BEN HILLMAN
AND GRAY TUTTLE

Columbia University Press
New York

Columbia University Press
*Publishers Since 1893*
New York   Chichester, West Sussex
cup.columbia.edu

Library of Congress Cataloging-in-Publication Data

Names: Hillman, Ben. | Tuttle, Gray.
Title: Ethnic conflict and protest in Tibet and Xinjiang : unrest in China's
   west / edited by Ben Hillman and Gray Tuttle.
Description: New York : Columbia University Press, 2016. | Includes
   bibliographical references and index.
Identifiers: LCCN 2015024326 | ISBN 9780231169981 (cloth) |
   ISBN 9780231169998 (pbk.) | ISBN 9780231540445 (ebook)
Subjects: LCSH: Tibet Autonomous Region (China)—Ethnic relations.
   | Xinjiang Uygur Zizhiqu (China)—Ethnic relations. | Ethnic
   conflict—China—Tibet Autonomous Region. | Ethnic conflict—
   China—Xinjiang Uygur Zizhiqu. | Borderlands—China. | China—Ethnic
   relations. | Ethnic conflict—China.
Classification: LCC DS786 .E735 2016 | DDC 305.800951/5—dc23
LC record available at http://lccn.loc.gov/2015024326

COVER DESIGN: Jordan Wannemacher
COVER IMAGE: ©PETER PARKS/AFP/Getty Images

# Contents

# Ethnic Conflict and Protest in Tibet and Xinjiang

**MAP 1.** Sites of unrest in Tibetan areas since 2008. Australian National University, College of Asia and the Pacific, CartoGIS.

# Introduction

## Understanding the Current Wave of Conflict and Protest in Tibet and Xinjiang

Ben Hillman

n the spring of 2008 the Tibet Plateau erupted in protest. On March 10 a group of monks demonstrated for the release of fellow clergy who had been detained by police since the previous year.[1] When police dispersed the monks, lay Tibetans gathered in support. Over the next few days street protests erupted across Lhasa. Thousands of monks, nuns, and ordinary Tibetans railed against Chinese policies. Some decried Chinese rule and called for independence. By March 14 the protests had turned into riots. Rioters attacked police stations, vehicles, and government offices. Some rioters attacked Han and Muslim Chinese persons and property, leading to the deaths of eighteen civilians and the destruction of hundreds of small businesses. Parts of Lhasa became like a war zone as the People's Armed Police responded with tear gas and gunfire. The protests spread to ethnic Tibetan areas in Qinghai, Gansu, and Sichuan provinces (map 1). An estimated two hundred Tibetans died, and two thousand or more were arrested in more than one hundred "mass incidents" (*qunti shijian*) across the region in what quickly became the most widespread unrest in Tibet since the founding of the People's Republic of China (PRC) (Barnett 2009).[2]

As unrest spread across the Tibet Plateau, trouble was also brewing in neighboring Xinjiang Uyghur Autonomous Region (Xinjiang, see map 2). On March 7, just three days before protests erupted in Lhasa, Chinese

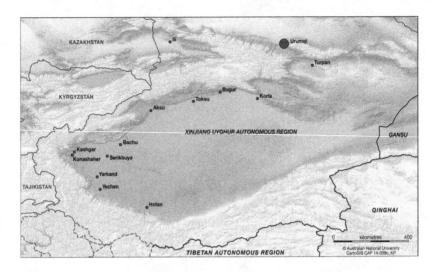

**MAP 2.** Sites of unrest in Xinjiang Uyghur Autonomous Region since 2008. Australian National University, College of Asia and the Pacific, CartoGIS.

authorities announced they had thwarted an attempted suicide bombing aboard a China Southern Airlines flight from Urumqi to Beijing. According to official media, a Uyghur woman was apprehended while attempting to ignite gasoline that she had smuggled aboard inside soft-drink cans. A few months later two Uyghur men launched coordinated attacks against local police in the predominantly Uyghur city of Kashgar. One of the assailants drove a truck into a group of seventy jogging policemen before attacking them with homemade explosives and a machete. Sixteen police officers died in the attack. At the same time, the other man attacked a nearby police station with homemade explosives.[3] A wave of popular unrest unfolded in the following months. In the summer of 2009 as many as one thousand Uyghurs took part in demonstrations in Urumqi. Demonstrators demanded a full investigation into the deaths of two Uyghurs at a factory in Shaoguan, Guangzhou. Over the following two days the protests escalated into riots that paralyzed the city. Dozens of vehicles and buildings were destroyed. In scenes reminiscent of Lhasa the previous spring, rioters attacked police and government property, as well as Han Chinese citizens and their property. Groups of Han Chinese vigilantes responded with force, attacking both Uyghur citizens and police. According to the Chinese government, 197 people died in the violence, and 1,721 people were injured.[4]

Since 2008 unrest has continued to flare throughout the region. The discontent has been characterized by "ethnic protest" (i.e., protests against the state and its policies), as well as by "ethnic conflict" (i.e., intercommunal ethnic violence).[5] In Tibetan areas there have been frequent clashes between Tibetan citizens and the police, leading to injuries, deaths, and multiple arrests. Ethnic protest is also taking new forms. Since 2009, and with increasing frequency since 2011, self-immolation has emerged in Tibetan areas as a new and extreme form of ethnic protest. At the time this book went to press (November 2015), 140 Tibetans had set themselves on fire in protest against Chinese government policies or Communist Party rule.[6] Elements within the Uyghur community have adopted increasingly violent forms of protest in recent years. Since 2008 in Xinjiang attacks against Chinese government targets, as well as against Chinese citizens, have increased.[7] More recently there have been attacks against Chinese citizens in other parts of the country. In October 2013 a sport utility vehicle ploughed into pedestrians before catching on fire near Beijing's Tiananmen Square, killing two tourists and injuring forty other people. The driver of the vehicle and his two passengers, all reportedly from Xinjiang, died in the incident.[8] In February 2014 eight people stormed the Kunming Railway Station, indiscriminately attacking people with knives and machetes, killing twenty-nine people and injuring 143 others. Police were quick to identify the assailants as Uyghur separatists. Media reported that police had found a hand-painted East Turkestan flag at the scene of the crime (Xinhua 2014a). A number of Chinese commentators described the event as "China's 9/11." In July 2014 Chinese state media reported that dozens were killed in an attack on a local police station in Shache County.[9] In September 2014 Chinese state media reported that forty suspected assailants were either killed by blasts or shot by police during a series of explosions in Xinjiang's Luntai County (AP 2014). And on June 23, 2015, as many as twenty-eight people were killed in an attack on a police checkpoint in Kashgar (RFA 2015).

The Chinese government blames all of the unrest and violence in Tibet and Xinjiang on separatists determined to weaken and split China by fomenting instability. In the case of Xinjiang, authorities blame attacks on separatists linked with the East Turkestan Islamic Movement (ETIM) and other hostile groups such as the World Uyghur Congress led by Rebiya Kadeer, a prominent Uyghur activist living in exile in the United States. China's leaders pointedly blamed Kadeer and her group for orchestrating the Urumqi riots of 2009.[10] In the case of Tibet, China's leaders blame the "Dalai clique" (a derogatory term for the Tibetan government-in-exile) and "hostile forces" (read Western supporters) for orchestrating and co-ordinating protests that spread across the Tibet plateau in the spring of 2008. Speaking at a televised press conference in the aftermath of the 2008 riots, China's then premier Wen Jiabao declared the existence of "ample facts and plenty of evidence proving that the incident was organized, pre-meditated, masterminded and incited by the Dalai clique" (Xinhua 2008). China's leaders have also accused the "Dalai clique" of promoting self-immolations for "political gain."[11]

Exile groups counter that the unrest is not the work of separatists but a reaction to marginalization and that Tibetan and Uyghur frustrations have reached a boiling point (ICT 2008). Exile groups and disaffected members of the wider ethnic communities charge that Tibetans and Uyghurs are being marginalized culturally and economically in their homelands and that their rights are being systematically violated. According to this view, ethnic unrest is triggered by a deterioration in "ethnic security"— people's perceptions of their ability to preserve, express, and develop their ethnic distinctiveness in everyday economic, social, and cultural practices (Wolff 2006; Horowitz 2000). An exile Uyghur group report accuses the Chinese government of wholesale demolition of Uyghur communities in the name of development.[12] Some have gone even further, accusing the Chinese government of "cultural genocide"[13] and claiming that radical Islam has emerged as a symbol of resistance following the failure of Uyghur nationalism. The Chinese government vehemently denies such accusations, claiming that state policies protect and promote ethnic traditions. China's leaders also routinely point out that Tibetans and Uyghurs have greatly benefited from Chinese Communist Party (CCP) policies, including preferential access to education, employment and welfare, and representation in regional government. According to the official line, any and all political unrest would be resolved if not for the actions of violent separatists bent on destroying China with the help of their foreign allies.

While acknowledging the desire for independence among some sections of the Uyghur and Tibetan communities, international analysts disagree with the proposition that recent unrest in Tibet and Xinjiang can be attributed to the machinations of separatists. International analysts generally agree that the unrest has been fueled by widespread grievances against state policies in these regions. However, there are important differences in how these analysts understand the primary sources of Tibetan and Uyghur discontent. One group emphasizes social and economic factors as the key to understanding the regional unrest of recent years.[14] Although China's western provinces have experienced more than a decade of double-digit economic growth, scholars point out that growth in Tibet and Xinjiang has been uneven, noninclusive, and destabilizing. Rapid growth based on mega infrastructure projects has attracted unprecedented numbers of migrants to the region. Because economic migrants generally have superior skills and training, they are able to out-compete the local population for jobs. Nearly all taxi drivers in Lhasa, for example, are non-Tibetan, as are the owners of most small businesses in the city. Similar trends can be observed in Xinjiang. As Tyler Harlan notes in his chapter in this volume, Uyghur entrepreneurs are absent in many industries because they are unable to compete with Han Chinese entrepreneurs who have superior access to local state networks and capital. Indeed, some argue that inequality and economic marginalization are the roots of the recent wave of unrest. Tellingly, more than one thousand Han and Hui Chinese-owned small businesses in Lhasa were reportedly destroyed in the March 2008 riots. In the Urumqi riots of summer 2009 Han Chinese-owned businesses were similarly attacked and destroyed.

Another group of scholars emphasizes cultural and religious factors in their analyses of the causes of the recent wave of ethnic unrest. They argue that government policies in the region have become increasingly intolerant of cultural and religious difference, stoking deep fears among Uyghurs and Tibetans about the survival of their ethnic and cultural distinctiveness (Barnett 2009). In Tibetan areas scholars point to increasing restrictions on monastic life, including the continued use of "patriotic education" for monks and nuns, as well as limits on the number of monks a monastery can recruit. There are also travel restrictions in place to certain monasteries, blocking access to nonlocal visitors. Scholars have also pointed to suicide notes left by several self-immolators as evidence that fears of cultural survival are fueling such desperate acts. In the case of Xinjiang, scholars have similarly observed heavy state intervention in religious life, including periodic restriction of access to mosques and banning of religious gatherings. Some argue that heavy-handed restrictions on Islamic practices have radicalized many Uyghurs (Hao and Liu 2012; Shan and Chen 2009).

Because of censorship Chinese scholarship is largely silent on the question of Tibetan and Uyghur grievances. By blaming unrest on separatists and other hostile forces, and by treating most forms of protest, including self-immolation, as criminal acts, the official discourse makes it politically difficult, if not impossible, for Chinese scholars to investigate the unrest from the perspective of Tibetan and Uyghur grievance. Chinese researchers who have attempted to do so have been censored, sacked, and in some cases, imprisoned.[15] In other cases research centers have been closed and funding stopped.[16] Because of the political difficulties faced by Chinese scholars, nuanced analysis of the unrest has been left to the international scholarly community.[17]

International scholars seeking greater understanding of the recent unrest in Tibet and Xinjiang are often hindered by a lack of access. Very few scholars are permitted to visit the region for the purposes of research, highlighting the importance and timeliness of this volume. Contributing authors represent part of a small cohort of international researchers who have gained unique access to the region in recent years. Contributing authors are deeply engaged with the region and have thorough knowledge of local communities. The authors emphasize the lived experiences of ordinary Tibetans and Uyghurs whose voices are seldom heard. Each of their chapters sheds new light on the causes of the recent wave of unrest, the state's response, and the evolving forms of protest and conflict across the region.

The chapter by Ben Hillman provides a broad analysis of Chinese government policies in the region and the role of local governments in formulating and implementing state policies. Hillman asks why local governments have been unable to use decentralized powers to experiment with policies that address local grievances in the same way that local governments in other parts of China have been able to drive policy innovation. Hillman argues that despite decentralization of significant decision-making powers to local-level governments, a complex system of formal and informal incentives deters risk taking and inhibits creative policy making among local government officials in conflict-affected areas. Drawing on extensive fieldwork in several Tibetan counties, Hillman explains that many local officials understand and sympathize with protestors. However, the politicization of unrest and the pressures of political competition compel local officials, especially ethnic minority officials, to take a hard line against protestors. Local officials are unable to acknowledge ethnic grievances or express sympathy for protestors, which would be a necessary first step in local policy innovation. Hillman explains how political incentives encourage local officials to distance themselves from any groups that might be linked to the protests, including local monasteries. Hillman explains how this diminishes citizen-official linkages and restricts the penetration of new ideas into local government thinking.

The chapter by Antonio Terrone examines a specific dimension of the CCP's response to the recent wave of unrest. Drawing on fieldwork in Tibet and Xinjiang, Terrone discusses the Communist Party's renewed propaganda efforts to promote Tibetan and Uyghur loyalty to the PRC. Terrone documents in rich detail the large-scale propaganda drives spearheaded by local governments in the region to remind Tibetans and Uyghurs (and other ethnic groups) of the sacrosanct notions of unity of the nation, territorial integrity, and interethnic harmony while discouraging any illegal activity aimed at separatism and the disruption of social stability. Terrone pays special attention to the propaganda essays, slogans, and messages that central and local governments display in public arenas in western China and argues that the propaganda campaign is more likely to exacerbate grievances than to galvanize loyalty to the PRC.

While CCP propaganda dominates physical public spaces, Françoise Robin's chapter documents the vitality of alternative discourses in the digital sphere. In an era of mass electronic communication Robin shows how young and educated Tibetans are increasingly able to use new media to discuss their plight. Specifically, Robin notes the increasing use of universal human rights terminology among Tibetans to debate Chinese government policies and the future of Tibet. Robin examines the use of the term *rights* (Tib. *thob thang*) that has appeared in slogans and on placards during several demonstrations in Tibet since 2008, including the Tibetan language–related protests in 2010. Robin weaves her observations into a discussion of the growing body of rights-related discourses taking place in print and online within Tibet, which highlights an increasing boldness and rights-awareness among a new generation of Tibetans. Robin finds that the writings of this generation are playing an important part in the continued unrest in Tibet. Understanding the changing attitudes and expectations of youth is critical to understanding the changing dynamics of ethnic protest and conflict in the region.

Youth, especially students, have been at the forefront of many protests in recent years. In many parts of Tibet students have rallied for changes to language and education policies. Tibetan-medium education offers an opportunity to master Tibetan literature and access a rich body of cultural and historical knowledge recorded in the Tibetan language. Attending Tibetan-medium schools, however, can limit young people's future career options as further education and employment opportunities require the skills and education that only Chinese-medium schools can provide. Using case studies of Yulshul (Ch. *Yushu*) and Tsolho (Ch. *Hainan*) Tibetan Autonomous Prefectures in Qinghai Province, Clémence Henry explores how individuals, families, teachers, and lamas devise and implement local strategies to balance and negotiate the imperatives of official educational programs, an ideal conception of what Tibetan education should be, and the reality of everyday living. Henry argues convincingly that Tibetan language and education policies are a site where CCP leaders' fears and Tibetan people's worries meet: a fear of resurgent nationalism on the one side and worries of losing one's cultural identity on the other.

As Tibetan and Uyghur protestors express their anxieties about loss of cultural identity, their protests play a part in shaping cultural identities. There is evidence that the protests of spring 2008 have galvanized ethnic consciousness (*minzu yishi*) among Tibetans from different parts of the plateau—people who speak different Tibetan dialects and who decades ago might not have readily identified with one another as members of the same group.[18] A similar phenomenon can be observed among Uyghurs, especially in places like Urumqi, where protests evolved into violent conflict between Uyghur and Han Chinese mobs. China's so-called stability maintenance measures also reinforce collective identities. Uyghurs and Tibetans are often targeted by security personnel and subjected to body searches and confiscation of their passports, smartphones, and literature. Tibetans and Uyghurs are also often subject to discriminatory profiling when traveling in China, including dedicated security lines at airports and refusal of service at hotels and restaurants.

China's leadership sees a rise in "ethnic consciousness" as a challenge to its authority and the legitimacy of its political institutions in the region.[19] Tom Cliff's chapter examines the state's efforts to counter the rise of "ethnic consciousness" in Xinjiang. Cliff observes that CCP authorities have taken an increasing interest in cultural policies in Xinjiang in recent years and that such policies can be used to shape ethnic and cultural identities. He draws on extensive recent fieldwork to highlight state efforts to comprehensively reshape Xinjiang's culture, including the culture of local Han and Uyghur communities, as well as the culture of government, private business, and state enterprises. Cliff shows how a variety of social and economic policies promote and facilitate new connections, identifications, and categories of belonging while simultaneously weakening or severing old ones. His chapter sheds new light on the CCP's cultural policies and the unanticipated consequences of state intervention in this domain.

Yonten Nyima and Emily Yeh's chapter extends the discussion on local government policies and their impacts on local communities. Focusing on environmental policies and natural resource management in Nakchu Prefecture, in the eastern part of the Tibet Autonomous Region (TAR), the authors examine the social and economic impacts of policies and relate their observations to the official discourse of the state as benevolent provider of development. Focusing on the grassland rejuvenation policy (*tuimu huancao*) that was implemented widely across the region, the authors observe that despite serious flaws in the assumptions behind the policy, as well as a lack of understanding among higher-level government officials of Tibetan pastoralism and indigenous practices, pastoralists in Nakchu have managed to negotiate with authorities to shape the outcomes of the policy in ways that suit their interests. The chapter examines local government incentives for implementing the policies, as well as the ways in which local pastoralists understand, resist, and manipulate policy to their own ends. Using comparative case studies of the implementation of pastoral policies in two Tibetan regions of Qinghai Province, the authors put to rest assumptions that Tibetans are passive victims of Chinese government policies. The chapter reminds us that levels of satisfaction with government policies vary greatly among Tibetan communities, a fact that probably has as much to do with demographics as it does with variation in local government policies. The concerns and priorities of Tibetan pastoralists, for example, are bound to differ from the concerns and priorities of formally educated urban Tibetans.[20]

Tyler Harlan's chapter continues the debate on livelihoods and economic factors that are relevant to the recent wave of unrest. His chapter investigates the emergence of urban Uyghur entrepreneurs in Xinjiang and the role of private business in shaping conflict dynamics between Han and Uyghur communities. Drawing on extensive fieldwork, Harlan argues that Xinjiang's private sector privileges Han-owned businesses linked to state networks, which results in Uyghur entrepreneurs being limited to fringe industries. Harlan observes that Uyghur entrepreneurs lack business experience and access to capital and that they cluster in specific industries where they hold a cultural advantage. Overcoming these barriers requires training, language skills, and state connections, which many entrepreneurs are unable to access. This in turn affects the ability of minority businesses to absorb surplus Uyghur labor, contributing to a stratification of labor that undermines ethnic relations and helps to explain why ethnic unrest in Xinjiang has been marked by a sharp increase in intercommunal ethnic violence.

Eric Mortensen's chapter continues the inquiry into local violence, noting the variation in levels of ethnic conflict and ethnic protest across the Tibetan region. Mortensen uses the case of Gyeltang (Ch. *Xianggelila/ Zhongdian*) in Yunnan Province, a region that escaped much of the pointedly political violence witnessed in most of Kham and Amdo to the north, to argue that violence in the region should not be simply construed as a reaction to Chinese government policies. Mortensen observes that Gyeltang is a violent place despite the absence of ethnic protest. His chapter explores why this is the case, raising questions about how we study ethnic unrest and ethnic-based violence.

The final chapter, by James Leibold, places the recent unrest in Tibet and Xinjiang in the context of overall ethnic relations in China. Leibold notes that the unrest in Tibet and Xinjiang has triggered new debates within China about the country's ethnic policies and institutions. Some scholars and officials have begun advocating for the removal of regional ethnic autonomy, arguing that special treatment of ethnic minorities has only served to harden ethnic boundaries. One influential and well-known scholar of China's ethnic politics argues, for example, that the identification of Tibetans, Uyghurs, and other groups as "minority nationalities" (*minzu*) has politicized ethnicity in China and undermined the PRC's nation-building efforts. He advocates replacing the term *minzu* with *zuqun* (ethnic group) as a step toward depoliticizing ethnicity. Proponents of a "second generation of ethnic policies" argue that political rights for ethnic minorities should be abolished in favor of a system based on equal citizenship and multiculturalism (Hu and Hu 2011).[21] Under this

second-generation ethnic policy, territorially concentrated ethnic minority groups such as the Tibetans and Uyghurs would have even less voice in
the governance of their homelands. Although other parts of the Chinese
scholarly community have warned against tampering with the system of
ethnic regional autonomy, arguing that forced assimilation could be disas-
trous for social relations,[22] proponents of second-generation ethnic policies remain an influential group in senior policy circles.

Leibold's chapter suggests that major changes in China's ethnic policies
are unlikely in the short to medium term. Drawing on a wide range of in-
terdisciplinary data—survey material, secondary and media reports, and
demographic and economic figures, among others—Leibold argues that
China's ethnic relations, on the whole, are not in crisis; nor do ethnic contradictions pose a significant threat to the political and social stability of
the PRC. He argues that, from a macro perspective, the unrest in Tibet and
Xinjiang is anomalous and unlikely to trigger a major shift in ethnic policies despite the scholarly debates it has generated.

It is apparent that CCP leaders have responded to the unrest by intensifying the party's carrot-and-stick approach to the region in which large-
scale subsidies and investments in the region's economic growth are accompanied by repressive measures against protest or unrest. In 2013,
63 percent of Xinjiang's budget was funded by transfers from the central
government (Chen 2014). For the Tibet Autonomous Region this figure
was 90 percent (ChinaTibetNews 2014). Central funding continues to pour
into the region for large infrastructure projects. Following the completion
of the world's highest railway, from Golmud to Lhasa, in 2006, authorities continue to expand the rail network in Tibetan areas with the aim of
connecting Lhasa to several neighboring provinces by 2020. The line from
Lhasa to Chengdu alone is expected to cost US$20 billion ("Tibet" 2014).
There are now six airports on the Tibet Plateau, four of which have opened
or been expanded since 2010. Plans to connect all county towns in Xinjiang
and Tibetan areas with paved roads are almost complete. Other benefits
include an increase in rural pensions and education subsidies, as well as
construction of lavish new schools. Such investments are intended to integrate the regions socially and economically with the rest of China, which
the party sees as an essential component of national security.

On the "stick" side of the equation Beijing has also invested heavily in scaling up so-called stability maintenance (*weiwen*) measures. This

includes increases in the number of security personnel (regular police, armed police, military, and intelligence), as well as expanded surveillance infrastructure. In Xinjiang spending on public security accounted for 12.4 percent of the region's budget in 2014.[23] In Tibetan areas People's Armed Police reinforcements that were sent as a response to the 2008 riots have been made permanent. In many rural areas, especially parts of eastern Tibet, where there have been a high number of self-immolations, local governments have stationed "volunteers" (typically township or country government employees) to monitor activities in the villages. In Lhasa and some other urban areas local authorities have divided neighborhoods into grids, appointing staff to monitor each grid and to report suspicious activities to the district administration or police. In Xinjiang provincial officials announced in early 2014 a similar plan to deploy two hundred thousand party cadres to spend a year at a time living with grassroots communities.[24]

Authorities have also placed increasing restrictions on Uyghurs' and Tibetans' movements and communications. Tibetans from outside the TAR, for example, are not permitted to travel to the TAR, and many Tibetans involved in earlier protests have been barred from leaving their home counties. Internet services in Tibetan areas are often only available through monitored Internet cafes, and 3G networks providing Internet access to mobile phones are unavailable in much of the plateau. Festivals and other cultural events have been cancelled indefinitely in order to prevent large public gatherings of Tibetans.[25] Checkpoints at all county borders are closely monitored by uniformed and plainclothes police reinforcements. China's total spending on domestic security now exceeds total spending on external defense (more than US$100 billion annually), and is the largest budget for domestic security of any country in the world (Reuters 2012). More recent figures on domestic security spending have been withheld (Reuters 2014).

Read together, the chapters in this volume provide the most comprehensive account to date of the causes of the recent wave of unrest in Tibet and Xinjiang. It is one of the richest collections of on-the-ground observations and interviews with Uyghurs and Tibetans to be published in recent years. The volume also provides thorough analysis of state responses to the unrest, the impacts of the state's response on local sentiments, and the prospects for policy change.

## Notes

1. March 10 is the anniversary of the Dalai Lama and his retinue's flight into exile in 1959.
2. Here *Tibet* refers to all Tibetan areas in China, including the Tibet Autonomous Region and Tibetan regions administered by Qinghai, Gansu, Sichuan, and Yunnan provinces.
3. Chinese authorities condemned both attacks as the work of Uyghur separatists living abroad.
4. The numbers of deaths and injuries are taken from Chinese government data; see http://politics.people.com.cn/GB/8198/160488/160489/index.html.
5. The distinction between "ethnic protest" and "ethnic conflict" follows Susan Olzak (1992). Olzak defines ethnic conflict as "a confrontation between members of two or more ethnic groups," and ethnic protest as a demonstration of public grievance by an ethnic group that "has the general public or some office of government as its audience" (8–9).
6. For a detailed analysis of the self-immolations as a new form of protest in Tibet see Shakya (2012); see also McGranahan and Litzinger (2012).
7. In August 2010 a Uyghur man detonated explosives in a crowd of police and paramilitary officers, causing seven fatalities and fourteen injuries. In July 2011 police killed twenty protesters during clashes in Hotan, according to exile sources. In August 2011 alleged terrorists killed thirteen people in an attack in Kashgar. Police reportedly killed eight of the alleged terrorists in response. In February 2012 rioters armed with knives killed ten people in Yechen. Later that same year six Uyghur men attempted to hijack an aircraft scheduled to take off from Hotan Airport. In April 2013 gunfights in Bachu County resulted in the deaths of fifteen police and community workers; six of the assailants were also killed. In June 2013 thirty-five people were killed when mobs attacked police stations and other government offices in Lukqun Township, Turpan.
8. Chinese authorities called the crash a "terrorist attack" and within hours had detained five other Uyghurs in connection with the incident. A spokesperson for the Uyghur World Congress dismissed claims of a terror attack and predicted that the incident would be used to justify further repression of Uyghurs. See AFP 2013.
9. According to a regional government report by official news media outlet Xinhua, "Police gunned down 59 terrorists and arrested 215 others" (Xinhua 2014b).
10. Rebiya Kadeer was once a prominent businesswoman in Xinjiang with close ties to the Chinese Communist Party. Kadeer was sentenced in 2000 to eight years in prison for leaking state secrets but was released on bail in 2005 to seek medical treatment in the United States. According to Wang Lequan, party secretary of the Xinjiang Uyghur Autonomous Region, once she was in the

United States, Kadeer "became involved with overseas terrorists, separatists and extremists forces" (Xinhua 2009).

11. On March 7, 2013 a panel of local officials reiterated these accusations during the annual meeting of China's National People's Congress. See, especially, comments by Wu Zegang, governor of Aba Prefecture, a Tibetan Autonomous Prefecture in Sichuan Province, where a large number of the self-immolations have taken place (Xinhua 2013). Chinese media outlets routinely reiterate the official position. English-language publications targeting an international audience similarly accuse Tibetan exiles of coordinating the self-immolations. According to one such publication, the self-immolations are to be blamed on "the shameless brutality of the 'Dalai clique' as the organizer and author of these crimes" (Yeshi 2013).

12. See Uyghur Human Rights Project 2012. At the end of the report is the following acknowledgment: "The Uyghur Human Rights Project would like to extend a special debt of gratitude to the Uyghurs of East Turkestan, whose dispossession necessitated the compiling of this report. Their deliberate marginalization from policy planning in East Turkestan has resulted in the gradual loss of a unique Uyghur cultural life and identity" (88).

13. See ICT 2012. Leader of the World Uyghur Congress Rebiya Kadeer has several times accused the Chinese government of perpetrating cultural genocide against Uyghurs; see, e.g., Kadeer 2012.

14. For examples of this scholarly perspective see chapters by Tyler Harlan and Tom Cliff in this volume; Dreyer 2006; Fischer 2013; and Hillman 2013.

15. Beijing-based Uyghur economist Ilham Tohti was convicted of "organizing and leading a separatist group" allegedly consisting of several of his students, for which he was sentenced to life in prison in September 2014. He is still there as of this writing.

16. Following its publication of an insightful report into the causes of the 2008 unrest in Tibet, the Beijing University–based Open Constitution Initiative was closed down. Its founder, academic and legal rights activist Xu Zhiyong, was recently sentenced to four years in prison, after being convicted of "gathering a mob to disturb public order" (Ch. *juzhong raoluan gonggong changsuo zhixu*). See Jacobs and Buckley 2014.

17. The exception is a handful of politically connected scholars engaged in debates about the future of China's ethnic policies, including the question of whether the current system of territorial ethnic autonomy should be replaced by multiculturalism. For further discussion of this debate, including its implications for China's ethnic policies, see the chapter by James Leibold in this volume; and Sautman 2010.

18. For more discussion about ethnic consciousness among Tibetans see the chapters by Françoise Robin and Ben Hillman in this volume.

19. This claim was verified by authors' interviews with police and local government officials in Yunnan and Sichuan, March 2013.

20. For a discussion of demographic factors in the analysis of grievance in China's Tibetan areas see Hillman 2014.

21. Hu Angang and Hu Lianhe argued that the CCP must cease recognizing difference along ethnic lines, abandon the regional autonomy system, and push for greater assimilation.

22. Liu Ling (2012) summarizes debates at a 2012 Chinese Academy of Social Sciences symposium to discredit arguments for a second generation of ethnic policies, noting, inter alia, that ethnic autonomy was not the reason for the breakup of the Soviet Union as is sometimes claimed. In a similar vein Qin Wenpeng (2009) highlights the experience of Mexico and Spain to note that assimilationist policies often backfire politically. He argues that the international experience suggests the most reliable way to accommodate territorially concentrated minorities is through systems of federalism of asymmetric autonomy.

23. Xinjiang's budget for public security in 2014 was 9.39 billion yuan (US$1.6 billion); see Chen 2014.

24. *Xinjiang Daily*, Feb. 15, 2014 (cited in Leibold 2014).

25. An example is the famous Lithang (Sichuan Province) horse race festival that was held every summer before 2008 but was canceled in subsequent years.

## References

AFP. 2013. "Uighur Group Scorns China's Tiananmen 'Terrorist Attack' Claim." *Australian*, Oct. 31. www.theaustralian.com.au/news/world/uighur-group-scorns -chinas-tiananmen-terrorist-attack-claim/story-e6frg6so-1226750669958.

AP. 2014. "China Says 50 Dead, 54 Injured in Sunday Terror Attacks in Restive Xinjiang." *SouthChinaMorningPost*, Sept. 26. www.scmp.com/news/china/article/1600583/ xinjiang-says-50-dead-54-injured-luntai-county-terror-attacks.

Barnett, Robert. 2009. "The Tibet Protests of Spring 2008: Conflict Between the Nation and the State." *China Perspectives*, no. 3, 6–23.

Chen Lina. 2014. "Public Security: How Much Will Xinjiang Spend?" [Gonggong anquan: Xinjiang yao hua duoshaoqian?] *Southern Weekly* [Nanfang Zhomou], August 29. www.infzm.com/content/103612.

ChinaTibetNews. 2014. "The State of Tibet's Public Finances in 2013 and Draft Report for 2014." Jan. 20. www.chinatibetnews.com/zhengwu/2014/0120/1318402_2 .shtml.

Dreyer, June Teufel. 2006. "Economic Development in Tibet Under the People's Republic of China." In *Contemporary Tibet: Politics, Development, and Society in a Disputed Region*, edited by Barry Sautman and June Teufel Dreyer, 129–51. Armonk, NY: M. E. Sharpe.

Fischer, Andrew Martin. 2013. *The Disempowered Development of Tibet in China: A Study in the Economics of Marginalization*. Lanham, MD: Rowman and Littlefield.

Hao Yufan and Liu Weihua. 2012. "Xinjiang: Increasing Pain in the Heart of China's Borderland." *Journal of Contemporary China* 2 (74): 205–25.

Hillman, Ben. 2013. "The Causes and Consequences of Rapid Urbanisation in an Ethnically Diverse Region." In "The Urbanisation of Rural China," edited by Ben Hillman and Jonathan Unger. Special issue, *China Perspectives*, no. 3, 25–32.

——. 2014. "Unrest in Tibet: Interpreting the Post-2008 Wave of Protest and Conflict." *Dalny Vychod* [Far East] 4 (1): 50–60.

Horowitz, Donald L. 2000. *Ethnic Groups in Conflict*. 2nd ed. Berkeley: University of California Press.

Hu Angang and Hu Lianhe. 2011. "Second-Generation Minority Nationalities Policies: Toward the Blending Together and Flourishing Together of Minority Nationalities as One Body" [Di erdai minzu zhengce: Cujin minzu jiaorong yiti he fanrong yiti]. *China Minority Nationalities and Religions Network*. http://mzb.com.cn/html/Home/report/293093-1.htm.

ICT. 2008. "The Spring Uprising in Tibet and China's Crackdown." International Campaign for Tibet, April. www.savetibet.org/wp-content/uploads/2013/06/Spring_Uprising_Tibet.pdf.

——. 2012. "60 Years of Chinese Misrule: Arguing Cultural Genocide in Tibet." International Campaign for Tibet, April 25. www.savetibet.org/wp-content/uploads/2013/05/Cultural-Genocide-in-Tibet-single-pages-2-1.pdf.

Jacobs, Andrew, and Chris Buckley. 2014. "China Sentences Xu Zhiyong, Legal Activist, to 4 Years in Prison." *New York Times*, Jan. 26. www.nytimes.com/2014/01/27/world/asia/china-sentences-xu-zhiyong-to-4-years-for-role-in-protests.html?_r=0.

Kadeer, Rebiya. 2012. "The World Holds Its Breath for China." *Wall Street Journal*, Nov. 8. www.wsj.com/articles/SB10001424127887323894704578106280566035950.

Leibold, James. 2014. "Xinjiang Work Forum Marks New Policy of 'Ethnic Mingling.'" *China Brief* 14 (12): www.jamestown.org/single/?tx_ttnews%5Btt_news%5D=42518&no_cache=1#.

Liu Ling. 2012. "Persist with the Basic Political System, Resolve Ethnic Issues Through Development—An Outline of the Symposium of the Association of Chinese Ethnic Theory" [Jianchi jiben zhengzhi zhidu—zai fazhan zhong jiejue minzu wenti—zhongguo minzu lilun xuehui zuotanhui jiyao]. Institute of Ethnology and Anthropology, Chinese Academy of Social Sciences, Beijing, Feb. 23.

McGranahan, Carole, and Ralph Litzinger, eds. 2012. "Self-Immolation as Protest in Tibet." *Cultural Anthropology Online*, April 9. www.culanth.org/fieldsights/93-self-immolation-as-protest-in-tibet.

Olzak, Susan. 1992. *The Dynamics of Ethnic Competition and Conflict*. Stanford: Stanford University Press.

Qin Wenpeng. 2009. "The Political Nature of Ethnic Theory" [Shilun minzu de zhengzhishuxing]. *Heilongjiang Journal of Ethnicity* 5: www.21ccom.net/articles/sxpl/sx/article_2011042734381.html.

Reuters. 2012. "China's Domestic Security Spending Rises to $111 Billion." March 5. www.reuters.com/article/2012/03/05/us-china-parliament-security-idUSTRE 82403J20120305.

——. 2014. "China Withholds Full Domestic-Security Spending Figure." March 4. www .reuters.com/article/2014/03/05/us-china-parliament-security-idUSBREA 240B720140305.

RFA. 2015. "At Least 18 Dead in Ramadan Attack on Police Checkpoint in Xin-jiang." *Radio Free Asia.* June 23. www.rfa.org/english/news/uyghur/attack -06232015182353.html.

Sautman, Barry. 2010. "Self-Representation and Ethnic Minority Rights in China." *Asian Ethnicity* 15 (2): 174–96.

Shakya, Tsering. 2012. "Self-Immolation, the Changing Language of Protest in Ti-bet." *Revue d'études tibétaines* 25:19–39.

Shan Wei and Chen Gang. 2009. "The Urumqi Riots and China's Ethnic Policy in Xinjiang." *East Asian Policy* 1 (3): 14–22. www.eai.nus.edu.sg/Vol1No3_Shanwei ChenGang.pdf.

"Tibet: Taming the West." 2014. *Economist.* June 21. www.economist.com/news/ china/21604594-communist-party-deepens-tibets-integration-rest-country -taming-west.

Uyghur Human Rights Project. 2012. "Living on the Margins: The Chinese State's Demolition of Uyghur Communities." Report, March. http://docs.uyghur american.org/3-30-Living-on-the-Margins.pdf.

Wolff, Stefan. 2006. *Ethnic Conflict: A Global Perspective.* Oxford: Oxford University Press.

Xinhua. 2008. "Premier: Ample Facts Prove Dalai's Role in Lhasa Riot, Door of Dia-logue Still Open." Xinhuanet, March 18. http://news.xinhuanet.com/english/ 2008-03/18/content_7813012.htm.

——. 2009. "Evidence Shows Rebiya Kadeer Behind Urumqi Riot: Chinese Gov't." July 9. http://news.xinhuanet.com/english/2009-07/09/content_11676293.htm.

——. 2013. "Government Blames Tibetan Self-Immolations on Overseas Instigation." Xinhuanet, March 7. http://news.xinhuanet.com/english/china/2013-03/07/ c_132215985.htm.

——. 2014a. "Commentary: High Time for West to See the Real Evil Face of 'East Turki-stan' Separatists." Xinhuanet, March 5. http://news.xinhuanet.com/english/ indepth/2014-03/05/c_133162664.htm.

——. 2014b. "37 Civilians Killed, 13 Injured in Xinjiang Terror Attack." Xinhuanet, Au-gust 3. http://news.xinhuanet.com/english/china/2014-08/03/c_126825972 .htm.

Yeshi Dorje. 2013. "The Self-Immolation Plot: The Dalai Clique Is Doomed to Failure." *China's Tibet* 24:22–25.

# 1

# Unrest in Tibet and the Limits of Regional Autonomy

Ben Hillman

L
ocal governments in China have been credited with much of the innovation that has propelled the country's modernization and development since the 1980s. Indeed, it is widely accepted that China's decentralization reforms provided the space and incentive for local governments to experiment with new social and economic policies, pioneering reforms that have subsequently been adopted and promoted nationwide by the central government. By contrast, local governments in China's Tibetan areas have been much less innovative. Widespread ethnic unrest in Tibetan areas in recent years has highlighted a failure on the part of local governments to formulate and implement conflict-sensitive policies and to use conflict-reduction strategies in the implementation of higher-level policies. In this chapter I examine the formal and informal incentive structures that shape local officials' behavior in Tibetan areas. Drawing on interviews with officials, religious leaders, businesspeople, representatives of nongovernmental organizations (NGOs), educators, farmers, and nomads in several Tibetan counties, I examine why local governments in Tibetan areas have so far been unable to use their decentralized powers to reduce ethnic tensions.

## Local Government in China

When the Chinese Communist Party (CCP) abandoned central planning in favor of decentralized economic governance in the late 1970s and early 1980s, local governments, particularly at the county and township level, acquired new powers and responsibilities.[1] They became responsible for delivering essential public services such as health, education, and social welfare, including pensions. To fund these new mandates, local governments were given a larger share of tax receipts and control over the profits of local state-owned enterprises. Subnational governments became responsible for an ever-increasing share of total public expenditure. In 2010 subnational governments were responsible for 82 percent of total public expenditure, up from 65 percent in 2000, making China, on this measure, one of the most decentralized countries in the world—more decentralized, even, than many federal states such as Germany, Australia, and the United States. The decisions made by local party and government leaders have a greater impact on Chinese society and economy than at any time since the founding of the People's Republic.[2]

By the early 1990s it appeared to many scholars that reforms had so empowered the localities that Beijing had little sway over them at all. Some analysts pointed to the emergence of local kingdoms (*xiao wangguo*) and dukedom economies (*zhuhou jingji*), warning that powerful localities could lead to a breakup of the People's Republic of China. In the mid-1990s central authorities began to reassert control over the localities by establishing a new tax regime and by strengthening the cadre management system. The new fiscal arrangements (which ensured the central government collected a higher portion of revenue before redistributing it to the regions) gave the central government more control over the purse strings, but widespread evidence of corruption and bureaucratic indiscipline continued to fuel debates about the capacity of the center to control its local agents. Even in very recent times corruption scandals have exposed the way in which some localities are run like personal fiefdoms by powerful local bosses.[3]

As in other parts of China, Tibetan-area governments have acquired significant autonomous powers in the reform era.[4] In the early years of the People's Republic the CCP sought to integrate Tibetans and other territorially concentrated ethnic groups through the adoption of a system of "regional ethnic autonomy," which was loosely modeled on the Soviet example.[5] Introduced gradually in many parts of western China since the 1950s, the system was ostensibly intended to give such groups a greater role in the way their localities were governed.[6] While "ethnic autonomy" turned out to be an empty promise, the so-called autonomous ethnic regions did acquire scope for autonomous decision making. For example, autonomy status gave local administrations greater flexibility in implementing central government directives. Ethnic autonomous regions were empowered to enact a wider range of laws (as long as they did not conflict with central government laws or policies) and to modify or oppose central government policies deemed unsuited to local conditions. When a central government law is deemed unsuited to local conditions, "autonomous" local governments can lodge a request for modification or delayed implementation.

The obvious weaknesses of China's system of ethnic autonomy have led sections of the scholarly community to dismiss the significance of local governments in Tibetan areas. But it is incorrect to equate a lack of ethnic autonomy with a total lack of local discretion. Generally speaking, CCP leaders in Beijing set only policy principles and directions (*fangzhen*), leaving policy interpretation and implementation to lower levels of party-state administration. Local governments in Tibetan areas are responsible for developing local economic policies, deciding which industries to support through tax incentives and access to subsidized credit. Local governments also have scope to develop social and cultural policies. County governments in Tibetan areas decide, for example, whether to apply a Tibetan or Chinese language–based curriculum in schools and how much to remunerate teachers.[7] Local governments also sponsor cultural events, such as major festivals, or ban such events, as they have often done since 2008. Prefecture and county governments are also responsible for managing relations with religious authorities and for responding to unrest. Why, then, have local governments not been able to use their autonomy to develop conflict-sensitive policies that address the sources of unrest? I argue that a combination of formal and informal incentives and constraints prevents creative policy making and reformist initiatives at the local level. In the next section of this chapter I examine the formal institutional constraints that shape local officials' priorities. In the subsequent section I explain how informal incentives align with formal institutional constraints in Tibetan areas to create a political culture characterized by risk aversion and the prioritization of politics and profits over policy innovation.

## Formal Constraints on Policymaking: The Cadre Assessment System

Students of Chinese politics generally agree that the center retains effective control of its local agents through the CCP's cadre management system. The cadre management system involves elaborate processes for screening and evaluating cadres for advancement and is administered by each level of government for the leaders of the level immediately below. The assessment process acts as a powerful incentive for career-conscious local officials. Career advancement for local officials depends, in large part, on regular performance evaluations. Individual performance evaluations (*kaohe*) are conducted annually and are based on a points system. During an annual assessment an official can receive a maximum of one hundred points across four categories: (1) integrity (*de*), (2) industriousness (*qin*), (3) capability (*neng*), and (4) performance (*Ji*).[8] All criteria are scored on the basis of opinions provided by superiors and colleagues. "Performance" becomes a quantifiable criterion when it is used to assess the performance of heads of local government (i.e., not ordinary cadres) against political responsibility contracts, which specify hard GDP growth and family planning targets. The number of points awarded for each of the four criteria varies by region, but performance generally accounts for fifty to sixty points out of the total one hundred.

While I have written elsewhere about the limits of the cadre management system in influencing local officials' behavior (Hillman 2010a, 2014a), here I argue that the system is more "effective" in Tibetan areas. The key difference lies in the emphasis and meaning given to the "integrity" component of the assessment in Tibetan areas. *Integrity* essentially means "political correctness," which in Tibetan areas is generally interpreted as "fealty" to the CCP. The CCP's concern for "loyalty" is highly visible in Tibetan areas. Billboards and public notices everywhere demand it. In other parts of China government billboards exhort people to obey traffic rules and avoid spitting and littering. In Tibetan areas a large amount of government propaganda exhorts people to be loyal citizens. In the center of Kantze (Ch. *Ganzi*) Tibetan Autonomous Prefecture (TAP), for example, a moving electronic script in front of the police station urges loyalty to the party and loyalty to the country (*shi yu dang, shi yu guojia*), in that order. Another large whitewashed wall in town is emblazoned with the lyrics to a ditty titled "Promote Patriotic Spirit."[9] The lyrics read, "the Communist Party is good, socialism is good . . . reform and opening up is good, the great motherland is good . . . every ethnic group's people are good." Such slogans are reminiscent of a much earlier period in China proper, yet they are common adornments of the urban landscape in Tibetan areas. They reflect a concern not just about ordinary people's loyalties but also about the loyalties of local state employees, especially ethnic Tibetan employees.

Because of party leaders' insecurity about the party's authority and legitimacy in many Tibetan communities, ethnic Tibetan officials are under constant pressure to demonstrate their loyalty. Officials use a variety of means to demonstrate their loyalty to the Communist Party. Joining the party and participating in its meetings and campaigns are among the most obvious means of doing so. Another important means of demonstrating loyalty is by becoming a role model for party policies. Ethnic Tibetan cadres who are entitled to have more than one child, might, for example, choose to have only one child—an action that serves as a strong symbol of personal commitment to the party's family-planning policies. In many parts of Tibet ethnic Tibetan officials and other state employees such as teachers have had to take additional steps to ensure their loyalty to the CCP by avoiding practices associated with Tibetan Buddhism, which the CCP sees as a competing source of legitimacy and authority in Tibetan areas. In many Tibetan areas this has meant dismantling Tibetan Buddhist altars in family homes. It also means avoiding monasteries and sacred sites.[10] Local officials must be particularly careful in their private associations with members of the Tibetan Buddhist clergy and in their observance of religious rituals.[11] In many areas monasteries and other religious sites are off limits to officials, except when they visit on official business—for example, to make announcements or to provide patriotic education.[12] Even when not explicitly prohibited from visiting religious sites, government officials are aware that such an action might be construed as sympathy for organized Tibetan Buddhism.

The need for Tibetan-area officials to constantly demonstrate their loyalty by avoiding association with Tibetan Buddhism severely constrains the effectiveness of local government. I have argued elsewhere that the avoidance of the monastic establishment greatly limits local officials' capacity to understand issues of concern to many ethnic Tibetans (Hillman 2010b). It also disconnects Tibetan officials from important channels of communication, which is particularly significant given the primacy placed on personal relationships (*guanxi*) in Chinese politics and society. And given that many Tibetan-area conflicts have a religious dimension (numerous eruptions of discontent have begun with demonstrations by monks and nuns), the lack of meaningful communication with Tibetan Buddhist clergy makes it difficult for local officials to understand the source of conflicts, which is a prerequisite for thinking about how to manage such conflicts in the present and how to prevent such conflicts in the future.

A related problem is the preferencing of Sinicized (*bei hanhua*) Tibetans for promotion in county and prefecture government. "Sinicized Tibetans" are ethnic Tibetans who have grown up in communities with long-established Han Chinese populations and who have either adopted Chinese as their first language or are as comfortable speaking Chinese as they are speaking Tibetan. Most of these officials have been trained in a Chinese-language education environment, and their values and priorities tend to be different from educated Tibetans who have been trained in a Tibetan-language educational environment. In recent years there is clear evidence that Sinicized Tibetans have been promoted ahead of other Tibetan officials because their loyalties are less suspect. The consequence of this has been that an increasing number of local officials have insufficient proficiency in the Tibetan language to communicate with local citizens. In Ngaba (Ch. *Aba*) TAP the party's Organizational Bureau recently issued a circular requiring lower level party units to organize Tibetan language classes for officials.[13] But such classes are unlikely to restore the language proficiency that has been lost. A more effective measure would be to uphold the generally ignored law that requires government communication in ethnic autonomous regions to be conducted in both languages. Another more effective means of ensuring Tibetan language competence would be to include a Tibetan-language requirement in the civil service entrance exams or, at least, to have a Tibetan-language component examination for a fixed number of positions. The current Chinese-language civil service examination system discriminates against many capable and educated Tibetans who attended Tibetan-language medium schools.[14]

Career-conscious officials need to keep more than just monasteries and monks at arm's length. NGOs are also regarded with suspicion, especially those with foreign links. This is because the CCP routinely blames unrest on manipulation by "hostile forces" (i.e., the "Dalai clique" of Tibetan exiles and their Western backers).[15] In Tibetan areas the relentless insistence that instability is the result of interference by external forces bent on destabilizing or splitting China has created a sense of paranoia among many local officials. Some Tibetan-area officials have come to believe that Western visitors to Tibetan areas can only be involved in mischief and refuse to have any contact with individuals or organizations that are foreign or that have foreign links.[16] Other officials have a more nuanced understanding of the reasons for instability, but for the sake of their careers, they cannot afford to be associated with the activities of any groups that might have foreign, especially American, connections. Even though the security apparatus keeps dossiers on local and foreign organizations, including a "black list," as one county official told me, "we cannot always be sure how people are connected. . . . Even if an activity appears innocuous we might later find out that a troublemaker is involved."

Many officials I have interviewed in Tibetan areas admit to being vigilantly wary of individuals who might be linked, however remotely, with foreign groups, especially those suspected of sponsoring activities deemed to promote Tibetan ethnic consciousness (*minzu yishi*). According to a retired county government official, the Communist Party considers Pan-Tibetan ethnic consciousness a major threat.[17] But many local and international NGOs are held in suspicion simply because they operate outside of the state in a region where the state is accustomed to dominating the sectors in which NGOs seek to make a contribution—e.g., the environment, livelihoods, education, and the "preservation" of cultural heritage. There is a common attitude among local officials in Tibetan areas that there is something suspicious about groups that do not seek to operate through state institutions or channels.

The pressure on local officials to demonstrate their loyalty by minimizing or avoiding links with nonstate actors disconnects local governments from potential sources of information and new ideas. For several years I was involved in developing vocational training programs for unemployed ethnic Tibetan youth. As cofounder of a local training institute in Deqen TAP I worked with local government and industry to develop a range of preemployment programs that helped more than one thousand young people across eastern Tibet to find employment and start new businesses. Because I was a foreigner, the program's success required a huge investment of time in building trust, even in the relatively open Deqen TAP. It also required additional regular reporting to various government agencies including the public security bureau, which is responsible for domestic intelligence. Even then, and despite the program's visible successes as well as praise from business groups and the Chinese media, senior local officials in Deqen always maintained distance from the program and refused to fund it, even though vocational training had become a national priority. The opportunities to share global expertise with local education authorities were always limited. Outside of the relatively open Deqen TAP the opportunities for policy-exchange ideas are even more limited. School principals refused to meet unless I had a letter of introduction from the county chief executive. One school principal said sympathetically that he would be interested to talk with me but that it would cause too many problems if he did.

Many ideas for improving local livelihoods, promoting inclusive economic growth, and managing the environment are generated by the NGO sector. Internationally funded NGOs, in particular, have access to the global marketplace of ideas. Yet it is very difficult for the NGO sector to engage with local government. The suspicion of foreigners and foreign funding means that, regardless of a cause's importance or value, Tibetan-area officials have little incentive to want to be involved. Braver local officials—especially those with powerful connections at higher levels—are sometimes more willing to engage, but such officials are usually too risk-averse to give an initiative formal approval or funding. At the very most, such officials might give their tacit approval to a group's activities if it can manage without overt or explicit government support. Some extremely cautious officials will simply refuse to have anything to do with any group or activity in which there is foreign involvement. It is one of the tasks of the greatly expanded internal security industry, spearheaded by the Public Security Bureau, to identify people and activities that are ambiguously labeled "problematic" (*you wenti*). In an environment characterized by low levels of trust and high levels of suspicion, it is no surprise that an increase in *weiwen* budgets and operations has been accompanied by an expanding list of suspects.

Another assessment criterion that acts as a powerful constraint on local officials' behavior, especially leading cadres' (*lingdao ganbu*) behavior, is "performance" or "achievement" (*Ji*). Unlike other assessment criteria, which are based on the subjective judgment of superiors, performance is more quantifiable. Performance is based on the meeting of hard targets set by the central government, with an overwhelming weight placed on achieving high levels of economic growth and maintaining social stability. Social stability, measured by the number of mass incidents (the lower the better), and economic growth, measured by regional gross domestic product (GDP), are key performance indicators for local heads of government and party branches. They are considered veto (*yipiao fojue*) issues, which means that failure to meet targets will preclude career advancement regardless of performance in other areas.[18]

Hard indicators for economic growth and social stability, combined with the "veto" factor, serve as a powerful incentive for heads of local government. On the economic front it explains why local officials pursue growth at all costs, even if it is achieved through reckless borrowing.[19] It also explains why local governments prioritize big-ticket infrastructure projects such as dams, roads, and bridges. Such projects add significantly to gross regional product (GRP).

Although investments in public infrastructure bring economic benefits to many people, the growth-at-all-costs model of development has had adverse consequences for economic equality and social stability in Tibetan areas.[20] In expanding urban areas rapid urbanization and the emergence of new industries such as tourism have provided new economic opportunities and higher material living standards for those with desirable skills and education. However, there is mounting evidence that rapid urban-led growth in Tibetan areas has been characterized by the increasing marginalization of ethnic Tibetans, especially in the urban economy where non-Tibetan migrants are outcompeting ethnic Tibetans for jobs.[21] When I first visited Lhasa in 2001, nearly all taxi drivers were non-Tibetan. So were nearly all owners of small businesses in the city. Across Tibetan areas billions of dollars worth of construction projects such as dams, airports, and roads employ nonlocal labor. Although many ethnic Tibetans have found work driving trucks and collecting building materials such as sand and rock for construction sites, the better-paid and higher-skilled jobs generally go to outsiders. In March 2013 I asked a group of young men in Chaktreng (Ch. *Xiangcheng*) County, Kantze TAP, why they were not working on a nearby airport project that was already in its fourth year of construction. One replied, "We Tibetans can't do Han's work." Even in sites of cultural tourism where one might expect to see ethnic Tibetans well represented, non-Tibetans are often able to outcompete Tibetans, especially when it comes to higher-skilled and higher-paid employment opportunities. In a 2012 survey of 147 enterprises in Deqen TAP, a popular destination for Han Chinese and foreign tourists, it was revealed that the ethnic composition of the workforce was largely representative of the composition of the population. Employers acknowledged in separate interviews, however, that Tibetans were underrepresented in higher-paid managerial and technical positions (Hillman 2013). Tyler Harlan's chapter in this volume discusses a similar phenomenon in Xinjiang, where Uyghur entrepreneurs struggle to compete against the superior social and financial capital of Han Chinese entrepreneurs.

The growth fetish has also been associated with insensitivity to local social and cultural concerns, undermining ethnic security—i.e. people's perceptions of their ability to preserve, express, and develop their ethnic distinctiveness in everyday economic, social, and cultural practices (Wolff 2006; Horowitz 2000). In cities such as Lhasa the Han Chinese–led modernization juggernaut has made many parts of the city unrecognizable to its indigenous inhabitants. Buildings and boulevards have made many parts of Lhasa and many other Tibetan towns look much like cities in China proper. Urbanization projects have also destroyed the Uyghur character of many cities and towns in Xinjiang.[22] While urban development in Beijing and other Chinese cities has been similarly destructive, the implications are different in Tibetan and other ethnic minority regions where such destruction transforms the social and cultural landscape that forms a core part of people's identities. When the destruction of cultural heritage is accompanied by economic changes that marginalize the traditional inhabitants, the sense of loss can be profound (Shakya 2012; Barnett 2009).

The performance-assessment criterion as it is presently evaluated creates few incentives for local officials to pay attention to the quality of economic growth or its inclusiveness. The assessment system's emphasis on GRP leads to disproportionate investments in physical construction and underinvestment in people. In the education sector, for example, local officials in Tibetan areas show a great passion for school building but much less interest in improving the quality of teaching or training programs.[23] I know this firsthand from my experience with education projects in Deqen TAP and from interviews with education authorities in other regions. The continued prioritization of hardware over software benefits construction companies, many of which hire nonlocal workers, without providing opportunities for locals to acquire the skills needed in the changing economy.

The focus on GRP (which is common across all of China) has also had deleterious environmental impacts on Tibetan areas, where the upland environment is particularly fragile. Since a logging ban was introduced in 1998, Tibetan-area governments have begun promoting new industries as a source of local tax revenue.[24] In Deqen TAP local authorities have successfully promoted tourism, but rapid growth in the number of visitors has strained infrastructure and put pressure on the natural environment. Every day thousands of liters of raw sewage are pumped into Napa Lake, a breeding ground for black-necked cranes and an important seasonal pasture for local transhumance agropastoralists. In Ngaba TAP local government has welcomed the arrival of heavy industries such as television and mobile phone manufacturers and a salt refinery. Approximately seventy new heavy polluting industries have been established in Ngaba TAP since 1998, emitting chemicals such as calcium carbide into ecologically important watersheds.[25] The long-term impacts on the livelihoods of local Tibetan farmers and pastoralists are difficult to assess because political sensitivities prevent objective environmental impact assessments of such industries. It is a problem driven by the GRP-growth targets of the formal cadre assessment system.[26]

A related constraint on local policy making is the funding mechanism for local development projects. Tibetan-area local governments rely heavily on fiscal transfers from above to fund operations. There are various types of fiscal transfers, but the most significant for Tibetan areas are the Tibetan-area fiscal transfers (zangqu caizheng zhuangyi zhifu), provided by the central government, and special-purpose transfers (zhuangxiang buzhu), provided by various line ministries on an ad hoc basis.[27] Special-purpose funds are earmarked for certain programs such as road construction, introduction of agricultural technologies, or housing construction for nomads. The pursuit of special-purpose transfers leads heads of local governments to prioritize development programs for which funding is being made available regardless of local development priorities. County government officials invest large resources in accessing the latest information about funding opportunities and maintain representative offices in Beijing for this purpose. Local government officials flock to Beijing when they anticipate the announcement of a new round of spending.

The prescriptive manner in which funding is provided to local governments does not encourage creative thinking about local public welfare. Officials are not motivated to ask themselves what kind of programs are needed to address local grievances. The pursuit of transfers fixes the gaze of local officials on higher levels and encourages them to be opportunistic. In one Tibetan county town I witnessed a single road repaved three times in ten years. When I asked the former head of the county finance bureau for an explanation, he told me "local government leaders will spend money on whatever they can find money for; if there is money for road building, you build a road. Even if there are no roads to build, you find one that needs fixing. Whether it is needed or not, the road becomes your personal achievement (*Ji*)." Officials are, of course, aware that road projects add significantly to GRP, which registers an increase even if a perfectly good road is wastefully replaced with a new one.

The other key performance indicator for local government leaders is social stability, defined by the lack of "mass incidents" (*qunzhongxing shijian*), which is officially defined as a protest, riot, or unauthorized gathering involving more than five hundred people. Throughout China local government and party leaders go to great lengths to prevent outbreaks of mass incidents.[28] In Tibetan areas stability maintenance has become the main priority for evaluating local government leaders' performance since 2008. Heads of township, county, and prefecture governments know that they will be given a better evaluation if they prevent unrest, regardless of anything else they do.[29] But because party secretaries and heads of local governments serve only short terms—a maximum of five years—there is little incentive or opportunity for them to think about long-term solutions to unrest.[30] Following decades of periodic unrest in Tibetan areas and the party's traditional intolerance of dissent, local officials in Tibetan areas are more familiar with the use of force and repression than they are with more sophisticated policy approaches. A recent *Legal Daily* report on mass incidents across China in 2012 grouped local government responses to unrest as either "positive" or "negative." Positive measures included official announcements (*guangfang shengming*), thorough investigations (*shenru diaocha*), dealing directly with responsible people (*chuli fuzeren*), consoling/

persuading/advising concerned parties (*weiwen/quanshuo/dangshiren*), and publicizing policies, laws, and regulations (*chutai zhengci faguan*). According to the report, positive measures were identified in 57.8 percent of reported mass incidents. "Negative" responses included such measures as information blackouts (*fengsuo xiaoxi*), forcible dispersal (*qiangying qusan*), and arresting and detaining concerned parties (*daibu/juliu dangshiren*). According to the report, negative measures were used in 62.3 percent of incidents in 2012.

Because unrest is officially blamed on forces hostile to China, local government leaders and security personnel are encouraged to use stern measures to prevent mass incidents. Repressive measures used by local security forces to prevent protests in Tibetan areas include the recruiting of large numbers of informants to spy on fellow citizens; the forcing of monks and other potential troublemakers such as returnees from India to sign contracts promising they will not engage in protests or demonstrations or to publicly express devotion to the Dalai Lama; the confiscation of passports to prevent Tibetans from traveling to India and other countries where hostile forces reside; the shutting down of Internet connections, denial of travel outside of one's home county;[31] and the frequent administrative detention and jailing of ethnic Tibetans for communicating information about unrest or promoting alternative interpretations of unrest.[32]

The strong incentive to prevent mass incidents has led local officials in a number of areas to severely restrict or very carefully control public events where Tibetans congregate in large numbers. In Lithang an extremely popular and well-known annual horse festival was cancelled in 2008 and for several years thereafter. Horse festivals and cultural events in other Tibetan areas are also frequently cancelled for fear they will lead to unrest. Many Tibetans, however, see such measures as restrictions on their freedom of ethnic expression. Even in the relatively stable Deqen TAP, where such festivals continue to be held, since 2008 local officials have deployed large numbers of military, armed police and armored personnel carriers on the streets during such events to deter antiparty behavior, but this too has a demonstrably negative effect on public sentiment. Law-abiding citizens report that they feel they are being unfairly targeted. Such actions strangle local creativity and expression and reinforce an us-vs.-them mentality between ordinary Tibetans and the state. The impact of such decisions is not only psychological. A local business owner in Lithang lamented the damage to the local economy of the cancelation of the horse festival and similar events.

## Informal Constraints on Policy Making: Patronage and Career Advancement

Career advancement within the party-state depends not only on formal assessments but also on an official's ability to navigate informal politics. In a system in which personal power relations trump formal rules, career opportunities are greatly affected by informal ties. Junior officials recognize very early in their careers that they cannot advance without the support of a well-placed patron. The patron provides support for their advancement, as well as protection from hazards encountered along the way. In return junior officials provide personal loyalty, which is a different kind of loyalty than loyalty to the party.

The practice of patronage is inextricably linked to the politics of spoils. Like in US cities such as New York and Chicago in the not-so-distant past, spoils have become a prominent feature of local politics in many parts of China, including Tibetan areas. In a political environment characterized by weak rule of law and an emphasis on revenue-generation, it is not surprising that politics has come to revolve around spoils. In local politics money is needed to buy influence and protection and to win friends and allies. A politics of spoils has flourished in reform-era China as local officials have been able to exercise a high degree of regulatory power with very few institutional constraints. Accountability mechanisms from below are weak or nonexistent, and supervisory mechanisms from above are vulnerable to capture by private interests.[33]

Patronage networks extract spoils via their control of positions in the local bureaucracy. As a result political competition at the local level involves constant contestation over bureaucratic appointments. The most sought-after positions are those responsible for large infrastructure projects, development programs, and environmental protection schemes, as well as positions that have influence on personnel appointments, especially leading cadre (*lingdao ganbu*) appointments.[34]

Local powerbrokers vie with one another to place allies (*zijiren*) in positions that will extend their informal control over the state's resources.

Although they are not formally organized, these groups are readily identifiable and are frequently spoken about in political circles. Local political decisions, such as which bureau leads a particular endeavor or which
locale will pilot a new program, are often the outcome of rivalries among
powerful groups within the local state. Such groups are often formed on
the basis of native place ties, but members are also recruited through other
means, such as shared experiences in the army or old school ties. Together
with their private sector partners, these state-based powerbrokers have
been labeled the new Tibetan aristocracy.[35] It must be noted, however, that
such local "aristocracies" can be found throughout contemporary China,
not just in Tibetan areas.

The accumulation of private wealth by local officials is evidenced by
officials' consumption habits. Officials' wealth can be seen in the houses
they own (the ones they live in, as well as their investment properties),
the cars they drive, the mistresses they keep (most officials are male), the
vacations they take (including to overseas destinations), the clothes and
watches they wear, and the way they entertain themselves. In Tibetan areas I have seen officials wager staggering sums of money at card games and
mah-jongg. During more than a decade of visits to Tibetan areas, I have
been able to observe firsthand the rapid self-enrichment of local officials,
whose wealth stands in stark contrast to the living standards of the rest of
the population.[36]

In Tibetan areas the spoils system has been fueled by large injections of
central government funds into local state coffers. Since the launch of the
Great Western Development Program in 2000, in particular, hundreds of
billions of *yuan* have been channeled to Tibetan-area local governments.
Many of the investments have targeted public infrastructure as a means
of lifting economic growth, extracting resources and integrating western
area economies with the dynamic markets of eastern China. Such spending
priorities suit spoils-seekers because public infrastructure and other construction projects provide multiple opportunities for collecting informal
fees—mostly in the form of kickbacks from subcontractors.

The combined incentives of formal growth targets and the informal
pursuit of spoils focus local officials' attention on big-ticket construction projects. In the education sector, as I noted above, there are already
strong incentives to build schools, regardless of whether there are teachers or students to fill them, rather than invest in education software such
as teacher training or new vocational training programs. This is where the

logic of the informal spoils system aligns with the formal policy emphasis on GRP growth.

The informal competition over appointments also aligns with formal pressures to avoid political risk; local officials are under pressure to actively demonstrate their loyalty to the Communist Party but also not to embarrass their patrons. The intensity of political competition also focuses officials' attention on intrastate political machinations at the expense of policy deliberation. Political competition between local power brokers requires time-consuming politicking and lobbying, which involves elaborate social rituals. Cadre rotations in large counties can be so frequent that local powerbrokers are often completely absorbed by their efforts to maximize the advantage of their allies. This leaves officials with little time to think about how they might serve the people better. This is not to say that all local officials are venal and uninterested in the people's welfare. Sometimes officials manage to look after their communities as well as themselves. For example, officials sometimes use their power to direct spending toward their home townships and villages. I have also observed a normative consensus emerge around such spoils sharing. Ordinary citizens in Tibetan areas tend to view state money as the government's money and not as the people's money. Local officials and villagers often express the view that informal fees are an appropriate reward for officials who manage to secure higher-level funding for a local development project.

In Tibetan areas I have encountered many local officials who are concerned about local social policies and interested in change. But such officials tend to be on the margins of political power, occupying positions in politically weak agencies. For example, ethnic Tibetan officials with an interest in cultural or religious policies are often relegated to the culture department or the state-run Buddhist association or to committees within the toothless People's Political Consultative Assembly, such as the culture and history committee (*wenshi weiyuanhui*). This is because career advancement beyond a certain level is virtually impossible in a spoils system unless one is willing to play by the unwritten rules of the game.

---

Formal and informal incentives for career advancement act as serious constraints on policy innovation within Tibetan-area local governments. The cadre assessment system ensures that local government leaders are focused on economic growth at all costs and the prevention of unrest. This promotes short-term thinking among local government leaders and leads to political decisions that undermine long-term stability. The need for local officials, especially ethnic Tibetan officials, to constantly demonstrate their loyalty to the Communist Party also cuts officials off from important channels of communication and sources of information. This problem is compounded by the civil service examination system and the current preference given to Sinicized Tibetans when appointing ethnic Tibetans to bureaucratically powerful positions.

The informal incentives of intrastate politics and political competition align with the formal incentives of the cadre assessment system to produce a political culture characterized by risk aversion and an emphasis on politics and profits over ideas. In a political system in which personal power relations trump formal rules, Tibetan-area officials become preoccupied with concerns of political survival and material gain. Energies are invested in intrastate machinations rather than in creative thinking about how to improve conditions and help ethnic Tibetans feel more secure about their futures.

China's leaders blame unrest in Tibetan communities on the meddling of hostile forces rather than on governance failings. The official line on the causes of instability justifies the use of harsh measures in responding to unrest. But harsh measures only suppress unrest and do not deal with its root causes. Harsh measures also add to local grievances. Unless there are fundamental changes to incentive structures, both formal and informal, it is likely that local governments will further alienate Tibetan communities and perpetuate the cycle of unrest.

## Notes

1. My definition of local government includes township, county, and prefecture government. Even though analysts frequently include the province in their definition of "local government" in China, I argue that provincial administration in China is too far removed from the localities to be properly considered "local." Most provinces are larger in population and territory than Western European countries such as France and Italy. And it is widely known that provincial leaders identify more readily with the pool of central government cadres than with officials at lower levels.

2. Between 2000 and 2013 subnational governments' share of total government expenditure in China increased from 65.3 percent to 85.4 percent (see China Statistical Yearbook 2014). Local government includes all subnational government expenditure, including provincial government. These figures do not include expenditure of off-budget revenues for which no data are available. The inclusion of such expenditures would further increase local governments' share of the total.

3. See, for example, the stories of corruption, including mafia-style tactics and arbitrary exercise of power, surrounding Bo Xilai's fall from grace as party secretary of Chongqing Municipality. For more detail on local bosses, patronage, and informal networks in China's local politics see Hillman 2014a.

4. Tibetan-area governments include the province-level Tibetan Autonomous Region, eight Tibetan autonomous prefectures in Qinghai, Gansu, Yunnan, and Sichuan provinces and two Tibetan autonomous counties in Gansu and Sichuan provinces. In two other prefectures "autonomy" is formally shared between Tibetans and other groups. They are the Haixi Mongol and Tibetan Autonomous Prefecture in Qinghai and the Aba Tibetan and Qiang Autonomous Prefecture in Sichuan Province.

5. An important difference was that the Soviet model provided a legal basis for secession from the Union. The Chinese Communist Party insisted that all regions over which the former Qing Empire claimed authority, including present-day Xinjiang and Tibet, formed part of the inalienable territory of the People's Republic of China. China's territorial integrity is a central pillar of contemporary Chinese nationalism.

6. In the first two decades of Communist Party rule four provincial-level territories and thirty prefecture-level territories acquired self-governing (zizhi) status. A number of county- and township-level units also acquired self-governing status.

7. On the variation in language and education policy between different Tibetan local government areas see the chapter by Clémence Henry in this volume.

8. This system has been in place since 1979. An elaboration of the assessment system is found in the Civil Service Law (2005). For an English translation of the law, see www.china.org.cn/english/government/207298.htm. Further assessments are carried out when a cadre is being assessed for promotion.

9. For a detailed treatment of public propaganda in Tibetan areas see the following chapter by Antonio Terrone.

10. As a major source of Tibetan cultural identity, as a competing source of legitimacy and authority, and as an occasional vehicle for political mobilization, organized Tibetan Buddhism is widely perceived as the greatest potential threat to Communist Party rule in Tibetan areas.

11. There are exceptions to this rule. A number of Tibetan Buddhist monks have reputations for being explicitly pro–Communist Party or, at least, Communist Party–friendly. Such monks are often feted by officials and used as an example

of healthy ties between the Communist Party and Tibetan Buddhism. As I have argued elsewhere, monks are also able to exploit such ties to the benefit of their monasteries or their monastic faction. See Hillman 2005 and Hillman 2009.

12. An exception to this general rule is Deqen TAP, where there are fewer restrictions on ethnic Tibetan officials. Local officials regularly visit the monastery and are frequently seen in the company of monks.

13. Interview with Ngaba Prefecture official Chengdu, March 13, 2013.

14. The Tibetan language is used as the medium of instruction in schools at all levels, from elementary school to university. Each Tibetan region determines where such schools will be offered as an alternative to Chinese-language medium education. Since 2008, however, the building of new Tibetan-language schools has been stopped. My interviews uncovered increasing frustration among Tibetans educated in Tibetan-language medium schools over the lack of career opportunities available to them in Chinese society. Opportunities for graduates of Tibetan programs are generally limited to the professions of teaching in Tibetan-language schools or Tibetan medicine.

15. As I pointed out in my introduction, the recent and tragic series of self-immolations has been blamed on "the shameless brutality of the 'Dalai clique' as the organizer and author of these crimes" (Yeshi 2013).

16. The exception, of course, is when foreign visitors are guests of the local government, such as technical experts working on government programs.

17. Interviews with local officials in Deqen, Yunnan, and Kardze, Sichuan, July 2012; see also Hillman 2014b.

18. Students of Chinese politics have noted how local officials tend to focus their energies on demonstrable hard-target achievements at the expense of other policies. See O'Brien and Li 1999.

19. Public finance specialists have observed how economic growth targets have driven cash-strapped local governments to borrow excessively from state banks. When the central government introduced rules to limit reckless borrowing by local governments, local governments created new financial vehicles, such as investment companies, to circumvent the regulations.

20. On the consequences for social equality of infrastructure-led development see Hillman 2008a.

21. On the challenge of inclusive growth in Tibetan areas see Fischer 2005; and Hillman 2008b. On economic inequality and marginalization in Xinjiang see the chapters by Tyler Harlan and Tom Cliff in this volume.

22. See Tom Cliff's chapter in this volume, as well as Cliff 2013.

23. In recent years teachers' salaries have been increased in order to attract better teachers to Tibetan areas. In Kantze TAP teachers are paid a generous "altitude allowance" (*gaoyuan buzhu*), which increases with altitude. Schools are also inspected more frequently to make sure teachers are actually giving classes. In Deqen TAP, families who send children to school are given an allowance of

RMB 700 per child per year. Deqen is also increasing the number of hours of Tibetan-language education at Chinese-language elementary schools. These are progressive developments for basic education, but they do not address fundamental educational challenges in Tibetan areas—namely, the poor correlation between formal education and employment opportunities.

24. Prior to 1998 commercial forestry was the main source of local tax revenue for Tibetan-area local governments, especially local governments in eastern Tibet.

25. Interview with Ngaba County official, March 2013.

26. A recent study of local government behavior in Beijing similarly demonstrated that the formal assessment system encouraged officials to overinvest in urbanization-related construction and underinvest in environmental protection schemes; see Wu et al. 2013.

27. Three main types of fiscal transfers are available to local governments in China. Tax return transfers (*shuihou fanhuan buzhu*) provide local governments with 30 percent of any increase in locally collected value-added tax (VAT) above a 1993 baseline. General transfers (*cailixing buzhu*) are redistributive transfers that are mostly provided to cash-strapped local governments in rural areas, including to all Tibetan-area local governments. General transfers include operating expenses for poor counties and ethnic minority counties, funds for wage adjustments, rewards for high-performing county governments, and subsidies to support rural tax-for-fee reforms. Special-purpose funds are additional transfers provided mainly to impoverished counties and ethnic autonomous regions. The National Development and Reform Commission (NDRC) is a key source of special-purpose funds. NDRC funds typically fund large public-works projects such as road and dam construction and irrigation. (The NDRC was formerly known as the State Planning Commission and as the State Development Planning Commission.)

28. In 2011 there were approximately 180,000 mass incidents in China. Drawing on 2012 data China's *Legal Daily* published a report in January 2013 summarizing the nature of mass incidents. According to the report, 8.9 percent of incidents involved ethnic conflict, 13.3 percent involved conflict between people and state officials, and 22.3 percent involved conflicts between people and the police.

29. One official told me that since 2008 local party secretaries and government executives have been told that all they need to do is maintain stability: "Forget about everything else."

30. Prior to c. 2005 average tenure for leading cadre positions was only three years.

31. Since 2012 an unwritten rule prevents Tibetans from outside the Tibet Autonomous Region (TAR) from traveling to the TAR. The rule is not propagated anywhere, but Tibetans know they will be turned back if they attempt to travel there. Han Chinese are allowed to travel back and forth as they please. The rule

is part of efforts to prevent translocal interactions between disaffected groups. It is a divide-and-rule tactic used by the CCP in other parts of the country such as in farmers' protests. Localized protests are tolerated as a valve for letting off steam, but there is zero tolerance for associations that unite and coordinate people from different localities, which is evident, for example, in the CCP's response to Falungong activities in years past.

32. Five teachers from a Tibetan-language high school in Ngaba TAP were jailed for terms of one to three years for various "offences," including giving one student a publicly available Tibetan-language history of the region written by the chief of the People's Court in Qinghai Province and for "allowing" a student to write a reflective essay on the unrest in 2008 and to print copies for other students. I personally know other Tibetans who were jailed for sending text messages to friends that relayed information about how protests were unfolding.

33. Anticorruption agencies such as the Discipline Inspection Commission have no independent authority because they answer to the party secretary at each level. The party secretary must approve all investigations into officials above a certain rank.

34. The primary influences on leading cadre appointments are the party secretary and members of the party Standing Committee at each level of government. In most parts of China the Standing Committee has five, seven, or nine members. In Tibetan areas there are thirteen members, a decision made at a time when a majority of Tibetan-area officials were dispatched from other regions. It was assumed that any time, half the members of the Standing Committee would be resting from their high altitude duties.

35. On the new Tibetan aristocracy see Gongmeng 2008.

36. For studies of official corruption in China see Lü 1999; Yan 2004; and Wedeman 2012.

## References

Barnett, Robert. 2009. "The Tibet Protests of Spring 2008: Conflict Between the Nation and the State." *China Perspectives*, no. 3, 6–23.

China Statistical Yearbook. 2014. www.stats.gov.cn/tjsj/ndsj/2014/indexeh.htm.

Cliff, Tom. 2013. "Peripheral Urbanism: Making History on China's Northwest Frontier." In "The Urbanisation of Rural China," edited by Ben Hillman and Jonathan Unger. Special issue, *China Perspectives*, no. 3, 13–23.

Danwei. 2013. "Legal Daily Report on Mass Incidents in China in 2012." Jan. 6. www.danwei.com/a-report-on-mass-incidents-in-china-in-2012/.

Fischer, Andrew Martin. 2005. *State Growth and Social Exclusion in Tibet: Challenges of Recent Economic Growth*. Copenhagen: NIAS Press.

Gongmeng. 2008. "Investigative Report into the Social and Economic Causes of the 3.14 Incident in Tibetan Areas." Gongmeng Law Research Center, Beijing University.   http://blog.foolsmountain.com/2009/06/02/an-investigative-report -into-the-social-and-economic-causes-of-the-314-incident-in-tibetan-areas/ all/1/.

Hillman, Ben. 2005. "Monasticism and the Local State: Autonomy and Authority in a Tibetan Prefecture." *China Journal* 54:22–52.

——. 2008a. "Money Can't Buy Tibetans' Love." *Far Eastern Economic Review* 171 (3): 8–16.

——. 2008b. "Rethinking China's Tibet Policy." *The Asia-Pacific Journal: Japan Focus.* http://japanfocus.org/-ben-hillman/2773/article.html.

——. 2009. "Ethnic Tourism and Ethnic Politics in Tibetan China." *Harvard Asia Pacific Review* 10 (1): 3–6.

——. 2010a. "Factions and Spoils: Examining Local State Behavior in China." *China Journal* 62:1–18.

——. 2010b. "China's Many Tibets." *Asian Ethnicity* 11 (2): 269–77.

——. 2013. "The Causes and Consequences of Rapid Urbanisation in an Ethnically Diverse Region." In "The Urbanisation of Rural China," edited by Ben Hillman and Jonathan Unger. Special issue, *China Perspectives*, no. 3, 25–32.

——. 2014a. *Patronage and Power: Local State Networks and Party-State Resilience in Rural China*. Stanford: Stanford University Press.

——. 2014b. "Unrest in Tibet: Interpreting the Post-2008 Wave of Protest and Conflict." *Dalny Vychod* [Far East] 4 (1): 50–60.

Horowitz, Donald L. 2000. *Ethnic Groups in Conflict*. 2nd ed. Berkeley: University of California Press.

Lü Xiaobo. 1999. *Cadres and Corruption: The Organizational Involution of the Chinese Communist Party*. Stanford: Stanford University Press.

O'Brien, Kevin J., and Lianjiang Li. 1999. "Selective Policy Implementation in Rural China." *Comparative Politics* 31 (2): 167–86.

Shakya, Tsering. 2012. "Self-Immolation, the Changing Language of Protest in Tibet." *Revue d'études tibétaines* 25:19–39.

Wedeman, Andrew. 2012. *Double Paradox: Rapid Growth and Rising Corruption in China*. Ithaca, NY: Cornell University Press.

Wolff, Stefan. 2006. *Ethnic Conflict: A Global Perspective*. Oxford: Oxford University Press.

Wu Jing, Yongheng Deng, Jun Huang, Randall Morck, and Bernard Yeung. 2013. "Incentives and Outcomes: China's Environmental Policy." Working Paper 18754. National Bureau of Economic Research (Feb.).

Yan Sun. 2004. *Corruption and Market in Contemporary China*. Ithaca, NY: Cornell University Press.

Yeshi Dorje. 2013. "The Self-Immolation Plot: The 'Dalai Clique' Is Doomed to Failure." *China's Tibet* 24:22–25.

# 2

# Propaganda in the Public Square

## Communicating State Directives on Religion and Ethnicity to Uyghurs and Tibetans in Western China

Antonio Terrone

*Strengthen the progress of ethnic unity, advance the propagation of religious policy.*
—PUBLIC SIGN IN CENTRAL SQUARE, XINING, QINGHAI

This chapter analyzes political propaganda in Tibet and Xinjiang in the context of the recent wave of ethnic unrest.[1] By examining public propaganda in Tibetan and Uyghur areas, we can gain insights into the Chinese Communist Party's (CCP) political imperatives and policy priorities in the regions. Local citizens' reactions to the propaganda further illuminate the grievances that underlie increasing levels of unrest. Findings from this study suggest that although CCP propaganda is designed to promote interethnic harmony, by highlighting difference and inequality, offending cultural values, and interfering in religious practice, political propaganda can serve to exacerbate social discontent and ethnic tension.

Data for this study was gathered from public posters, billboards, slogans, and signs displayed on streets and university campuses in the Tibet Autonomous Region (TAR), Qinghai Province, and the Xinjiang Uyghur Autonomous Region (Xinjiang). Four towns provided data for the study: Lhasa, the provincial capital of the TAR; Xining, the provincial capital of Qinghai, where many ethnic Tibetans as well as Hui live; Urumqi, the provincial capital of Xinjiang; and the old Silk Road town of Kashgar in eastern

Xinjiang. Since 2008 all of these cities have experienced various forms of unrest allegedly instigated by extremist Tibetan and Uyghur political activists, religious fundamentalists, or separatists. Additionally, these cities offer extensive evidence of large-scale state propaganda encouraging social harmony and admonishing unlawful political activism, religiously motivated violence, and "splittist" activities.[2] In addition to propaganda material in the form of street signs, posters, and billboards documented between 2009 and 2011 in China, my data also include information from interviews and conversations with ordinary Tibetans and Uyghurs, as well as with researchers living and working in the region.[3]

My analysis is informed by the notion of "thought management" that Anne-Marie Brady has applied to her analysis of propaganda in China (Brady 2012a). While "thought management" refers to the ideology behind China's policies, I suggest a companion term *praxis management* to help us understand how citizens are expected to comply with the state's directives in the practice of their daily life. The aim of this chapter is to show how policies on religion, social order, and ethnic harmony articulated in state-sanctioned propaganda billboards often come in the form of limitations and prohibitions, which fuel resentment among Tibetans and Uyghurs toward the state.

## Propaganda Posters in Western China

In China political propaganda appears in many forms. Among the most pervasive media used for propaganda purposes are billboards, banners, posters, and street signs.[4] The CCP has a long tradition of using such media to communicate state policies, ideologies, and political imperatives. Strategically placed propaganda posters characterize the urban "décor" of many Chinese cities and towns, but in areas with large ethnic minority populations (and much cultural and religious diversity) billboards and posters play a magnified role in publicizing "national unity" policy imperatives. In Uyghur and Tibetan areas propaganda slogans (*kouhao*) are a hallmark of the urban landscape. Posters and billboards celebrate economic development and progress and promote patriotism. They also proclaim the government's zero tolerance of any attempt to contradict the party, interfere with social stability, or disrupt China's territorial integrity.

Propaganda signs appear along streets, in public squares, and at intersections but also on college campuses, in apartment courtyards, religious institutions, official buildings, and often along the facade of buildings un- der construction. Frequently, posters, signs, and banners combine text with bright color backgrounds, graphics, and photos to attract the atten- tion of drivers, pedestrians, and casual observers alike. They tend to sum- marize and strategically condense in short phrases and slogans otherwise lengthy policy positions and narratives articulated via mainstream me- dia outlets. An important difference between propaganda in the national media and that communicated via billboards and posters is that whereas the former is aimed at immediate consumption, the latter is typically dis- played for long periods to maximize its impact. Furthermore, while pro- paganda in the news media is filtered and shaped by journalists, state pro- paganda in the streets comes directly from party officials, cadres, and the *nomenklatura* at the local level and is thus unmediated by the cosmetics of general news coverage.

Propaganda posters at colleges, temples, monasteries, mosques, and so forth reach out to large segments of the population with messages de- signed to deter unlawful or otherwise "incorrect" behaviors and activi- ties. Propaganda targeting Uyghur and Tibetan communities tends to deemphasize local traditional values, level cultural differences, disregard local concerns, and demonize the "enemy"—that is, proponents of sepa- ratism. My conversations with Tibetans and Uyghurs suggest that this rhetoric fuels local resentments and the potential for confrontation be- tween the state and the communities targeted by the propaganda. In the following section I examine the content of propaganda and local reactions. My analysis is organized around three key themes that appear repeatedly in public propaganda in the region: religion, separatism and terrorism in Xinjiang, and social harmony.

## RELIGION

Religion is a universal theme in the propaganda posters displayed in urban areas of both Xinjiang and the TAR that I observed between 2009 and 2011. Religion—Islam in the case of Uyghurs and Buddhism in the case of Ti- betans—is integral to Uyghurs' and Tibetans' cultural identity and is pro- foundly rooted in their cultural history. According to the Chinese Consti- tution, religious beliefs and activities are protected if they comply with a broad set of state regulations, support social harmony, and do not interfere with education.[5] However, organized religious activity and religious practices are tightly controlled and regulated by the state. Religious practice falls under the jurisdiction of the local religious affairs bureau (*zongjiao shiwuju*), which in some areas is a combined ethnic and religious affairs agency known as the Nationality and Religious Affairs Bureau (*minzu zongjiao shiwuju*) (Chan and Carlson 2005, 6–7). Ethnic minorities' religious activities are monitored and regulated in accordance with specific policies aimed at preventing any attempt to trigger social unrest, threaten China's territorial integrity, or disrupt national unity (State Council 1999).

The CCP leadership is aware that ethnicity and religion are closely intertwined in the histories and identities of several ethnic minorities. For many of these, religion constitutes a cohesive and nonnegotiable element of ethnic self-identification and cultural self-representation. In the summer of 2011 a propaganda display was set up in Central Square in Xining, the provincial capital of Qinghai. Several posters, signs, and banners communicated the central government's stance on ethnic and religious issues. The slogans read, "Strengthen the progress of ethnic unity, advance the propagation of religious policy" and "Patriotic education as principal ethnic religious policy." The slogans demonstrated that the notion of "religion" is an essential element in the government's articulation of cultural and political difference. In this regard the state continues to apply a "Marxist view" (*makesizhuyi de guan*) to the regulation of religion. For example, a Chinese-language public notice displayed in 2010 in Xining, Qinghai, read, "The Five Views of Marxism: the view of country, the view of nation, the view of religion, the view of culture, and the view of history."[6] This emphasis on the Marxist view of religion highlights the tension between the secular state and religious communities.

Students in Tibet and Xinjiang receive extra training in Marxism-Leninism-Mao Zedong Thought (Zhang and Hou 2010). Political propaganda aimed at students in China tends to emphasize "correct" attitudes toward religion, including that religion should be considered only as a personal interest. Students are reminded that public communications with religious content are forbidden without prior approval. They are also reminded that while the state protects their right to practice religion, the state also upholds the rights of those who do not practice religion. In a large poster located on the Xinjiang University campus in Urumqi, students were reminded that article 36 of the Chinese Constitution holds that "no state organ, public organization or individual may compel citizens to believe in, or not to believe in, any religion; nor may they discriminate against citizens who believe in, or do not believe in, any religion."[7] Non-believers are promised strong ideological support and protection, while religious practitioners are urged to adhere to the state's version of "normal" religious activities. Expression of patriotism, support for the power of the state, and a joint effort for ethnic unity and stability are preconditions in China for any religious institution, group, or organization to exist (Koesel 2014, 131; Saich 2011, 18).

On November 20, 2004, the State Council issued Decree 426, titled "Religious Affairs Provisions" (*zongjiao shiwu tiaoli*). After March 1 of the following year, when they became effective nationwide, these provisions were distributed by local propaganda departments and other state offices, such as the Public Security Bureau, in the form of pamphlets and billboards in both Chinese and local languages. The provisions detailed responsibilities of agencies in charge of controlling and administering religious activities such as the State Administration for Religious Affairs (SARA, *guojia zongjiao shiwuju*) and the Religious Affairs Bureau (RAB, *zongjiao shiwuju*), as well as registered religious organizations. Printed posters or pamphlets listing the 2004 provisions can still be found in many Buddhist monasteries and mosques in Uyghur and Tibetan inhabited areas of western China. Printed banners and flags marking the official visits of cadres and local authorities to promote the provisions adorn the guest rooms of many religious institutions. In the past decade, during campaigns to enforce the 2004 provisions, cadres would often pay visits to Buddhist monasteries, nunneries, churches, and mosques to distribute the propaganda products and to discuss their content with religious communities. Since 2004 the state has released several other documents that address religious affairs, including "Working Points for the National Religious Affairs Bureaus," published in 2011 (*guojia zongjiao shiwuju 2011 gongzuo yaodian*), specifically intended to further implement the regulations on religious affairs.[8] These regulations reiterate that control, administration, and supervision of all religious communities and their activities are the responsibility of the government.[9]

Religious propaganda is especially pervasive in urban areas such as Lhasa, where monasticism still characterizes the cultural texture of the Buddhist tradition, and monks are typically at the forefront of public expressions of discontent, including in nonviolent confrontations with local authorities. Following the 2008 violent riots in Lhasa and other Tibetan urban areas across western China, local officials displayed propaganda posters promoting patriotism and recommendations for a "safe" monastic life. These were displayed in monasteries and historical temples that were popular destinations for pilgrims. My interviews and conversations with local Tibetans, including Tibetan monks and laypeople, suggest that many consider such political propaganda an intrusion into their religious life and a reflection of state attempts to curb religious freedom.

At the same time public propaganda confirms that religion in Tibet can be socially beneficial and a lawful activity, as long as it is practiced "correctly." A bilingual Chinese and Tibetan language poster displayed in 2011 at Ramoché monastery, one of the oldest Buddhist centers in the historic center of Lhasa, pressed citizens to "support, according to the law, the administration of religious affairs and positively guide the mutual adaptation of religion and socialist society."[10] Exhortations of the link between patriotism and religious fervor appear frequently in the aftermath of public demonstrations and during official anniversaries. The ubiquitous slogan "Love the country and love religion, protect the country and benefit the people" reminds citizens that patriotism is a sine qua non of religious practice.

Posters and signs address not only religious practices but also the administrative affairs of religious institutions. New regulations such as those promoting the implementation of the "Tibetan Buddhist temple management approach" (zangchuan fojiao simiao guangli banfa) apply to nearly every Tibetan Buddhist monastery, nunnery, and religious institute. Additionally, the SARA regularly organizes workshops and seminars to train religious leaders in new regulations on monastery and temple management (simiao guanli) (SARA 2014). The new regulations, posted throughout monasteries, remind religious practitioners to conduct themselves "according to law, democratic governance and social management."[11] Propaganda posters continually remind devotees, visitors, and tourists of the presence of the state in religious buildings and monastic complexes. Often, the local Religious Affairs Bureau (RAB) and SARA offices require monasteries to print the "regulation system" (guizhang zhidu) specific to that monastery and display it next to the main entrance of assembly halls and in the vicinity of guest rooms. Numerous state decrees, including those concerning monastic financial management, maintenance of public order, and assembly hall security, are publicized in this way.

Another characteristic of propaganda posters is the format and the style of the language used. In many instances slogans tend to be short and metrically organized in verses of four or more characters. These are frequently arranged in lists of rules and regulations, such as the ubiquitous "eight honors and eight shames" (*ba rong ba chi*) and the "four protections" (*sige weihu*).[12] This structure is designed to facilitate reading and prompt memorization. At the entrance to the Jinta Temple in Xining, a Sino-Tibetan Buddhist temple that caters primarily to local urban Chinese Buddhist devotees, various painted slogans and rules cover both walls of the hallway opening into the courtyard. These include "monastic discipline rules" that require monks to "respect the constitution and the law, carry out related patriotic and religious policies, uphold the dignity of the law, protect the interests of the people, protect ethnic unity, and protect territorial integrity."[13] Thus, the sacredness of the religious space, once rigorously devoted to monastic education and ritual practice, is now also a channel to disseminate political information. As a Tibetan Buddhist monk from Drepung monastery near Lhasa told me in a visit in 2009, "Nowadays politics is everywhere [in the monastery]. If once we had religion and [Tibetan] politics, now we have religion and Chinese Communism!" My research findings suggest that Tibetan monks' frustrations at such interventions in monastic life are a major trigger of unrest. Many of the street protests that have taken place since 2008 began with demonstrations by monks against state policies toward monastic life and organized Tibetan Buddhism. In many instances ordinary people joined the protests, especially when monks were arrested by police or when local citizens perceived that monks were being mistreated by the police (Hillman 2014). This can be appreciated also in the more recent events of self-immolations as suicides, which started within monastic circles and later expanded to the civilian population (Terrone 2014a, 2014b).[14]

If we consider some of the examples discussed above, it appears that the ultimate goal behind much of the public propaganda in Tibet and Xinjiang is the promotion of a secular society where the expression of religious identity is confined to local ethnic contexts. Although the Chinese constitution guarantees protection of lawful and normal religious beliefs and activities, the central government and its local branches discourage any public display of symbols and signs of religious fervor. This is particularly true for employees in the government and public sector, as well as college students and professors (*Taipei Times* 2014). The Chinese state considers this measure a rightful approach to limiting expressions of religiosity that would otherwise conflict with the Chinese state's commitment to atheism and the equal protection of the rights of both religious and non-religious citizens. Some of the propaganda announcements specifically list prohibitions and legal or disciplinary repercussions for those individuals who disregard the regulations by carrying religious items such as prayer beads and by wearing headscarves, beards, or Muslim hats in public institutions, government buildings, and offices, as well as schools (Reuters 2014). Of particular concern for Chinese authorities seems to be the exhibition of religious markers (*zongjiao biaozhi*) of ethnic identity. The "Provisional Regulations Concerning the Prohibition of Any Kind of Religious Activity and Religious-Hinting Actions Within Xinjiang University" detail that "it is prohibited for students to wear religious attires and carry religious symbols." The regulations further state that "all students wearing religious clothes and symbols will be forbidden from entering classrooms, libraries, and other places of learning."[15] The regulations also warn that ignoring directives regarding the display of religious insignia might prompt disciplinary measures. Several young Uyghur college students I spoke with in the fall of 2011 indicated they felt threatened by the state's intrusion on campus life in the form of propaganda, political study, and the presence of undercover informants. Some students expressed resentment at the bans on Islamic dress, including headscarves for women and the *doppa*—the traditional Uyghur hat—for men.

## SEPARATISM AND TERRORISM IN XINJIANG

Unlike Tibetan areas in China, Xinjiang has been the source of increasingly violent and deadly terror attacks organized by groups and individuals inspired by extremist ideology. Independent and critical assessments of the events are difficult to achieve. Official Chinese media reports typically attribute these riots and attacks to various brands of fundamentalist Islam including the East Turkistan Islamic Movement (ETIM). Terrorist attacks attributed to Islamic radicals have targeted state institutions and offices such as police stations and government buildings, as well as ordinary citizens (*China Daily* 2014a, 2014b). More recently attacks have spread from Uyghur urban areas to other parts of China.[16] These attacks are of great concern to Chinese authorities and to Chinese citizens obviously worried about the rise of violent and terrorist attacks in their country (Zhao 2007, 1). However, a number of scholars outside China have observed that such concerns underline a tendency within China to apply the "terrorist" label to all forms of ethnic protest (Economy 2013; Roberts 2013; Cook 2013; and Hillman, this volume). State propaganda confirms that authorities make insufficient distinction between antistate terrorism and everyday protest against state policies (*Wall Street Journal* 2013). This delegitimizes and, in some cases, criminalizes ethnic protests, which further fuels resentments and undermines the CCP's nation-building efforts in Xinjiang and Tibet.

Similarly, in the case of Tibetan discontent, state propaganda frequently associates various forms of ethnic protest and unsanctioned expressions of religious fervor with separatism and hostile forces led by the Dalai Lama and Tibetan exile groups. What is increasingly evident in the propaganda material about religion and ethnic harmony in western China is the link between domestic insurgency (and "terrorist" violence) and hostile forces intent on weakening China and "splitting" the motherland. In both Tibetan and Uyghur cases episodes of self-immolation and urban violence are rarely attributed to local Tibetans or Uyghurs alone (Terrone 2014b). In other words there is an implicit conviction in Chinese official rhetoric that protests and discontent are instigated by outside forces aimed at destabilizing the country.[17] The group most commonly blamed for instigating unrest among Tibetans in China is the so-called "Dalai clique"—a term that refers to the Dalai Lama and his affiliates in India and supporters in the West.[18] Since the 2008 violent uprising in Lhasa and many other Tibetan areas of western China, billboards and posters calling for "a common fight for unity and joint prosperous development for all ethnic minorities" and a "strengthening of ethnic unity and a joint construction of a prosperous Lhasa" have been erected in several areas in downtown Lhasa. According to a poster titled "Important Tasks in Constructing a Safe Tibet," displayed in 2011 in the courtyard of Ramoché monastery in Lhasa, one of the five resolutions for building a safe Tibet is "to uphold the work for a stable situation, thoroughly develop opposition to separatist struggle, and uphold national safety and social stability." By exhibiting such propaganda and regulations in a monastic environment, the state makes a clear link between religious activities and ethnic separatist intent. And this message is not lost on Tibetan Buddhist clergy, as many report deep offense at such intrusions into their places of worship and religious devotion.

In the decades since the end of the Cultural Revolution in the late 1970s, the relative thaw in prohibitions against religious practices among ethnic minorities fueled the emergence of nationalistic sentiments and separatist interests among sections of the Uyghur and Tibetan communities, seemingly more so than among other ethnic groups in the PRC. However, following the al-Qaeda-backed terrorist attacks on the World Trade Center in the United States in 2001 and the subsequent launch of the Global War on Terrorism or "war on terror" by then-US president George W. Bush, China reframed its own struggle against domestic separatism as part of that war (Chung 2002). Since that time, the PRC's propaganda machine has consistently used the language of terrorism to describe Uyghur unrest. In a public statement reproduced in a poster displayed at Xinjiang University in September 2011 titled "Secretary Zhang Chunxian's Speech at the Ninth Section of the Seventh General Committee Meeting of the Autonomous Regions Party Committee (Summary)," Zhang Chunxian, party secretary of Xinjiang since 2010, announced that to maintain harmony in Xinjiang, it is necessary to crack down on "three fronts" (sanfu shili): separatist activities (fenlie huodong), terrorism (baoli kongbu), and religious extremism (zongjiao jiduan). The "three fronts" narrative articulates China's own version of the "war on terror" and strategically justifies its commitment to bringing restive Uyghurs under control. Regional secretary of the Xinjiang committee of the CCP since 2010 and newly appointed Political Bureau member of the eighteenth CCP Central Committee, Zhang Chunxian thus launched a vigorous campaign against the "three fronts." The same poster provided this additional quote from Secretary Zhang: "We must cater to new circumstances, research new features, and keep as a current goal a resolute curbing of the ongoing emergence of violent terrorist cases, a resolute curbing of large incidents of collective nature that violent terrorism triggers, and keep a high-level crackdown on terrorists' crimes."

Party cadres are encouraged to take an active role in administration, to engage with the people, and specifically "to resolutely prevent unlawful religious activities, and resolutely crackdown on the use of religion to instigate and carry out terrorist activities." These directives converge in the often overstated, albeit contested, goals of classic patriotic propaganda slogans such as "love your motherland with ardor and build a beautiful homeland," and "uphold the efficiency of Xinjiang, develop Xinjiang civility," which are among the most ubiquitous public slogans found in Uyghur areas.

CCP attitudes toward Uyghur unrest are related to oft-stated concerns that organized Islam in Xinjiang has close links to separatist organizations outside China, such as ETIM (Xinhua 2013). One such poster articulating this concern was displayed at Xinjiang University. Entitled "'The Three Fronts' Are the Greatest Threat to the Fundamental Interests of National Security and the People of All Nationalities," the poster advised "in Xinjiang, although each of the 'three fronts' has its own characteristics, nevertheless [they all] equally hold the reactionary flag of 'East Turkestan Independence.'"[19] The same poster continued to assert that "'Pan-Islamism' (fan yisilanzhuyi) is their religious vision; 'pan-Turkestanism' is their ethnic vision; the 'theory of East Turkestan Independence' is their nationalist vision; the fabrication and distortion of historical idealism is their vision of history; a 'theory of common Turkic culture' is their cultural vision; and opposition to the Chinese Communist Party and its guiding socialism is their political vision."

Xinjiang party secretary Zhang Chunxian's narrative of the three fronts as "problems" for economic stability in Xinjiang concretizes them as entities in their own right with an internal structure and a defined objective. They are represented as possessing "political spirit, organizational spirit, deception, and ruthlessness." "Political and organizational spirit" signifies terrorists' intent to harm national unity, split the country, and establish a theocratic rule through merging religion and politics. In this discourse religion and ethnicity become charged with deception (qipian) and ruthlessness (canren). In this regard the poster read: "Their [the Three Fronts' terrorists] deception manifests in their constant use of the banners of 'ethnicity' and 'religion.' Giving themselves the air of representing 'ethnic interests,' domestically they deceive the masses while abroad they deceive international public opinion, thus they possess a very strong deceptive and instigative nature. Their ruthlessness manifests by using bomb attacks, assassinations, arsons, throwing poison, and other terrorist means in the name of holy war (shengzhan)."

Although this rhetoric refers to a small minority of violent Uyghurs, such statements often offend law-abiding Uyghurs who are concerned not with holy war but with preserving their religious and ethnic distinctiveness within China. The vast majority of Uyghurs are moderate Muslims who abhor the violence perpetrated by extremists in the name of religion or nation.

## SOCIAL HARMONY CONFUCIAN STYLE

Another recurring motif in propaganda posters aimed at Uyghur and Tibetan populations is the maintenance of "harmonious socialist well-being" (*hexie shehui zhuyi de xiaokang*). Inspired by the ideal of a harmonious and stable society elaborated in the Confucian classics, the socioeconomic principle of harmonious socialist society was revived by President Hu Jintao as part of his vision to accelerate China's scientific development (*kexue fazhang*). His scientific development concept aims at creating a humanistic society that enjoys social welfare, sustainable development, success, and harmony (*People's Daily* 2008). Despite the CCP's somewhat troubled relationship with Confucianism, several elements of its classic ideas have found new meaning in the contemporary Chinese sociopolitical landscape. This is especially evident in political propaganda that promotes New Confucianism, or "Confu-talk" as Valérie Niquet (2012) calls it, as a unifying ideology for the Chinese nation.

Political propaganda posters emphasize that multiethnic harmony, social stability, and territorial integrity are essential for the successful "development of the country and progress of society."[20] The strong emphasis on national unity underlines the Chinese leadership's claim that "all business flourishes, when political power brings human unity."[21] Without national unity, China's authorities claim, the country would be taken over by "social unrest, progress stagnation, and suffering for the people of all of China's 56 nationalities."[22] Hence, hundreds of patriotic slogans, propaganda posters, and colorful wall hangings adorn many Tibetan and Uyghur towns from Lhasa and Xining to Urumqi and Kashgar, proclaiming statements such as "Strengthening ethnic unity protects social stability"; "Strengthening ethnic unity [is a way] to build a harmonious society"; "We must uphold an unshakable protection of territorial integrity"; and "The collective creation of harmony lies in national cohesion." For many Tibetans and Uyghurs such slogans devalue ethnic difference and highlight majority Chinese distrust of their ethnic group. This distrust is reinforced by heightened security and discrimination, such as dedicated lines at airport security for Tibetans and Uyghurs (Hillman 2014). The idea of a unified Chinese nation also often appears to be one that embraces Uyghurs and Tibetans only under strict conditions. A poster in Xining in 2011 reflects the nationalist project behind this vision of ethnic unity: "The important meaning of strengthening national unity is to protect social stability and territorial integrity in the highest interest of every people of each nationality in the country. It affects the comprehensive construction of a prosperous society while shaping a harmonious socialist society and realizing the great revival of the Chinese nation."[23]

In contrast to the Maoist period, when Chinese society was explained exclusively through the lens of Marxism-Leninism in terms of socialist theory, the CCP's post-Maoist approach to national identity building seems to incorporate more and more traditional values often associated with Confucian ideals. Goals of national unity and social stability remain, but the methods and rhetorical tools used to advance these goals have been updated (Sun 2013; Qing 2013; Brady 2012b; Niquet 2012; Bell 2010). A manifestation of this new trend in China was the use of Confucian aphorisms and Confucius-inspired dance during the 2008 Olympic Games opening ceremony in Beijing. Another visible manifestation is the rise of "Confucius Institutes" around the world that promote Chinese language and culture, as well as projecting China's soft power in the context of international relations and politics (Cheng 2009; Brady 2012b, 57–75; Kurlantzick 2007). The promotion of Confucian ideals in CCP propaganda and political discourse has been a focus of recent scholarship (Brady 2012b). However, the impact of this rhetoric on non-Han Chinese citizens has not been systematically studied. While further research is needed to definitively test this hypothesis among Tibetan and Uyghurs in China, my preliminary findings suggest that the promotion of Han-centric political ideals exacerbates tension among Tibetans and Uyghurs, many of whom have expressed concern about their ability to preserve their ethnic distinctiveness and ways of life (Hillman 2014). These findings are consistent with the work by Hugh Forbes on multiethnic societies. His international comparative study finds that the acknowledging of ethnic difference is a major cause of prejudice and discrimination in multiethnic societies (Forbes 1997, 40).

Through its propaganda campaigns the Chinese state communicates rules and directives to its citizens. But the language used in state propaganda conveys much more than a sociopolitical narrative; it asserts the institutional presence of the state within local society. This is characterized by the sheer number of political boards and banners displayed throughout Chinese urban areas. In many instances, however, the language in propaganda materials reflects attitudes that many observers find discriminatory (Mackerras 2004, 221).[24] My interviews among Uyghurs and Tibetans suggest that such daily reminders of the ethnic pecking order are a major source of resentment—resentment that lies at the heart of the recent unrest. They also suggest that propaganda aimed at national unity and nation building often has the opposite effect: it leaves Uyghurs and Tibetans feeling like targeted outsiders. Discriminatory language in state propaganda can fuel resentment in its target audience. In my own experience among ethnic minorities in western China since 1997, particularly among Tibetans and Uyghurs, I have heard many complaints about the disdain they perceive in official propaganda.

Furthermore, my findings suggest that the language used on propaganda posters and billboards serves to distance Uyghurs and Tibetans from the state. "Propaganda-speak" is impersonal and "methodologically defines and categorizes thoughts and experiences" (Pennebaker 2011, 285). The formality of the language and the complexity of its structure and terminology aim to deter rather than encourage, enforce rather than suggest. Ji Fengyuan's (2004) discussion of "linguistic engineering" is instructive on this point. According to Ji, the state's manipulation of language has had a profound impact on citizens' ideas and beliefs. It has constituted the CCP's "attempt to remake people's minds by compelling them to participate in a totalizing discourse—a discourse that touched all aspects of reality and expressed a single worldview to the exclusion of all others. It required people to use the 'correct' revolutionary terms to say the 'correct' revolutionary things, emphasizing linguistic form as well as political content" (Ji 2004, 4). Developed under Mao Zedong, this form of language engineering and sociopolitical control through the medium of language was active in Deng Xiaoping's reform era in the early 1980s and can still be seen today. The CCP uses specific types of language to guarantee the transmission of "correct" ideology and political content among both party members and society as a whole. The various moral concepts, political slogans, and formulaic verses appearing in street signs and propaganda posters represent the CCP's goal of enforcing a specific worldview and engraining an unambiguous discourse in people's daily lives. The "three fronts" (*sanfu shili*) campaign can be seen as an example of this type of linguistic strategy in which leaders' formulas become guiding paradigms and dominant discourses. However, the effectiveness of such language in promoting national unity among Uyghurs and Tibetans is debatable. Indeed, the Han chauvinism, moral patronization, and intolerance of difference inherent in the language of official propaganda serve to highlight the concerns of many Uyghurs and Tibetans for the future of their ethnic distinctiveness and unique cultural heritage.

---

The ubiquity of propaganda posters and billboards throughout Tibetan and Uyghur areas suggests that China's leaders consider such communication tools to be an effective part of political efforts to win the hearts and minds of the country's ethnic minorities. Despite the advancement in technology, communication, and media marketing, China's authorities remain committed to Maoist-era forms of political communication. One reason for continuing to exhibit propaganda posters is the enormous number of people who are regularly exposed to them. The state can be sure that its political ideology and its imperatives are publicly and continually visible. Unlike news outlets and the media, whose audience must choose to seek out, purchase, and listen to its short-term messages, nothing can match the immediacy, ubiquity, and duration of posters and banners. In the already tense areas of western China, however, my research suggests that propaganda targeting ethnic and religious identities undermines China's nation-building efforts.

Whereas public propaganda in other parts of China communicates general policy imperatives, in Uyghur and Tibetan areas it focuses predominantly on religion and ethnicity. The emphasis reflects the state's overriding concerns about social instability in these regions. But by serving to highlight ethnic difference and inequality, such propaganda has become a cause as well as a symptom of ethnic tensions in the region.

## Notes

1. I am indebted to many people for this chapter, some of whom cannot be named herein. Several Tibetans and Uyghurs in China have over many years helped me understand their relationship with the Chinese state and have patiently an-

swered my questions. I also want to express my gratitude to Gulnisa Nazarova, who kindly helped me refine some of the translations from Uyghur contained in this chapter. I would also like to thank Thomas Cliff and Robert Barnett for reading an earlier version of this chapter and for offering valuable comments.

2. See, for instance, the recent cases of Gartsé Jikmé, a young Tibetan Buddhist monk arrested in May 2013 and sentenced to jail for five years for writing a short book on self-immolations titled *Chinese Government and Tibetan Self-Immolations*; and the high-profile case of Ilham Tohti, a prominent Uyghur scholar and university professor who was sentenced in 2013 to life in prison for allegedly inciting separatism. On Gartsé Jikmé's arrest see TCHRD 2013b; on Ilham Tohti see Wong 2014.

3. My ethnic Tibetan and Uyghur interviewees included monks, shopkeepers, taxi drivers, restaurant owners, hotel managers, university professors, academic researchers, bookshop owners, and a number of students. All the names of my informants related to this study have been purposely omitted to honor their request of anonymity.

4. *Merriam-Webster's* defines *propaganda* as "the spreading of ideas, information, or rumor for the purpose of helping or injuring an institution, a cause, or a person" and also "ideas, facts, or allegations spread deliberately to further one's cause or to damage an opposing cause" (*Merriam-Webster's Collegiate Dictionary*, 11th ed., s.v. "propaganda"). Willcox (2005) defines propaganda as "the conscious or unconscious attempt by the propagandist to advance their cause through the manipulation of the opinion, perception and behavior of a targeted group" (17).

5. For a White Paper on religion in the PRC see Ch. II ("The Fundamental Rights and Duties of Citizens"), Article 36, in the Constitution of the People's Republic of China (adopted on Dec. 4, 1982), http://english.people.com.cn/constitution/constitution.html.

6. All the primary source materials used for this study, namely Chinese posters, signs, billboards, and slogans, were publicly displayed and accessible to the public and were photographed by the author during numerous field trips to Tibetan and Uyghur inhabited areas of the TAR, Qinghai, Sichuan, and Xinjiang provinces between 2009 and 2011.

7. "Students should not engage in any religious activities" (poster on campus of the Xinjiang University, Urumqi, Xinjiang, Sept. 2011).

8. For the Chinese version of this document see China's State Administration for Religious Affairs (SARA) website: www.sara.gov.cn/xwzx/xwjj/7090.htm.

9. The full Chinese text of the "Provisions on Religious Affairs" (*Zongjiao shiwu tiaoli*) is available on the website of the State Administration of Religious Affairs of the People's Republic of China (www.sara.gov.cn/zcfg/xzfg/531.htm). For an English translation of the text see "Regulations on Religious Affairs" on the website of the US Congressional-Executive Commission on China (www.cecc.gov/resources/legal-provisions/regulations-on-religious-affairs).

10. Poster at Ramoché monastery, Lhasa TAR, August 2011.

11. "Working Points for the National Religious Affairs Bureaus," www.sara.gov.cn/xwzx/xwjj/7090.htm.

12. "The eight honors and the eight shames," also known as "the eight honors and the eight disgraces," slogan was launched by President Hu Jintao in 2006 to promote social morality among Chinese citizens. The Xinhua News Agency offers a translation in an article titled "CPC Promotes 'Core Value System' to Lay Moral Foundation for Social Harmony." The eight honors and shames are:

Love the country; do it no harm.
Serve the people; never betray them.
Follow science; discard superstition.
Be diligent; not indolent.
Be united, help each other; make no gains at other's expense.
Be honest and trustworthy; do not sacrifice ethics for profit.
Be disciplined and law-abiding, not chaotic and lawless.
Live plainly, work hard; do not wallow in luxuries and pleasures.

The four protections are "protect respectability for the law; protect the interests of people; protect national unity; and protect territorial integrity." The entire document can be seen at http://news3.xinhuanet.com/english/2006-10/18/content_5220576.htm.

13. "Regulation System of the Jinta Temple" (*Xining jintasi de guizhang zhidu*) poster at the entrance to the Jinta Buddhist temple in Xining (Sept. 2011).

14. For a detailed discussion of the self-immolations in Tibet see McGranahan and Litzinger (2012); and Buffetrille and Robin (2012).

15. Poster titled "Provisional Regulations Concerning the Prohibition of Any Kind of Religious Activity and Religious-Hinting Actions Within Xinjiang University" (Xinjiang University, Urumqi, Xinjiang, Sept. 2011).

16. Two of the most tragic incidents outside Xinjiang occurred in Beijing and Kunming. In the first case, on Oct. 28, 2013, a car of three apparently Uyghur people drove directly into a crowd of pedestrians practically in Tiananmen Square in Beijing bursting into flames and causing casualties (including the passengers) and several injuries among the bystanders (Wan 2013). The second episode occurred in the southwestern city of Kunming in Yunnan Province, where on March 1, 2014 approximately ten individuals suspected to be Uyghurs randomly attacked people at the railway station armed with long-bladed knives apparently leaving at least twenty-nine people dead and injuring 130 (*China Daily* 2014c).

17. See, e.g., "Self-Immolations in Tibet Manipulated: Tibetan Legislators," Xinhuanet.com, http://news.xinhuanet.com/english/china/2013-06/21/c_132474793.htm.

18. For more on the anti-self-immolation campaign launched by the Chinese government in 2013, see the India-based Tibetan Centre for Human Rights and

Democracy (TCHRD) report about a document reportedly published in the PRC in January 2013 titled *Zhenxi shenghuo zunshou shoufa* (Cherish life, abide by Law). This document purportedly addresses the self-immolations and the legal consequences for those instigating or supporting self-immolations (see also TCHRD 2013a).

19. "'The Three Fronts' Are the Greatest Threat to the Fundamental Interests of National Security and the People of All Nationalities." Poster on the Xinjiang University campus, Urumqi, Xinjiang, Sept. 2011.
20. "The Collective Creation of Harmony Lies in the Unity of Nationalities." Propaganda poster on display in Xining, Qinghai, Sept. 2011.
21. "The Collective Creation of Harmony Lies in the Unity of Nationalities." Public sign in Central Square, Xining, Qinghai, August 2011.
22. "The Collective Creation of Harmony Lies in the Unity of Nationalities." Propaganda poster on display in Xining, Qinghai, Sept. 2011.
23. "Strengthening National Unity Helps Create a Beautiful Future." Poster on display in Xining, Qinghai, Sept. 2011.
24. For a discussion on Han racism toward Uyghurs see Kaltman (2007); and Devonshire-Ellis (2009).

## References

Bell, Daniel A. 2010. *China's New Confucianism: Politics and Everyday Life in a Changing Society*. Princeton, NJ: Princeton University Press.

Brady, Anne-Marie, ed. 2012a. *China's Thought Management*. Abingdon, UK: Routledge.

——. 2012b. "State Confucianism, Chineseness, and the Tradition in CCP Propaganda." In Brady 2012a, 57–75.

Buffetrille, Katia, and Françoise Robin, eds. 2012. "Tibet Is Burning—Self-Immolation: Ritual or Political Protest?" Special issue, *Revue d'études tibétaines* 25 (Dec.).

Chan, Kim-Kwong, and Eric R. Carlson. 2005. *Religious Freedom in China: Policy, Administration, and Regulation: A Research Handbook*. Santa Barbara, CA: Institute for the Study of American Religion.

Cheng, Xiaohe. 2009. "Education: The Intellectual Base of China's Soft Power." In *Soft Power: China's Emerging Strategy in International Politics*, edited by Mingjiang Li, 103–23. Lanham, MD: Lexington Books.

*China Daily*. 2014a. "Deadly Terror Attacks 2011–2013." ChinaDaily.com.cn, March 2. www.chinadaily.com.cn/china/2014-03/02/content_17315492.htm.

——. 2014b. "China Fights Terrorism and Violent Attacks." ChinaDaily.com.cn, n.d. www.chinadaily.com.cn/china/2014crackdownterrorists/.

——. 2014c. "At Least 29 Dead, 130 Injured in Kunming Violence." ChinaDaily.com.cn, March 2. www.chinadaily.com.cn/china/2014-03/02/content_17315179.htm.

Chung, Chien-peng. 2002. "China's 'War on Terror': September 11 and Uighur Separatism." *Foreign Affairs*, July/August.

Cook, Sarah. 2013. "Be Skeptical of the Official Story on the Tiananmen Car Crash." *Freedom House*, Nov. 4. www.freedomhouse.org/blog/be-skeptical-official-story -tiananmen-car-crash#.

Devonshire-Ellis, Chris. 2009. "China's Minority Ethnic, Racism and Sensibility Issues." *China Briefing*, July 8. www.china-briefing.com/news/2009/07/08/chinas -minority-ethnic-racism-and-sensibility-issues.html.

Economy, Elizabeth C. 2013. "China's Xinjiang Problem." *CNN Global Public Square*, Nov. 5. http://globalpublicsquare.blogs.cnn.com/2013/11/05/chinas-xinjiang -problem/.

Forbes, Hugh D. 1997. *Ethnic Conflict: Commerce, Culture, and Contact Hypothesis.* New Haven, CT: Yale University Press.

Hillman, Ben. 2014. "Unrest in Tibet: Interpreting the Post-2008 Wave of Protest and Conflict." *Dalny Vychod* [Far East] 4 (1): 50–60.

Ji Fengyuan. 2004. *Linguistic Engineering: Language and Politics in Mao's China.* Honolulu: University of Hawai'i Press.

Kaltman, Blaine. 2007. *Under the Heel of the Dragon: Islam, Racism, Crime, and the Uighur in China.* Athens: Ohio University Press.

Koesel, Karrie J. 2014. *Religion and Authoritarianism: Cooperation, Conflict, and Consequences.* New York: Cambridge University Press.

Kurlantzick, Joshua. 2007. *Charm Offensive: How China's Soft Power Is Transforming the World.* New Haven, CT: Yale University Press.

Mackerras, Colin. 2004. "What Is China? Who Is Chinese? Han-Minority Relations, Legitimacy, and the State." In *State and Society in 21st-Century China: Crisis, Contention, and Legitimation*, edited by Peter Hays Gries and Stanley Rosen, 216–34. New York: Routledge Curzon.

McGranahan, Carole, and Ralph Litzinger, eds. 2012. "Self-Immolation as Protest in Tibet." *Cultural Anthropology Online*, April 9. http://culanth.org/fieldsights/ 93-self-immolation-as-protest-in-tibet.

Niquet, Valérie. 2012. "'Confu-talk: The Use of Confucian Concepts in Contemporary Chinese Foreign Policy." In Brady 2012a, 76–89.

Pennebaker, James W. 2011. *The Secret Life of Pronouns: What Our Words Say About Us.* New York: Bloomsbury.

*People's Daily*. 2008. "Scientific Development and Social Harmony." People's Daily Online, Oct. 31. http://english.peopledaily.com.cn/90002/91580/.

Qing, Jiang. 2013. *A Confucian Institutional Order: How China's Past Can Shape Its Political Future.* Princeton, NJ: Princeton University Press.

Reuters. 2014. "China Bans Beards, Veils from Xinjiang City's Buses in Security Bid." Oct. 2. www.reuters.com/article/2014/08/06/us-china-xinjiang-idUSKB N0G60AA20140806.

Roberts, Sean R. 2013. "Tiananmen Crash: Terrorism or Cry of Desperation?" *CNN*, Oct.31.http://edition.cnn.com/2013/10/31/opinion/china-tiananmen-uyghurs/.

Saich, Tony. 2011. *Governance and Politics of China.* Basingstoke: Palgrave Macmillan.

SARA (State Administration for Religious Affairs). 2014. "Guojia zongjiaoju juban zangchuan fojiao simiao guangli gongzuo yantaoban" (The State Administration for Religious Affairs Holds Workshop on Tibetan Buddhist Temple Management). www.sara.gov.cn/xwzx/tplb/170983.htm.

Sun, Anna. 2013. *Confucianism as a World Religion: Contested Histories and Contemporary Realities*. Princeton, NJ: Princeton University Press.

*Taipei Times*. 2014. "Xinjiang Schools Set to Discourage Religion at Home." Oct. 30. www.taipeitimes.com/News/world/print/2014/10/30/2003603274.

TCHRD (Tibetan Center for Human Rights and Democracy). 2013a. "Anti Self-Immolation Propaganda Now Part of China's 'Patriotic Education' Campaign." Feb. 8. www.tchrd.org/2013/02/anti-self-immolation-propaganda-now-part-of-chinas-patriotic-education-campaign/.

——. 2013b. "Tibetan Writer Sentenced to 5 Yrs in Prison for Writing Book on Self-Immolation." May 21. www.tchrd.org/2013/05/tibetan-writer-sentenced-to-5-yrs-in-prison-for-writing-book-on-self-immolation/.

Terrone, Antonio. 2014a. "Suicide Protesters in Eastern Tibet: The Shifting Story of a People's Tragedy." *Asia Pacific Memo*, June 6. www.asiapacificmemo.ca/suicide-protesters-eastern-tibet.

——. 2014b. "Burning for a Buddhist Cause in Tibet: Self-Immolations, Rationality, and the Issue of Terrorism." Paper read at the conference "Buddhism and Politics," organized by André Laliberté, University of British Columbia, June 6–7.

*Wall Street Journal*. 2013. "China's Desperate 'Terrorists': Human Rights Abuses in Xinjiang Create a Cycle of Violence." Nov. 4. http://online.wsj.com/articles/SB10001424052702303936904579177382991370134.

Wan, William. 2013. "Chinese Police Say Tiananmen Square Crash Was 'Premeditated, Violent, Terrorist Attack.'" *Washington Post*, Oct. 30. www.washingtonpost.com/world/asia_pacific/chinese-police-say-tiananmen-square-crash-was-premeditated-violent-terrorist-attack/2013/10/30/459e3e7e-4152-11e3-8b74-d89d714ca4dd_story.html.

Willcox, David R. 2005. *Propaganda, the Press and Conflict*. London: Routledge.

Wong, Edward. 2014. "China Sentences Uighur Scholar to Life." *New York Times*, Sept 23. www.nytimes.com/2014/09/24/world/asia/china-court-sentences-uighur-scholar-to-life-in-separatism-case.html.

Xinhua. 2013. "Investigations Reveal Details of Xinjiang Terror Attack." Xinhuanet.com, July 6. http://news.xinhuanet.com/english/indepth/2013-07/06/c_124966189.htm.

Zhang, Xinfeng, and Hou Liangjian, eds. 2010. *Mao zedong sixiang he zhongguo tese shehuizhuyi lilun tixi gailun*. Beijing: Gaodeng jiaoyu chubanshe.

Zhao Bing-zhi and Wang Xiu-mei. 2007. "Countermeasures Against Terrorism Through Criminal Justice in China." Paper presented at the "First World Conference of Penal Law: Penal Law in the XXIst Century," Guadalajara, Mexico, Nov. 18–23. www.penal.org/sites/default/files/files/Guadalajara-Zhao.pdf.

# 3

## Discussing Rights and Human Rights in Tibet

Françoise Robin

O n "askbodyig.org," a relatively new participatory online encyclopedia to which queries about any field of knowledge can be
sent in Tibetan language, someone asked on April 4, 2012: "Do
'human rights' refer to an ethical standard or is there another way to look
at them?"[1] A blogger going by the pseudonym of Sapuché replied on the
same day that human rights were the most crucial element of all rights,
and explained the Rooseveltian fourfold division (freedom of speech, of
religion, from want, and from fear).[2] I was very surprised to read this exchange because it is widely considered unsafe in the current Sino-Tibetan
environment to use publicly the term *human rights*. Discussion of this topic
and other sensitive issues such as the "Dalai Lama" or "independence"
is monopolized by Chinese state discourse and propaganda.[3] Thus, such
an exchange in the currently sensitive Sino-Tibetan context begs several
questions. Does it reflect a relaxed state of expression in Tibetan public
spaces today, or is it an exception that somehow escaped the scrutiny of
censorship? Another question immediately follows: if Tibetans in Tibet
nowadays do discuss human rights, in what terms do they do so, and how
often, and since when? How do they appropriate the human rights discourse, and what is their focus or angle of discussion? Do social networks
play a part in this ongoing discussion, and if so, which ones? This chapter
will look into the ambit of human rights discursive practices among Ti-

betans in post-2008 Tibet and will conclude by reflecting on the possible sources, reasons and consequences of this inflation in rights-discourse in Tibetan language.[4]

## "Rights" in Tibet until the 1950s

As is well known, Tibet was never colonized by a Western imperialist power. Although a British military expedition reached Lhasa in 1904, it did not wield any deep influence on the Tibetan political or cultural realm. Moreover, Westerners' access to central Tibet was severely controlled between the mid-nineteenth and mid-twentieth century, mainly as a result of Manchu imperial influence and, after 1911, of pressure from the conservative side of the Tibetan monastic population. Few intellectual exchanges on such political concepts as democracy, humanism, rule of law, and other Western political and social notions had a chance to flourish there.[5] As controversial Tibetan intellectual Zhogs dung (2009, 6) wrote in reference to pre-1950 Tibet, "under the system of 'religious and secular authority combined' . . . most people did not even know whether secular values like 'freedom,' 'equality,' 'rights' and 'democracy' were things to be eaten or drunk. . . . Freedom and equality, rights and democracy and so on are fundamentally political concepts, by no means comprehensible in a country with little sense of political, territorial or national awareness."[6]

Tellingly, pre-1980s Tibetan dictionaries yield little in the field of "rights": Jaeschke's Tibetan-English dictionary (1881), Desgodins's (1899), or Das's (1902) do not include *thob thang* or *khe dbang*—the two words that currently translate as "rights" in Tibetan.[7] Tharchin's English-Tibetan-Hindi dictionary (1965) has no entry at all for "rights." The pocket Tibetan dictionary *Dag yig gsar bsgrigs*, compiled from 1973 onward and published in 1979 in Xining, does include *thob thang* but not with the definition of "rights," and it has no entry for either *khe dbang* or *dbang cha*.

The first Tibetan dictionary where the term appears is Dge bshes Chos grags's 1949–57 Tibetan-Chinese dictionary, which features the entry *thob thang*, with the following translations: "1. privilege; 2. rights." Two hypotheses can be made here: Dge bshes Chos grags, a Mongolian monk, had a circle of friends in Lhasa who included the mostly lay, intellectual and reforming strata of Tibetan elite interested in new and Western political

ideas in the late 1930s and 1940s. Spom gda' tshang Rab dga', a Tibetan reformer, kept in his library in Tibet in the late 1940s such books as G. G. Wil-
son's *International Law* (1949), Stalin's *Problems of Leninism* (1946), and, above
all, Sun Yat-sen's *The Three Principles of the People* (*Sanmin Zhuyi*), an anno-
tated copy of which McGranahan (2005, 266) discovered in his library. Spom
gda' tshang Rab dga' declared he had himself translated the latter into Tibetan[8] and, in 1975, explained why: "the Sanmin Zhuyi was intended for
all peoples under the domination of foreigners, for all those who had been
deprived of human rights. But it was conceived especially for the Asians.
It is for this reason that I translated it. At that time, a lot of new ideas were
spreading in Tibet" (Stoddard 1985, 86). If it ever existed, this Tibetan version still remains to be seen. This does not mean that there was no early
Tibetan translation of the text: according to Jagou (2011, 169), "the ninth
Panchen Lama made a reference, in a letter from his Qinghai office to the
Mongolian and Tibetan Affairs Commission, to a Tibetan translation of the
'Three Principles of the People' undertaken by his Xining staff in 1929."
Tuttle (2005, 201–2) considers it to be the first Tibetan translation of that
text. British sources explored by Stoddard (1985, 87) also mention a trans-
lation by the influential Dge gshes Shes rab rgya mtsho (1884–1968), a bilingual Tibetan-Chinese edition "published by the Guomintang office . . .
several copies [of which] circulated in Lhasa in the following months."

In summary, *Sanmin Zhuyi* seems to have been translated in Tibetan before 1949 (although not in Tibet proper), before three other translations
were subsequently produced in Taiwan (Jagou 2011, 172). The work makes
frequent references to the term *rights*—I counted sixty-seven in the online English translation.[9] At roughly the same time as *Sanmin Zhuyi* was
circulating in eastern Tibet and Han China, the young communist "Ba" pa
Phun tshogs dbang rgyal (1922–2014) was discovering Lenin's *Concerning
a Nationality Right of Self-Determination*. In his memoirs, Ba recalls, he "was
especially impressed by Lenin's idea that individual nationalities should
have the *right to their own identity and freedom*" (Goldstein, Sherap, and
Siebenschuh 2004, 30; my emphasis). There is thus a possibility that the
term *rights*, translated as "*thob thang*," might have found its way into this
Tibetan dictionary as early as the late 1940s.

During the first three decades of the Chinese takeover (early 1950s to
late 1970s) there is no doubt that Tibetans raised in the new Maoist political and educational system did come across the concept of "rights" and as-

sociated terms. To begin with, the third article of the Seventeen-Point Plan (1951) reads in part: "The Tibetan people have the right of exercising national regional autonomy under the unified leadership of the Central People's Government." Here, *right* is translated as "*dbang cha*," which nowadays carries the meaning of "power" or "authority." This suggests that in 1951 today's favored terms *thob thang* or *khe dbang* were yet to gain currency.

The Chinese Constitution of 1954 was a turning point in many respects: not only did it show a departure from the more basic 1949 "Common Program,"[10] but its chapter 3, titled "Fundamental Rights and Duties of Citizens," enshrined and elaborated on the notion of rights, with eighteen articles dedicated to the term. We know that it was translated into Tibetan in the summer of 1954.[11] In her doctoral dissertation Lauran Hartley (2003, 70) wrote that during the course of this translation, "according to one account, more than 2,000 terms were individually discussed and standardized by the translation team, which included scholars from across the Tibetan region. At the same time, selected works of Chairman Mao were also translated. With subsequent translation ventures, the number of new terms soon grew to 4,000." The Chinese term *quanli*, used consistently throughout the Chinese text, might have been translated literally as *khe dbang* in Tibetan. It is indeed this term that is found in the Tibetan translation of the 1982 Constitution.[12]

## Rights Discourse in Exile

In March 1959 the Dalai Lama and his immediate entourage fled into exile in India followed by tens of thousands of Tibetans. They had hardly settled down and established their new government before their Foreign Affairs Department, then called *Spyi srid khang* (literally "House of Foreign Politics"),[13] translated into Tibetan the 1948 Universal Declaration of Human Rights (UDHR). Tibetan authorities might have been convinced of the importance of this task by lawyer-diplomat Ernest Gross, who apparently "advised the Tibetans to make a plea to the world community to protect human rights in Tibet" (Sobisch and Brox 2010, 168–69). This option was recommended over the claim for independence, which few countries were willing to support even then, given the fuzzy status of Tibet in the international arena. This insistence on human rights might have been reinforced by the fact that the International Commission of Jurists wrote two reports (1959, 1960) accusing China of genocide and making ample use of the notion of "rights" (Römer 2010, 183). Thus, the notion of human rights might have appeared as a promising and potent one to Tibetan authorities to put forward their case to the international community. In 1961 the Dalai Lama presented his "People's Constitution" (Dmangs gtso'i rtsa khrims), or "Future Constitution of Tibet" (Ma 'ongs Bod kyi rtsa khrims) to his fellow Tibetans in exile: this text introduced the key principles of a full-fledged constitution for a future Tibet (back in 1961 the prospect of a quick return to Tibet was considered realistic). In the preamble the Dalai Lama clearly writes that this short, six-page programmatic text is based on two sets of thinking: the Buddha's teachings, on the one hand, and the UDHR, on the other (Dalai Lama 1961, 60–61). Interestingly, he refers to the UDHR in his explanatory preamble as "'dzam gling rgyal spyi'i 'gro ba mi'i kun spyod thob thang gsal bsgrags"—literally "Declaration of the Morals and Rights of Humans in the International World." This would seem to indicate that, in 1961, the title of the UDHR was not yet firmly established in Tibetan. On the basis of this provisional "People's Constitution" a more thorough and definitive "Draft Constitution for Tibetans" was elaborated in 1963, in which the first articles include a commitment to adhering to UDHR principles—a commitment that was to be reaffirmed in the revised, second version of the Draft Constitution in 1991.[14] The first translation of the UDHR was reviewed in 1970 under the supervision of the Secretary of the Ministry of Foreign Affairs (phyi srid drung che) Bstan 'dzin don grub, and led to the publication of a small, bilingual handbook, aimed at promoting the awareness of this text among exile Tibetans. The UDHR in Tibetan bore then the title it retains today in exile—*Yongs khyab gsal bsgrags 'gro ba mi'i thob thang*—although we will see in the course of the present chapter that this formulation has been criticized by Zhogs dung.

In the 1970s, for a number of reasons that have been aptly described elsewhere (Römer 2010), Tibetans in exile came to realize that the case of Tibet stood extremely little chance of being discussed at the UN general assembly. At roughly the same time, human rights gained ground as a core component in international relations (and diplomacy), notably under Jimmy Carter's presidency of the United States (1977–81). Tibetans in exile accordingly shifted their action toward international grassroots associations, international representations, or NGOs, in the hope that they could relay their rights-oriented demands in the international sphere. For instance, the US-Tibet Committee, which was founded in 1977, explains on its website that its primary aim is to "further the Tibetan people's nonviolent struggle to restore independence to Tibet . . . [and] educate Americans on the occupation of Tibet, and to mobilize them into action against this injustice."[15] The Tibetan Women's Association was established in 1984, in a move to secure a Tibetan presence in international women-related institutions, thus compensating for their lack of representation in major international policy bodies (Römer 2010, 183–85). Directed primarily at international agencies, human-rights-oriented discourse percolated among youngsters in exile, finding its way into school curricula and in slogans shouted during demonstrations that Tibetans regularly hold in exile. In short, Tibetans in exile, government officials and governed alike, embraced, with little reservation, the concept of the universality of human rights and the plan to plead the case of human rights for Tibetans on the world scene.

On June 15, 1988, the Dalai Lama addressed members of the European Parliament, saying, "The whole of Tibet . . . should become a self-governing democratic political entity founded on law by agreement of the people for the common good and the protection of themselves and their environment, in association with the People's Republic of China."[16] This shift was obviously made in the hope of winning support from the Chinese Communist Party (CCP) after four years of stalemate in the Sino-Tibetan dialogue and in the wake of proindependence demonstrations in Lhasa in the previous year. The Dalai Lama's comments were interpreted as relinquishing independence in favor of autonomy within the PRC. But this entirely new proposal was met with silence from the Chinese government. As a consequence, in 1991 the Tibetan leader cancelled the Strasbourg Proposal and started advocating for what later became known as the "'Middle Way' approach." The Middle Way is inspired by Mahayana Buddhism's "Madhyamaka" (dbu ma), which refers to the avoidance of extreme views such as essentialism and nihilism. In the case of Tibet and politics it means neither independence nor complete assimilation within China. This radical departure from what had been a consistent, thirty-eight-year political demand, was not met with unanimous enthusiasm by Tibetan exiles; some interpreted it as an unacceptable compromise made to the CCP and PRC authorities. Still, Tibetans active on the international scene increasingly

framed their claims and grievances on the international arena in a depo-
liticized human-rights-oriented discourse, which did not contravene the
Dalai Lama's new approach.

## Rights Discourse in Tibetan: 1987–2008

From September 1987 to March 1989 Lhasa became a hotbed of ethnic and
political contest, recording around two hundred demonstrations, three of
which turned into riots (Barnett 2012, 52). These demonstrations are today remembered as part of a proindependence movement led mostly by
clerics and followed by laypeople from central Tibet. Slogans shouted on
the streets also included references to human rights and the right to self-
determination. For instance, on their release from prison in January 1988,
politicized Drepung Monastery monks who had taken part in the September 1987 demonstrations decided one of their first projects would be "to
print and distribute a Tibetan translation of the Universal Declaration of
Human Rights" (Schwartz 1994, 125). It is not clear whether this project was
actually implemented or whether the original text came from Dharamsala,
which is likely. Furthermore, a large demonstration was organized in Lhasa
on December 10, 1988, to coincide with the anniversary of the UDHR. Thus
in the late 1980s, while human rights discursive practices were already
well-established in exile in both lay and religious circles, young and old,
they were slowly gaining ground among Lhasa demonstrators, especially
among clerics. Can it be deduced that the exile government was the only
instrumental force in awakening fellow Tibetans to this concept, as suggested in the following accusation directed at Ngag dbang phul byung,
leader of the Drepung monks resistance movement? He was sentenced in
1990 to nineteen years in jail, accused, among other things, of "crimes . . .
[that] demonstrate that the so-called human rights, freedoms and democracy played up by the separatists both at home and abroad are nothing
but a pack of deceitful lies" (Schwartz 1994, 125). Ironically, information
about the UDHR and Human Rights Day had been provided by the Chinese
authorities themselves. According to Schwartz, the Chinese government
publicly acknowledged, for the first time, the existence of a Human Rights
Day on December 10, 1988, as the fortieth anniversary of the celebration
of the UDHR was under way (Schwartz 1994, 137). This acknowledgment

did not fall on deaf ears. One monk interviewed by Schwartz said, "We heard that December 10 was the fortieth anniversary of International Human Rights. This reminded us of our country. To encourage our people and to commemorate this day, we decided to hold a peaceful demonstration" (Schwartz 1994, 138). By trying to secure a legitimate presence on the world scene, through adhering to world political standards, China had also opened a Pandora's box.

In March 1989 the Chinese government decreed martial law in the Tibet Autonomous Region (TAR). In June the Tiananmen crackdown triggered international outrage. In December the Nobel Peace Prize was awarded to the Dalai Lama. These events made the prospect of celebrating Human Rights Day in Tibet and China even more remote and hardened China's stance on the international scene with regard to the Tibet problem. Still, Tibet aside, China's leaders could not entirely ignore the human rights question as they were regularly confronted with it in international talks in which they were increasingly participating. This prompted the release in 1991 of the *White Paper on Human Rights*, the first in a series of nine to date (the most recent edition was published in 2009). Specialists diverge in how to interpret this gesture: did the PRC only pay lip service to the international community, feeling compelled to include human rights in its external communication efforts, to reconcile with international expectations or, as Li Peng claimed, as a "response to Western hostile forces who were attacking China" (Foot 2000, 152)? Or did human-rights-related concepts and ideas slowly become palatable to the Chinese authorities, as Chen (2005) asserts? The fact remains that the PRC did begin to make frequent mention of human rights in its official rhetoric, leading to an amendment of the Constitution in 2004, to include a reference to the protection and safeguarding of human rights by the state (Chen 2005, 156), revealing the importance that Chinese leaders placed on their international image.

Tibetans in Tibet, between the mid-1990s and the 2008 Tibetan crisis, do not seem to have been involved in discussions about human rights. There has generally been no political writing in the TAR since the late 1980s, and Amdo (northeast Tibet) intellectuals, considered to be the most active thinkers in Tibet today, only started to become more prominent in intellectual exchanges since the 1990s. Interestingly, human rights does not seem to have been a burning issue until quite recently. The most convincing proof of this can be found in the work of one of Amdo's leading intellectuals, Zhogs dung. First, he admitted in his 2009 book that he had only discovered the Dharamsala Tibetan translation of the UDHR a few years before. Second, as late as December 2007 his views on human rights, published in the magazine *Dus rabs kyi nga* (The I of the century),[17] confirm his initial disinterest in the concept of human rights. This interview forms the last chapter of *Rigs shes kun grol* (Liberating reasoning consciousness), a collection of twelve articles and speeches by Zhogs dung. Under the title "Replies to the Questions of the Editor of the Magazine *The I of the Century*," this forty-page interview enables Zhogs dung to clarify the iconoclastic views of Buddhism that characterize his thinking (Zhogs dung [2008] 2010). I will not deal with these views in the present article but instead will focus on the beginning of the interview, where he develops his original views about human rights. As far as I can tell, the opening of this interview is the only part in his collection where he mentions human rights—another indication that human rights did not at that time play a central role in his thinking. In "Replies to the Questions of the Editor of the Magazine *The I of the Century*" Zhogs dung mentions human rights, using his own rendering of the term—*mi bu'i khe dbang* (rights of the individual), which he clarifies by adding in parentheses the more conventional Tibetan translation, *'gro ba mi'i thob thang*. This suggests that his neologism was not that widespread among Tibetan readers. I will return to this neologism below. In summary, Zhogs dung explained that rights can be divided into two kinds: the first group consists of outer (or external) freedoms (*phyi'i rang dbang*) and outer (or external) equalities (*phyi'i 'dra mnyam*): these are freedom of belief, of expression, of publication, and of meeting, and equality of individual life, of individual dignity, and of the individual right to possession. These correspond roughly to universal rights that are globally accepted among democratic countries. He contrasts them with the second group, which he calls "rights to freedom and equality of inner thoughts" (*nang bsam blo'i rang dbang dang 'dra mnyam gyi khe dbang*). By this he means the right to emancipate oneself from the influence of one's tradition in a given culture. Through this concept he aims at denouncing the moral pressure that he claims bears on Tibetans' minds: according to him, the burden of traditional thinking, predominantly religious, weighs so much on Tibetans that it prevents them not only from developing a clear understanding of basic ideas such as rights but also from developing independent thought. According to Zhogs dung, Tibetans' staunch faith in Buddhism, and in such key concepts as no-self, emptiness, and impermanence, mean that they cannot be open to the idea of the individual. Because of this, he continues, the idea of universal rights and freedoms based on a solid sense of the value of the individual cannot take root in Tibetan thinking. As a consequence, he concludes, Tibetans should struggle for inner rights more than for outer rights, since the development of the former is a prerequisite to the flourishing of the latter. In other words Tibetans must embrace secularism as a step prior to embracing global ideas such as human rights. Events in 2008 proved him wrong: ordinary (and hence highly religious) Tibetans came to the streets in masses to demand rights. This came as a shock to Zhogs dung (2009), he admits in the introduction to *The Demarcation of Sky and Earth*, written one year later. He consequently dropped prioritizing "inner rights" over "outer rights" and began focusing on human rights.

The situation in the Tibetan exile community in India was all the while totally different. In 1996 the Tibetan Center for Human Rights and Democracy was officially established, possibly as a response to the creation, in January 1993, of the state-sponsored China Society for the Study of Human Rights in the PRC. Like its Chinese counterpart, the Tibetan Center for Human Rights and Democracy has the status of an independent NGO, but it is well known that it emanates directly from the Tibetan government-in-exile.[18] This center has been extremely active since its inception, regularly publishing news, statements, and thematic briefs on different aspects of human rights issues in Tibet. It has published a thirty-one-page introduction to human rights in the Tibetan language, as well as a longer English version.[19] To my knowledge, most of the center's publications are in English, a point to which I will return in my conclusion.

## The 2008 Turn: Tibetans Discuss Rights in Books and on the Internet

While the Chinese authorities displayed a decreasing reluctance to discuss human rights on the international and national level, the anthropologist Mette Halskov Hansen, in her study of Han migrants in Amdo in the early 2000s, experienced a different story. The level of tolerance of human rights discourse, on the part of a foreigner at least, in relation to Tibet was still very low then. She writes: "I felt that in order to be able to pursue my research in Tibetan Xiahe, I had to agree to an *official request never directly to employ the concept of 'human rights' in publications describing the localities of my fieldwork* . . . because local officials were acutely aware of the potential negative local consequences of publications about their area employing *a concept so heavily loaded with political connotations*" (Hansen 2005, 13; my emphasis). This was taking place in the Tibetan Autonomous Prefecture of Kan lho (Ch. *Gannan*) in Gansu Province, a place far enough from Lhasa to be usually spared from the tense political atmosphere that reigned in the TAR. A rig 'Gyur med, a Tibetan from Amdo born in 1977 who fled into exile in the early 2000s, confirms that human rights, for him too, were not a widely discussed topic when he was still in Tibet. His short opinion piece on women's rights, published in exile in 2010, begins: "It is only after I reached exile that I finally became aware of human rights, women's rights, children's rights, and many other similar terms. I felt that these expressions were widespread and strong in the exile society" (A rig 'Gyur med 2010, 96). Of course, it could be surmised that while still in Tibet, he showed no interest for such topics. However, as someone who eventually left Tibet to undertake the long journey into exile, he was no doubt interested in politics before his departure and would have been exposed to human rights discourse had it existed. Moreover, he had been a monk for some time. This would indicate that at least some of the monastic community in Amdo had no serious grasp of the notion of human rights in the late 1990s. The plea by Zhogs dung in favor of secularism as a prerequisite to the dissemination of the concept of human rights, described above and written as late as 2007, tends to confirm this. Although it was a "hot topic" among politicized clerics in the Lhasa area in the late 1980s, it took years (perhaps as long as two decades) for the discussion about human rights to reach the increasingly active Amdo intellectual circles and to carve out a space for itself in the Tibetan-language public arena.

Can we generalize and surmise that, although talking about human rights might have felt less (and decreasingly) problematic overall in China since the early 1990s, and more and more innocuous for Han Chinese citizens in bigger Chinese cities, the picture was different for Tibetans? Not only did they apprehend belatedly the concept of human rights, but also it seems they felt excluded from the state rhetoric on this subject, of which they were increasingly becoming aware. Mgar mi, a Tibetan writer, wrote in 2008 that although the PRC government did handle such concepts as human rights, it did not guarantee equality to its citizens on that matter:

> Does the government not claim that "The *human rights* situation is in the best period ever known in the history of the Tibetan nationality"? Does it not claim that "You (the nationality) have the *legal right* to self-protection"? However, in this civilized era when world governments voluntarily respect human rights, *the improvement of human rights under the Socialist system may have happened somewhat for the Chinese people, but Tibetans living under constant bullying and oppression never get to even hear the words "human rights,"* and ultimately *legal rights* are only written on paper, and although we have tongues in our heads we do not have the power to speak out, indeed it is before the law that misfortune usually strikes us. (Garmi 2009, 101; my emphasis)[20]

This comment was written in reaction to the PRC authorities' crushing of the 2008 Tibetan uprising. Let us remember here that in the spring of 2008 a new generation of Tibetans took to the streets—this time not only in Lhasa but across the entire Tibetan Plateau, in contrast with the late 1980s political demonstrations.[21] Proindependence slogans did not completely disappear, but they came after other demands: appeals to the Chinese government to allow the Dalai Lama's return to Tibet, freedom (of an unspecified type) in Tibet, and truth about the disappeared Panchen Lama. The demand for equality of rights gained even greater visibility in 2010, 2011, and 2012, when a second wave of protests involved Tibetan students and teachers in Qinghai. They gathered to protest against announced reforms that could, in their view, lead to the eradication of Tibetan medium education in Qinghai middle schools (see Clémence Henry's chapter in this volume). Slogans written on their banners showed that their requests were based on the notion of equality (*'dra mnyam*) of rights for Tibetans in China. They also asked for democracy (*dmangs gtso*) and freedom (*rang dbang*). Finally, at least five Tibetan self-immolators in 2011 and 2012 referred to rights, or rather the lack thereof, in their testaments. Nangdrol, an eighteen-year-old Tibetan who self-immolated on February 19, 2012, is reported to have left a note stating that he resorted to self-immolation "because the pain of not enjoying *any basic human rights* is far greater than the pain of self-immolation."[22] Dgu grub, the only Tibetan considered an intellectual or writer to have committed self-immolation so far, also linked his desperate gesture to rights: "The CCP . . . arrested and tortured those who demand *rights* for Tibetans." He added: "His Holiness [the] Dalai Lama advocates for a non-violent middle-way policy for the *right to Tibetan autonomy*. Six million Tibetans have been following His Holiness' teaching. But the CCP shows no support. Instead, they *arrested and tortured those who demand Tibetans' rights*."[23] Mkha' dbyings and Chos 'phel, two former monks from Kirti Monastery, also reportedly cried for human rights and freedom at the time of dying, on October 7, 2011: "Tibet has no freedom, *we have no human rights!*"[24]

When Bsod nams (twenty-four years old) and Chos 'phags skyabs (twenty-five years old) self-immolated in 'Dzam thang (Sichuan Province) on April 19, 2012, they were reported to have shouted, before taking their own lives: "We self-immolated [*sic*] for our misery and *lack of basic human rights*, as well as for world peace. The suffering of Tibetans *deprived of basic human rights* is much greater than our self-immolation."[25] Clearly, the question of rights, and, more particularly, human rights, has become gradually integrated in discursive practices of Tibetan demonstrators today. In contrast with the situation in the 1980s, these concepts are now being discussed by young, lay intellectuals and even common people, and no longer only by monks. I will show below that such concepts are also being debated in Tibetan public fora by older and politically savvy Tibetans.

## Rights in Print and Onscreen

I will provide here a chronology of significant post-2008 public documents that I have found that include references and discussions about rights and human rights in Tibetan language. I will evaluate their mutual influence, as well as their importance in the evolving Tibetan intellectual landscape.

### MAGAZINES

To my knowledge the first important document to emphasize human rights is issue 21 of the magazine *Shar dung ri* (East Conch Mountain), published in June 2008 by a group of Tibetan students from the Northwest Nationalities University in Lanzhou. According to Woeser (2009, 20), it "contained nine articles relating to the incidents of March 2008." The magazine was soon banned, its editor and some contributors arrested, but circulation continued illegally, and some articles were translated into English. The articles at my disposal extol the importance of the respect of rights (along with freedom and democracy) and denounce the double standards applied to Tibetans with respect to individual rights. For instance, Don kho's (penname "Gnyan") text—"What Human Rights Do We Have over Our Bodies?"—condemns the repression by Chinese authorities during the 2008 unrest. His text is structured in eight parts and begins with "1. Have you ever heard that our land does not have the benefit of *human rights*?" He continues:

> The Tibetan people, without refuge or protector, without forces or allies, have risen up out of desperation, *for the cause of human rights. . . . Human rights* apply to the political, economic, social and cultural spheres; their essential characteristic is freedom and equality, and their basic nature and concern is human life and progress. Since people cannot live or progress as humans without freedom and equality, it is hardly worth saying that this is even truer of *human rights. . . .* We should recognize not only that *human rights* always and in all aspects are something we ourselves strive for, but that this struggle is for the benefit of tomorrow's generation, and that it is ensuring that tomorrow's generation can live a life dignified with *human rights*, freedom, equality and happiness that gives meaning to our present lives. (Nyen 2009; my emphasis)[26]

Sonpo ("Alive"), another writer who contributed an essay to the same journal, insisted for his part on different standards in terms of rights, depending on whether one belongs to the majority (Han) or to a minority nationality:

> Equality means equality of living standards, equality of spoken and written language, equality of rights, equality of opportunity, equality in all aspects of social life. Is there any such equality for the 56 nationalities in this country? I dare to say in a loud voice that there is not. Why? For a start, there is no equality of spoken and written language. The official language of government in a minority nationality region is not the language of that minority, so the minority people have less chance of work

and official positions than Han Chinese. With less opportunity, their rights are diminished, and with this inequality of rights, equality disappears. (Sonpo 2009, 76)

A piece by Blun po Smyug thogs (The fool holding a pen) titled "The Force of Truth Spreads Its Wings" also mentions the double standards Tibetans face in accessing rights (Lünpo Nyugtog 2009). *Shar dung ri* was soon shut down, highlighting official intolerance for such debates. In September 2008 another magazine, *Courage of the Emperor* (*Btsan po'i snying stobs*), was published by a monk-cum-writer called 'Gar rtse 'Jigs med. The magazine has been described on an exile Tibetan website as including articles about "the real situation inside Tibet today, that is the tragedy of the past, present and future of the Tibetan people who live under imperialism, oppression, bullying, discrimination. It is a small book that collects essays written in a clear manner about human rights, about the rights of nationality; there is also a diary of misery and oppression, and opinions about the way to fight for the Tibet question, among others. It includes eight texts and a legal text and some speeches about 'rights of life.' It covers ninety-four pages, including the editor's conclusion."[27]

Although I could not obtain this issue, 'Gar rtse 'Jigs med's introductory note has been reprinted on another exile website. I translate it in its entirety here:

> I have gathered here writings that illustrate the true mental suffering of 99 percent of the Tibetan people. I have used my own money to publish some writings that reveal this suffering. I had to accomplish this without taking into consideration the possibility, in the conditions of the dark surroundings *which do not abide by the law* and do not look into actual reality, of being imprisoned, or having to undergo torture and beatings, or even risking my life. The reason for doing so is that I am aspiring and hoping for genuine peace, devoid of strife (*zhe 'khon*) and quarrel. It is also because I am aspiring to and hoping for a genuine harmony devoid of bloody fight and struggle. At the time of publishing this book now, I have experienced all sorts of pain and I have cried so much, that my whole mind is drenched with tears.[28]

From both the summary and the editor's introduction, it is obvious that the questions of rule of law, rights, and human rights play a major role in his commitment to producing this magazine. In an English publication mentioning this book, 'Gar rtse 'Jigs med is quoted: "As a Tibetan, I will never give up the struggle for the *rights* of my people. As a religious person, I will never criticize the leader of my religion. As a writer, I am committed to the power of truth and actuality. This is the pledge I make to my fellow Tibetans with my own life" (Gartse Jigme 2009, 91).

*Courage of the Emperor* was censored and 'Gar rtse 'Jigs med, as he had foreseen, was arrested and reportedly tortured in April 2011. He launched a second issue of his magazine after his release, which resulted in his second arrest in 2013. He was subsequently sentenced to a five-year jail term.[29] According to an exile Tibetan website, this second issue of *Courage of the Emperor* included twenty-four articles, dealing mainly with the wave of self-immolations in Tibet, and ended with a strong plea for human rights: "In summary, until Tibetans obtain genuine *human rights*, I will definitely express thus my mental agony. If this does not work out, I will definitely express the Tibetan people's ordeals until my life is interrupted. But I cannot express these by holding guns or explosives, only by speaking out, holding my pen and my *khata* of fame."[30]

## ZHOGS DUNG'S BOOK, *THE DEMARCATION OF SKY AND EARTH*

Next came a controversial iconoclast-cum-nationalist writer and intellectual, Bkra rgyal (b. 1963), known to multitudes of readers as Zhogs dung (Morning Conch). We have seen above how his views on rights were very specific to his perception of the Tibetan environment, lamenting until 2007 the lack of "inner rights" for Tibetans. He is the leader of the "New Thinkers" school, greatly inspired by the May Fourth Movement in China in 1919. This group of radical, anticlerical intellectuals has been active since the late 1990s in Amdo and promotes the spread of such values and concepts as freedom, democracy, and science among Tibetans. The New Thinkers present such concepts as remedies to Tibet's current sorry situation and a counterweight to the centrality of religion in Tibetan culture and of Tibetans' love of tradition. The proponents of these views have a sizable following among students, and they form a visible and significant intellectual movement in Amdo today (Wu 2013). While Zhogs dung had long lamented in his essays the ascendancy of "old thinking" over Tibetans, and his main writings have strived to establish a link between strong religiosity, lack of national awareness, and the decline of Tibet, in 2009 he launched a strident appeal in favor of human rights in *The Demarcation of Sky and Earth*, which was published illegally. Although the essay failed to attract attention outside of Amdo circles, it was the major topic of conversation among young educated lay Amdowas in the summer of 2010, when I was doing fieldwork there. Most of them were curious to know if I had read the book, and they were eager to comment on it themselves, without my raising the topic. It had by then been confiscated from shops, Zhogs dung having been taken away to an unknown location and his privately run bookshop near the bus station in Xining locked up by the police. The book circulated all the while: many people kept a copy in a cupboard or in a drawer, and all seemed impressed both by the content and the boldness displayed by its author. This 250-page book helps us understand the shift in Tibetan liberal intellectuals' attitudes toward politics, and it shows a so far unseen maturity in independent, nonreligious, political thinking in Tibet.

It is divided into four parts: "Joy" is an appraisal of the 2008 Tibetan revolution, which Zhogs dung calls the "peaceful revolution of the Earth Rat year" or the "Tibetan saffron revolution," drawing parallels with the Jasmine revolution in the Arab world and the Saffron revolution in Burma. "Joy" is followed by "Sorrow," where Zhogs dung recalls the most violent episodes of the last six decades of Sino-Tibetan encounter, especially the 1950s to the 1970s and the 2008 quelling of the Tibetan uprising. The third chapter, "Fear," deals with his terror of both the nature of the Chinese autocratic regime and of the rise of ultranationalism among Han Chinese, as well as the foreseeable extreme reactions on the part of Tibetans and the inevitable catastrophe that this would entail for the latter. The fourth, and final, part of Zhogs dung's book introduces three related concepts that are familiar to Westerners but are undoubtedly new to Tibetans, at least in Tibetan language: beginning with "civil disobedience," and the right to exert it, he also explains in a didactic way the Gandhian concept of "Satyagraha," for which he suggests *bden pa'i u tshugs* ("truth insistence"); he also introduces the notion of nonviolent noncooperation. Quoting Thoreau and Gandhi (but not Emerson), Zhogs dung's contribution to the rights debate among Tibetans in late 2000 is threefold: first he takes on himself the task of educating his readers in political science, introducing the hitherto neglected or unknown concepts quoted above. Second, he introduces individual rights, a dimension often ignored by Tibetans when discussing rights, a tendency that Ronald Schwartz had already noted in the mid-1990s. For Tibetans, Schwartz wrote, human rights "are conceived as a condition of collective freedom rather than as abstract individual liberties. The Tibetan concept of human rights is substantive rather than formal" (Schwartz 1994, 129). Although Zhogs dung does not mention it explicitly, he appears to endeavor, through this book, to anchor a clear understanding of the scope and field of application of these rights for Tibetans, both at the collective and individual level. His third contribution lies in explaining these notions within a linguistic Tibetan environment, framing them in a well-selected usage of Tibetan language and cultural references. For instance, he explains his translation of "civil disobedience" as follows:[31]

> First, we used to translate the Chinese term "gongming bufu cong" [civil disobedience] into Tibetan as "spyi mang gi brtsi bkur mi byed pa" [literally: nonrespecting as far as civilians are concerned], but thinking that this did not exactly meet the lexical standard of being easily pronounceable and succinct in meaning, I have amended the translation to "spyi mang gi mi ston pa" [civil nonfollowing]. This is because, according to Btsan lha Ngag dbang tshul khrims' Golden Mirror Lexicon, "ston pa is suffixed to 1. confidence, 2. desire, 3. following after, and so on, in archaic usage," and this archaic form, with the negative prefix, does convey the sense of the Chinese term.[32]

Zhogs dung endeavors to coin appropriate and, from what he says, clear, brief, and transparent neologisms for new political notions, neither too constrained nor artificial—although his choice of an archaism for "nonfollowing" may entail difficulties for some readers. In spite of his harsh criticism of the ascendancy of Buddhism within the minds of his fellow Tibetans, he is also careful in establishing links with Buddhist terms and views that fit the cultural mind-set and worldview of Tibetans. For instance, regarding his translation of civil disobedience, he is aware that the verb chosen to express "obey," ston pa, is also used in a Buddhist cultural environment. He explains: "'Ston pa bzhi' [four reliances] and 'Mi ston pa bzhi' [four nonreliances] are terms familiar from our religious recitations." The same concern is at work when he explains "Satyagraha," from a Gandhian point of view, adapting it to a Buddhist audience. He reminds his readers that Gandhi said, "Since God pervades all, He is also in the heart of each human being. That is why each human being is a manifestation of God," and he relates and adapts it to a Buddhist view: "Sentient beings are buddhas, but instantly defiled by obscurations. Once these defilements are cleansed, they are actual buddhas," or, "What we call people are buddhas. The Bhagavan is not different from them." Zhogs dung continues: "If we alter a couple of syllables to make it 'Every human being is God, but instantly defiled by sin. Once the sinful mind is purified, they are actually God' and 'What we call people are God. The divine realm is not other than them,' this is both consistent with Gandhi's view and more easily comprehensible for Tibetans." The utmost care with which Zhogs dung endeavors to transfer in Tibetan language some political notions thus far little commented on, is quite apparent. This concern for language is appreciated by Wu Qi, a Tibetan from Amdo whose doctoral thesis reflects on the tension between tradition and modernity in Amdo. Wu describes this tension both from an ethnographic point of view (focusing on material culture and kinship) and from his study of the New Thinkers group, to which he dedicates more than one hundred pages. While being otherwise very critical of Zhogs dung and his group's theories, Wu (2013, 268) writes that "the New Thinkers have had a positive influence on Tibet's publication language. The New Thinkers have tried to build new terms into the Tibetan language."

Zhogs dung's book was politically loaded, and it got him into trouble. He was arrested on April 23, 2010, and charged with "instigating to split the motherland." Unusual for a Tibetan, he hired a Chinese lawyer, Li Fanping. Li is a prominent human rights lawyer in China, and Zhogs dung's choice of him may reveal the network developed by Zhogs dung and possibly his connections with rights advocates in China. He was released on bail after six months. His stature has, if anything, been enhanced by his book and his arrest, especially among young university graduates. The number of young authors who use a penname beginning with *Zhogs* (Morning) is an indication of Zhogs dung's popularity. As a gesture of support to him, a book was released in April 2011 called *Zhogs dung snying stobs* (Zhogs dung's courage), hinting at one of Zhogs dung's other books, *Dogs slong snying stobs* (The courage of skepticism).[33] The self-named "Dur khrod" (Funeral site), one of the editors of the volume, explained in a blog post calling for contributions that he and a group of admirers had decided to pay homage to "The Honorable Mr. Zhogs dung" (*Sku zhabs Zhogs dung lags*), making use of an unusual honorific form in Amdo. He requested essays that analyzed Zhogs dung's "courageous thoughts and brave criticism." Still, aware of the sensitivity of the topic, he begged potential contributors "not to discuss [Zhogs dung's] political courage," which indicates that, in addition to a cultural reformer, he is also perceived to be a political thinker. The book was apparently published the following year and included numerous essays by authors such as 'Gar rtse 'Jigs med, A rig Dge mthong (an exile monk),[34] and Rno sbreng (who runs the opinion website New Youth, known for its sympathy for the "New Thinkers" school of which Zhogs dung is the leader) (Wu 2013, 201–2). Less famous writers, mostly going by pen-names ('Od 'dzin, Myi gson po, Om sras Bde grol, Snyug bcud len, Sge'u khung, Dur khrod, Khro gtum, Sgo yon, Srin po, O rgyan Nyi ma, Bis mdo ba Chos skyong), also contributed pieces. Essays discussed such topics as humanist thinking, courage, analysis, patriotism, and audacity.[35] The introduction of the book was reprinted online in the exile newspaper *Tibet Times*: it insists on the responsibility incumbent upon writers belonging to a minority nationality in danger of disappearing: "reflecting upon the situation of a nationality whose survival arms have been cut off is necessarily the life-long responsibility of those endowed with letters [i.e., writers], that is, brave analysts, patriots and thinkers." In late December 2012 a new blogpost titled "Discussing Zhogs dung, Master of a New Generation" (Tib. "*mi rabs gsar ba'i ston pa Zhogs dung gleng ba*")[36] appeared on the Tibetan-language website New Youth. The blogger, using the pseudonym "Solitary Thorn" (*Tsher ma kher skyes*), explained why a segment of the new generation of Tibetans, mostly laypeople but also a few clerics, considered Zhogs dung worthy of the title "Master" (*Ston pa*), an epithet for the Buddha in the Tibetan tradition: he argued that Zhogs dung had opened new venues for thought and reflection anchored in modernity. This blog post triggered many reactions, many of which were hostile to the use of "Master" to refer to someone who is famous for his anticlerical views.

## 'BA' PA PHUN TSHOGS DBANG RGYAL'S ANALYSIS OF THE RIGHTS OF NATIONALITIES ACCORDING TO MARXISM

On November 26, 2009, the same year that Zhogs dung's essay was published, the Tibetan website "Butter Lamp"—another Tibetan-language cultural, literary, and social website—posted a lengthy Marxist analysis of the right of nationalities by the famous Tibetan Communist Phun tshogs dbang rgyal. The text was published in eighteen installments during December 2009 and January 2010. The introduction begins as follows: "Aristotle said: 'I like my teacher, but I like truth even better,'" which implies that Phun tshogs dbang rgyal was intent on evaluating and investigating freely Marxist theory about the rights of nationalities, applying personal critical judgment to it.[37] I do not know when this analytical text was originally written—the Tibetan version is a translation from Chinese. With references to Engels, Belinsky, Feuerbach, Gandhi, Voltaire, Montesquieu, Washington, and the US Declaration of Independence, Phun tshogs dbang rgyal extends Zhogs dung's self-assigned task of educating Tibetan readers about secular and, more specifically, political topics from a Tibetan point of view. By appropriating concepts to the Tibetan cause, concepts with which Chinese leaders and political scientists may be familiar, he puts at his readers' disposal a set of tools intended to enable them to identify possible contradictions between the right to autonomy in theory and its actual implementation, from a theoretical background that is acceptable within the Chinese intellectual framework, as it relies on a reading of Marxist views.

One reader commented that Tibetans, however deep and ancient their culture may be, have long satisfied themselves with praying and taking refuge "in gods and demons," ignoring and considering heretical all thinking about the *samsara*. "Just reflect upon what happened!" this reader concludes.[38] He is obviously blaming an excessive interest in otherworldly concerns for the current political situation of Tibetans. In this he echoes a typical Zhogs dung-ist view, according to which strong Buddhist faith is the root of the current plight of the Tibetan nation.[39] At the end of his short note Zhogs dung wrote the following regarding the UDHR: "I myself saw the Tibetan version of this Declaration only in the last year or so [i.e., 2007 or 2008]. From this, it appears that people who have been praised as politicians, experts and scholars have ignored the necessity of pushing ahead with this fundamental text. Is it because of their love of religion? Or because religious pressure is too strong?"

It is not clear to me who are the "politicians, experts and scholars" that Zhogs dung accuses of having not relayed the UDHR: he seems unaware of the text having been strongly supported by monks in Lhasa in 1988 and of its currency in exile, where all politicians, experts, and scholars take it for granted. From what can be understood of Zhogs dung's view, it could well be that he implies that some people were aware of the existence of this text in Tibetan but were reluctant to put it forward for religious reasons. It can be surmised here that he believes that the centrality of the individual and of the human in the text, as well as its secularism, does not fit with the Buddhist views that put religion at the core of everything.

## OTHER PUBLICATIONS OF THE UDHR IN TIBETAN

One year before Zhogs dung included the UDHR in his book *The Demarcation of Sky and Earth*, another translation of this text had appeared in the appendix of a clandestine collection of interviews of survivors of the 1958 anti-"Democratic reforms" uprising, which swept over large parts of Amdo. The text indicates that this version was "translated and arranged from the internet" (Rin bzang 2008, 201), meaning that Rin bzang took some liberty with the original, interspersing the articles with explanations and comments. The UDHR was also posted five times online on different Tibetan websites, which can hardly be a coincidence: the first occurrence, in April 2010, was posted by someone going by a woman's name, Tshe skyid g.yang 'dzoms, who posted the Dharamsala translation. From the way her name is spelled in the weblink, "Caiji," she might be living in the PRC and not in exile as the *pinyin* spelling system is hardly used or even known in exile. Several posts by this blogger showing an interest in women-related topics (famous Tibetan women, women's health and safety), point to her being a woman. Her posting of the UDHR attracted only eighty-six views in three years.[40]

The UDHR was again posted apparently twice by someone going by the name Gyarikthar on the same website on September 30, 2010, and deleted twice.[41] The deletion could indicate the unease of the censors with regard to such a text. Both the spelling of the blogger's name and his self-description on his blog ("[Living] in a remote place, faraway, I am prevented from [going] back to my homeland") indicate that he lives in exile. His blogger pseudonym could be reconstituted into "Rgya rigs thar," an Amdo-sounding name meaning "Liberation from the Han Nationality," in which case it leaves little doubt as to his personal political opinions regarding the Sino-Tibetan encounter.

On November 6, 2011, another Amdo Tibetan blogger living in exile, going by the penname of Dug lce (Poisonous Tongue) but revealing also his real name, Bstan 'dzin, posted a commentary about the famous Buddhist text *Shes rab snying po* (The heart sutra). Of interest for this present chapter is that he quoted in his exegesis the ninth and nineteenth articles and the second point of the twenty-seventh article of the UDHR.[42] Half a year later, on April 8, 2012, he posted the full Dharamsala translation of the UDHR in three installments.[43] The first and second parts of the text attracted ninety viewers, while the third one received 150 visitors. This compares unfavorably with Dug Ice's previous posting, which had attracted more than twenty-two hundred viewers. That popular blog post was entitled "A Western Woman Talks About the Difference in Love Making Between Asian[s] and Westerners."[44] It is the transcription of a conversation between Dug Ice and a Western woman, who compares her sexual experiences with Tibetans and Westerners. Given the scarcity of open, Tibetan-language sex-related writings, it is no wonder it was welcomed by Internet users, many of whom are male.

While interviewing Dug Ice for this chapter, I asked him what prompted him to post the UDHR on his website: he replied that he realized that few Tibetans in Tibet were aware of the concept of human rights. As far as he was concerned, his first realization of the importance of spreading the UDHR among his fellow Tibetans had come three years earlier, in March 2009, after a monk from Ra rgya monastery, where Dug Ice came from, had jumped into the river either to escape a police search or to commit suicide.[45] Still, it took Dug Ice three years to post the UDHR on the Internet. It is also interesting that, although Dug Ice had by then lived in Dharamsala for more than fifteen years and reached exile many years after the Tibetan Center for Human Rights and Democracy was established, and in spite of his being an educated and heavily politicized Tibetan, he had only become aware of the UDHR relatively recently and had not seemed to have felt the urge until recently to propagate its Tibetan-language UDHR version. A possible explanation for his belated realization of the existence and content of the UDHR while in exile might be twofold: first, human-rights-related material produced in exile is mainly in English, which Tibetans born and bred in exile have no problem engaging with but which few Tibetans coming from the PRC are able to master; second, notions of human rights are introduced to Tibetan children in exile through the school curriculum, which means that the newly arrived Tibetans, often reaching India in their twenties, do not have access to this material.

In May 2012 a previously unseen Tibetan translation of the UDHR appeared on another Tibetan website.[46] The author of the post was none

other than Nags tshang Nus blo (b. 1941), a retired judge and elderly author of a censored autobiography about his childhood in the 1950s, when
he was a firsthand witness to the violent Sino-Tibetan armed confrontation. This book can be considered a best seller, as an estimated forty thousand copies (legal and illegal) have been circulating in Tibetan areas, notably Amdo, from where the author originates and where he still lives.[47] Nags
tshang Nus blo's posting of the UDHR in Tibetan, on a website of which he
is partly in charge, deserves attention for three reasons: first, the translation is quite different from that of the exile version, indicating it might
have been translated from the Chinese. The reason for the publication of
this new translation is also worth exploring: according to Zhogs dung, the
1961 Tibetan translation is convoluted, difficult to understand, and sometimes flawed. At the end of his book *Demarcation* he "urges repeatedly all
people with a broad knowledge [to engage in a revised Tibetan translation
of the UDHR] because we definitely need to know the meaning of world
documents and we must provide water, manure and heat at the right time
for the seed [of political awareness to grow]" (Zhogs dung 2009, 285). It
is a possibility that Nags tshang Nus blo, a likely reader of Zhogs dung's
book, decided to undertake a new translation. Second, this new translation
is preceded by a short foreword by Nags tshang Nus blo. Third, it has generated a number of comments, a selection of which will also be presented
below for what they reveal about Tibetan web users' reactions to this kind
of posting.

Nags tshang Nus blo's foreword begins: "Our country is a permanent
member of the [Security Council of the] UN. It is the responsibility of all
member-states to publicize (*khyab bsgrags*) the documents of the UN, their
functioning, etc., and to highly value and ensure the implementation of
human rights and other rights. Please read the UDHR that I have posted
below." This statement can be read as a *sotto voce* indictment of the nonim-
plementation by the PRC authorities of the UDHR or, at least, of its failure
to publicize it in "minority" languages.

The comments of the readers vary from praise for this initiative to cyni-
cism. The first to react, someone going by the name Rta mgrin, applauds
Nus blo, saying that "all Tibetans will undoubtedly welcome such a good
piece. Thank you for your website." This comment is immediately followed
by a lengthy reply by Nags tshang Nus blo, which is enlightening for our
discussion and is more important than his foreword because it reveals his
intention for posting the text. I will translate it in its entirety:

Talking from the point of view of a human being, not only should each and every one of us be aware that they possess fundamental rights, but they should also be aware that such rights must be guaranteed legally. Whether living in a country that is free, or a colony, or a country that does not govern itself politically, each person must initially study well the law of their country. Each person's rights and so on are guaranteed by the law of one's country, on a legal basis. In many places, legal discourses are nice but are not implemented: this is first due to a minority of bad leaders who have no mercy, and secondly to some people knowing only how to pocket state money but ignore the official legal system. Whatever the case may be, however, the legal system of a sovereign country may have a strong capacity to protect its citizens and most laws may be honest and fair, and the national legal system may be fine, but a few aggressive sovereign countries shamelessly fail to implement the law. This is obvious. This question depends on each individual's capacity to know extensively their country's legal system and their own needs in terms of guaranteeing one's own rights. It is erroneous to think that one's country's legal system has nothing to do with oneself [as an individual]. As someone living in this country, whether you ignore it or not, whether you like it or not, the whole legal system is above your head, there is absolutely no doubt about it. People who know how to protect themselves through legal means face few problems, while those who do not always face many problems. It may happen that some unlawful speech, hitting, and dragging befall you, for no reason. But if you do not know who to talk to, or what to say, well then, mercy be upon you, who will be gobbled up like a worm! This is why it is certain that there is a necessary time when every individual, high or low in the society, must somehow study law in relationship with one's own situation.[48]

This insistence on the need to develop legal awareness among Tibetans is presented with authority by Nags tshang Nus blo. As someone who worked in the legal field for his entire career, he knows that the legal framework does exist in theory and that ignorance of it on the part of Tibetans only makes it easier for the state to not apply it. Although resorting to the usual Chinese official discursive practice of blaming the few to spare the system (problems are ascribable to a handful of evil-intentioned people, not to the Communist Party per se), it is quite transparent that he means that citizens in China, and Tibetans in particular, would be well advised, in order to maximize their chances for real justice, to acquire a knowledge of the legal system, so as to hold the state accountable to it.

But some readers simply shrug off Nags tshang Nus blo's insistence on the importance of knowing one's rights: one person comments that no law at all would be better than a legal system if it is not to be implemented, reflecting the disillusionment felt by Tibetans, and indeed most PRC citizens, with the current state of the legal system in China. Not only is the lawlessness of the Chinese legal system lamented as a whole, but one commentator apparently from Rnga ba, Rnga ba Skal bzang, complains bluntly that Tibetans are particularly underprivileged in the PRC: "What level of guarantee does the PRC offer in terms of human rights? What is so difficult with being able to guarantee human rights of one's own citizens? Where are the ones protecting the rights of Tibetans? Can someone answer these questions?" Another reader, Tre hor Dpa' dga', concurs on the topic of the ethnically biased judicial system, thus returning to the complaints voiced in 2008 in *Shar dung ri* and other opinion magazines surveyed above: "Who guarantees the rights of Tibetans? There is no one who can implement them. Who repressed, who killed this year and last year, during the numerous events that happened in Tibetan localities belonging to Dkar mdzes, Brag mgo, Rta bo, Rdzogs chen, Gser thar, Rnga ba, 'Dzam thang, etc.? Who were the protectors? No need to say it, it is extremely clear. This is not due to the country's laws being bad, but because of a few shameless extremists who do not implement the country's laws. . . . All Tibetans know this." A blogger calling himself Bsam bzang gives a more moderate opinion, beginning skillfully with a praise to the legal system in Qinghai, and then blaming merciless and ignorant authorities rather than the overall system: "Qinghai does have laws that guarantee the rights of Tibetans. And it has done a good job about it. Whatever happens, basing oneself upon people's rights, problems can be solved in a peaceful way. In a few lawless areas, law is not even applied on the tip of the blade and, there, inhabitants receive only words for solace and are oppressed without restraint. . . . Everyone also knows that it is not a matter of knowing or not knowing the law, but whether people who apply the law are kind or not."

This tone is not to the taste of someone calling himself Rdza ba Bsam rdor, whose dejected rejoinder brings ethnicity again into the debate: "Nags tshang Nus blo is right. He says that the legal system of a country must absolutely guarantee an individual's rights. If authoritarian [*btsan drag*] and unlawful policies are enforced upon minorities of a sovereign state, will the law be in a position to guarantee the rights of the masses? It is fine that our country often talks about law, but when something, [even] small, happens, where is law? We only meet authoritarian violence."

Finally, at least at the time of writing this chapter, the Dharamsala translation of the UDHR was posted a fourth time online on a site that specializes in news and public opinions within Tibet, Ranggrol.[49] Presented with a pretty, flowery Tibetan design in the background of the document, "Tibetanizing" and embellishing the outlook of the text, it had recorded 476 hits four months after its posting online, which is higher than most other postings (one hundred to two hundred hits on average).

---

In this discussion on the spread of the terms and concepts of human rights in Tibetan, in Tibet, one should not ignore the Chinese social and political environment and context in which these Tibetan debates take place. Rights and human rights discourses have been on the increase and have even become internalized in China proper, especially since the 1980s, in response to international and domestic pressure. Moreover, intellectuals and law professionals have also become more active. To name but a few instances, Liu Xiaobo's Charter 08 made ample references to the notion of rights and human rights.[50] In February 2013 calls were made by influential intellectuals, among them (Han Chinese) rights specialists, for the National People's Congress to ratify the International Covenant on Civil and Political Rights, signed in 1998.[51] Ordinary Chinese citizens have also become more rights-conscious. Starting in the early 2000s, the development of largely informal social movements called *weiquan yundong* (rights defense movement), popularly known as the "civil rights movement," testifies to the rise of a legally aware stratum among Chinese citizens.[52] This has led, according to Feng, to "the Chinese government . . . becoming increasingly tolerant of rights assertion, in spite of the fact that it continues to selectively crack down on individual rights defence lawyers and human rights activists" (Feng 2009, 158).

This chapter has shown that Tibetans' rights awareness is on the increase, too, in some segments of the young and educated lay population as a result of a combination of several factors. On the occasion of the "Tibet spring" of 2008, followed by the self-immolation movement from 2011 to 2014, many Tibetans were faced with what they interpreted as proof of inequality of legal treatment after the crackdown on Tibetan demonstrators. Robert Barnett (2012, 64–66) has provided a list of everyday "restrictions" upon basic rights imposed on Tibetans in the TAR since 1994. His list shows that Tibetans in the TAR have been suffering from breaches of the regime of rights for twenty years, without what might be called a rights-based reaction on their part.[53] But the Tibetans calling for the respect of their rights surveyed in this chapter do not hail from the TAR but from Qinghai, Sichuan, and Gansu provinces. The 2008 demonstrations and the 2011–14 immolations also took place mostly outside the TAR. In these areas Tibetans had not previously been subjected to, educated about, or used to such intense "restrictions" as in the TAR. Severe measures imposed on many sections of the Tibetan society outside the TAR fueled intense frustration in these thus-far relatively liberal parts of Tibet where intellectual debates about the current state of Tibet were brewing. Moreover, it coincided with a shift in the intellectual discourse of the group of Amdo intellectuals called the "New Thinkers." As Wu (2013, 253) argues convincingly, "Universal values have become the core of the New Thinkers' argument and their dream," because they have realized they have little hope of acquiring many followers among Tibetans if they directly attack traditional Tibetan society. It is thus no coincidence that Zhogs dung dedicates twelve points, covering five pages, to his interpretation of the concept of universal values in his 2009 book. The fact that this short exegesis has been reprinted on several Tibetan-language websites is an indication of the interest that some educated Tibetans show on the matter of what the current Chinese regime does not favor.[54] We are thus witnessing educated Tibetans attempting to equip their fellow Tibetans with an awareness of the importance of knowing international and national law and rights, and they are giving them access, in Tibetan, to ideas and knowledge in the fields of rights, including the UDHR. This movement was started around 2008–9 by a small, educated, legal, political, and rights-savvy segment of the Tibetan population, among whom were three senior Tibetan thinkers from Amdo. Nags tshang Nus blo has reacted by sharing a didactic posting, offering a new translation of the UDHR and explaining the importance of rights awareness for any citizen of China. Zhogs dung, who does not have a legal background but who is an avid reader of Western political science, has for his part undertaken to anchor the concept of civil disobedience in his Tibetan readers' minds and has urged them to offer a new translation of the UDHR. Phun tshogs dbang rgyal, a staunch senior CCP member, has striven to explain the Marxist view on the right to autonomy for minorities.

What the China law scholar Sam Crane says regarding the impact of rights advocates in China could equally be applied to Tibetans: in spite of their lack of effective power, "they could be influential in how others understand power and how power-holders use their power at critical junctures."[55] The Foucauldian formula that knowledge is power is certainly not applicable here, but an increasingly rights-aware new generation of educated Tibetans—who have witnessed and sometimes participated in massive ethnic street protests, who have grown up using the Internet where the New Thinkers' views are amply introduced, who are aware of their Han fellow citizens' growing boldness in terms of expressing rights grievances, and who can no longer tolerate the double standard to which they feel they are submitted in terms of rights—will arguably be less pliable than the previous generation.

Moreover, the development of rights discourses among Tibetan intellectuals, described in this chapter, may likely be interpreted as a reaction to the increase of Han Chinese thinkers who have been termed nationalists, neoconfucianists, or exceptionalists. In the last decade these intellectuals have been increasingly vocal in pushing toward a more China-centered vision of political and economic change. Such "citizen intellectuals" are described by William Callahan (2013, 56) as favoring "Confucianism's hierarchical system that values order over freedom, ethics over law, and elite governance over democracy and human rights." Needless to say, Tibetan thinkers presented in this chapter do not adhere to these Sinocentric values. On the contrary, their strong emphasis on the universality of rights could be interpreted as an effort to detach Tibet from the Chinese cultural realm and the proponents of assimilationist policies that have gained ground under the aegis of such specialists as Ma Rong.

Finally, the present findings do little to confirm the "outside instigation" (read Dharamsala and the "Western hostile forces") theory usually favored by the Chinese government to condemn most pro-Tibetan protests as having ulterior motives and being instrumentalized by Western neoimperialism: it appears quite clearly that the new generation of educated lay Tibetans has increasing access to notions of the respect of human rights and the rule of law through their Chinese education and through official discourses by Chinese authorities themselves rather than through the instigation of exile; remember that Zhogs dung, one of the most avid readers of political science among today's Tibetans, had not come across the 1961 Dharamsala version of the UDHR until 2007 or 2008.

The frequent insistence on equality (*'dra mnyam*) is a further indication that the trend is being driven by the Chinese situation and by Tibetans within the PRC intent on making use of their agency, not by exile society. What pleads in favor of an "endo-Tibetan" development of the UDHR discourse is the fact that equality is seldom taken up or put forward by Tibetan exiles or in the Tibetan Center for Human Rights and Democracy publications. One possible reason for this silence outside Tibet is that "equality among nationalities," an oft-trumpeted slogan within the PRC, has lost currency and even relevance in the third millennium. Most multi-ethnic empires have crumbled, meaning that the question of ethnic minority rights within multinational polities is now superseded by other and more pregnant global topics, such as gender inequality and class-based discrimination. Last, judging from online information, human rights discourses in exile tend to be more frequently presented in the English language than in Tibetan, an indication that they are aimed at both the exile Tibetan schooling system (where English has long prevailed) and, more likely, at potential Western supporters of the Tibet cause. It is Tibetans in Tibet proper who experience breaches in the state rhetoric of "equality among nationalities" that is not experienced by their exile brothers.

It is thus safe to interpret the current rise in discourses about human rights, equality, and rights in general, among Tibetans in Tibet, as more characteristic of a "China's Tibet" than of an "exile Tibet" discourse and a further indication that, if exile Tibetan society may provide resources and ideas to Tibetans in Tibet, the latter are becoming increasingly self-reliant and, ironically, able to develop a rights-oriented discourse with the unwilling help of the Chinese regime itself.

## Notes

1. The question was posted at http://ask.bodyig.org/?question/view/3872.html. The post is no longer available.
2. These "Four Freedoms" were put forward by Franklin Roosevelt in his 1941 State of the Union address. They seem to be of special interest to Tibetans,

as on January 2, 2014, a Tibetan possibly from The bo (Kan lho Tibetan Autonomous Prefecture, Gansu Province), going by the name of The bo Sangs rgyas, posted a replica of the 1943 painting by Norman Rockwell, representing these "Four Freedoms," with an explanation of the meaning of the painting (see www.tibetcm.com/html/hist_04/201401025884.html).

3. Emily Yeh mentions a local party secretary in the TAR asking her, as a local interpreter for an "Aid-Tibet" project, to "ensure that the foreign experts asked nothing sensitive or 'political,' a category that according to him included questions not only about birth control, but also infectious diseases, human rights, the Dalai Lama, and military headquarters" (Yeh 2013, 48).

4. Tibet is understood here in the wide sense of the Tibetan Plateau in its entirety, encompassing all Tibetan autonomous areas according to the PRC administrative system.

5. Gray Tuttle concurs: "Central Tibet remained free of colonization or even the semicolonization of countries such as China. . . . The Tibetan elite was not forced to adopt the universal rhetoric and practice of modernization and the universal enlightenment values of the now-global West" (Tuttle 2005, 305).

6. Unless otherwise stated, quotations from Zhogs dung are reproduced from the unpublished translation of his *Demarcation of Sky and Earth* (2009), but the pages given in my notes refer to the original Tibetan version. I thank the translator for having shared it with me.

7. As far as I can tell, the former is preferred in exile and central Tibet and the latter in Amdo. Bhutan, which is translated in Dzongkha (a Tibetic language lexically close to Tibetan) the Universal Declaration of Human Rights only in 2010, has opted for the term *thob dbang*, literally "acquired powers/strength/rights," a combination of the two terms previously mentioned (see Institute of Language and Culture Studies 2010). This term seems to have been accepted in Bhutan as the common translation for "rights": the "right of information," a hotly debated topic in 2013 in Bhutan, is translated in Dzongkha as *gnas tshul thob dbang*. According to Ngag dbang, researcher at the Institute of Language and Culture Studies, who coordinated it, the Dzongkha translation was made both from the Tibetan 1961 version (about which see below) and the English original (personal communication, Thimphu, Sept. 2013).

8. This translation has not surfaced yet. I thank Gray Tuttle for this information.

9. See HYPERLINK "http://larouchejapan.com/japanese/drupal-6.14/sites/default/files/text/San-Min-Chu-I_FINAL.pdf" http://larouchejapan.com/japanese/drupal-6.14/sites/default/files/text/San-Min-Chu-I_FINAL.pdf. For an interesting survey about how the text was translated into Tibetan (in China and Taiwan), see Jagou 2010.

10. The text of this Common Program can be found at www.e-chaupak.net/database/chicon/1949/1949e.pdf. Citizens' rights are mentioned but do not feature as an essential part of the text.

11. "By the end of the summer of 1954, the political tides sweeping across China brought Tshe tan zhabs drung to Beijing, where he participated in translating the new Chinese Constitution into Tibetan" (Willock 2011, 18). The bilingual English/Chinese text of the 1954 Constitution can be found at http://e-chaupak.net/database/chicon/1954/1954bilingual.htm#j. I wish to thank Stephanie Balme (Science Po/CERI, Paris) for reading my chapter, for sharing her comments on the Chinese Constitution, and for stressing the importance of the 1954 version.

12. See http://ti.tibet3.com/politcs/2009-04/03/content_370194.htm for the Tibetan translation of the headings and chapters of this 1982 Constitution.

13. The Department of Information and International Relations was created later, in 1972; for a short history of this department see http://tibet.net/information/.

14. For the 1963 and 1991 Constitutions see www.tibetjustice.org/materials/.

15. See www.ustibetcommittee.org/ustc/ustc.html.

16. For the English translation of the entire Strasbourg Proposal see www.dalailama.com/messages/tibet/strasbourg-proposal-1988. Note that the notion of "association" put forward in this proposal is not precise.

17. The editors of the journal were arrested in 2010 in relation to pro-Tibetan writings in another journal, *Shar dung ri* (East Conch Mountain).

18. See Bentz (2008, 167n92); and Römer (2010, 191).

19. Original source: www.tchrd.org/tibetan/report/topicalreport/tibethuman rights.pdf. This document is no longer available online.

20. In this quote *autonomy* would be a better term than "self-protection" (rang skyong). The confusion may be due to the fact that the Tibetan word for *autonomy* does literally mean "self-protection." In the political sphere, though, it conveys the meaning of autonomy.

21. For an assessment of the 2008 movement see Barnett (2009).

22. See www.rfa.org/english/news/tibet/burnings-02202013095047.html (my emphasis).

23. See http://globalvoicesonline.org/2012/11/23/china-last-words-of-19-tibetans-who-committed-self-immolation/ (my emphasis).

24. See www.rfa.org/english/news/tibet/alight-10072011082911.html (my emphasis).

25. See http://globalvoicesonline.org/2012/11/23/china-last-words-of-19-tibetans-who-committed-self-immolation/ (my emphasis).

26. According to the Tibetan Centre for Human Rights and Democracy, the author had worked in the state-run Ngaba Regional Historical Research Centre. He was reportedly arrested by security officials on June 21, 2010, for "reactionary" writing and has not been seen since. See TCHRD (2010, 106).

27. See www.tibettimes.net/news.php?id=2331.

28. Quoted on http://youshun12.com/?p=2549.

29. For details (in Tibetan) see www.thetibetpost.com/bo/news/tibet/3404-china-jails-tibetan-writer-for-five-years-over-his-writings.

30. See the Tibetan original at www.thetibetpost.com/bo/outlook/reviews/3448 -my-words-are-not-tainted-by-lies-and-deception-a-writer-in-tibet. The last term, *bsgrags dar*, is not clear and "khata of fame" (ceremonial scarf) is a tentative translation.

31. This term appears in the *Three Principles of the People* by Sun Yat-sen. It remains to be seen whether Zhogs dung has been inspired by this work, which is possible. Still, he does not mention it explicitly in the book surveyed here.

32. The book referred to is *Brda bkrol gser gyi me long* (Beijing: Mi rigs dpe skrun khang, 1997), about which an online commentary says the following: "To date only one work has been published which can be properly called a dictionary of Old Tibetan, this being that by Btsan lha Ngag dbang tshul khrims (1997). This work carefully quotes and cites its sources, however not specifically enough to afford confirmation. Citations have been culled from Dunhuang texts as well as the *Bdra gsar rnying*, and commentarial literature" (http://en.wikibooks .org/wiki/Research_on_Tibetan_Languages:_A_Bibliography).

33. See www.tbnewyouth.com/article/show-7/201110191582.html. The same announcement was posted on the Tibetan website http://blog.amdotibet.cn/ grave/archives/39632.aspx, but it has since been removed.

34. Apparently, his contribution to the volume, which he had posted online, was blocked from the Internet by censors.

35. See www.tibettimes.net/blogs.php?id=88&post_id=19882.

36. See www.tbnewyouth.com/article/call/201212152143.html.

37. See www.tibetcm.com/html/list_24/7334f352f5f0d7187435fb9c3cf19197/.

38. See www.tibetcm.com/html/list_24/9694a61e305161d2ffb60894ef8cb593/.

39. In *The Demarcation*, though, Zhogs dung expresses a so far unseen appreciation of the role of clerics in the "Tibetan saffron revolution." This can be interpreted either as a shift in his views on Buddhism or perhaps as a strategic move or gesture to reconcile himself with a substantial portion of the educated Tibetan population—that is, those who cannot accept Zhogs dung's position because of its antagonism toward Buddhism. Wu (2013, 247) confirms this hypothesis.

40. See http://blog.amdotibet.cn/caiji/archives/504.aspx.

41. See http://blog.amdotibet.cn/gyarikthar/archives/2276.aspx.

42. See http://blog.amdotibet.cn/arrow/archives/42229.aspx.

43. See http://blog.amdotibet.cn/arrow/archives/50447.aspx.

44. See http://blog.amdotibet.cn/arrow/archives/44469.aspx.

45. See www.phayul.com/news/article.aspx?id=24251&article=Monk+kills+self+in +Ragya percent2c+residents+protest&t=1&c=1; and www.chinadaily.com.cn/ china/2009-03/22/content_7603753.htm.

46. See www.bodrigs.com/literature/prose/2012-05-10/367.html.

47. Personal communication, Xenia de Heering (EHESS-Inalco), Paris, December 2012.

48. I am unsure of the precise meaning of "*lgug pa'i bu ngam zos pa bzhin*," which I have decided tentatively to translate as "gobbled up like a worm."

49. See www.ranggrol.com/reading/other/2013-03-29/423.html.
50. For Charter 08 see www.charter08.com/eng/charter08.pdf. It has been translated into Tibetan under the title "Rtsa 'dzin 08 ma" on an unknown date. The
Tibetan translation can be found on the widely read exile opinion website
Khabdha (www.khabdha.org/?p=1386). Its translator goes by the pseudonym
of 'Brog myi (Herder), the spelling of which indicates that he (or she) is from
Amdo.
51. See    www.nytimes.com/2013/02/27/world/asia/chinese-intellectuals-urge-
ratification-of-rights-treaty.html?_r=0.
52. On this topic see Benney 2013.
53. Barnett (2012) explains:

At least four of the most important restrictions on religious activity
introduced into Tibet [i.e., the TAR] in the mid-1990s *did not conform
to the norms used to naturalize the state's exercise of its authority in contemporary China*, did not apply to ethnic Chinese citizens, and were not
explained. Even the existence of three of these restrictions—the ban
on worship of the Dalai Lama among the general public, that on religion among students and officials, and the spatial zoning of monks
and nuns—has not been acknowledged by the state, as far as is known,
*perhaps because these orders could be seen as illegal in inland China* or because they are seen as natural consequences of other public measures.
(95, my emphasis).

Emily Yeh (2013, 37–41) provides another list of such breaches in the egali-
tarian, nondiscriminatory state rhetoric. She writes that this "differential
guilt" of Tibetans in PRC "is a technique of sovereign power that helps produce
the state effect" (37). While this is certainly true, it also leads to an abhorrence
of the state and to an irreconcilability between the Tibetan citizen and the
Chinese state.
54. In *Demarcation* the passage on universal values can be found on pages 263–67.
Bao Tong, former director of the Office of Political Reform of the Communist
Party of China Central Committee (CPCCC), policy secretary of Zhao Ziyang,
premier of the State Council, mentioned in 2013 "universal values" as forming part of what he refers to as the "seven taboos." Others are press freedom,
civil society, citizens' rights, the historical mistakes of the Chinese Communist
Party, the financial and political elite, and judicial independence" (www.rfa
.org/english/commentaries/baotong/cultural-revolution-09122013103217
.html?utm_source=twitterfeed&utm_medium=twitter). The site Ranggrol,
mentioned previously, seems to have taken on itself to educate its readers
about the topic of "universal values": to the best of my knowledge, Ranggrol
is the only private-run Tibetan-language website in Tibet that offers a tab labeled "Universal Values" (yongs khyab rin thang), presenting a selection of
about thirty texts, mostly translated from the English and the Chinese, about

rights (it contains texts by Orwell, Aun Sung Suu Kyi, Nehru, and the US Declaration of Independence, among others).

55.  See  http://uselesstree.typepad.com/useless_tree/2013/01/confucian-consti
tutionalism-in-defense-of-freedom-of-expression.html.

## References

A rig 'Gyur med. 2010. "Bud med tsho / Chos nyid go ldog ma byed ang." *'Khrig gtam
dmar rjen ma*, 96–105.

Barnett, Robert. 2009. "The Tibet Protests of Spring 2008: Conflict Between the Nation and the State." *China Perspectives*, no. 3, 6–23.

——. 2012. "Restrictions and Their Anomalies: The Third Forum and the Regulation
of Religion in Tibet." *Journal of Current Chinese Affairs* 41 (4): 45–107.

Benney, Jonathan. 2013. *Defending Rights in Contemporary China*. London: Routledge.

Bentz, Sophie. 2008. *Les réfugiés tibétains en Inde: Nationalisme et exil*. Paris: Presses
universitaires de France.

Callahan, William A. 2013. *China Dreams: 20 Visions of the Future*. London: Oxford University Press.

Chen, Dingding. 2005. "Explaining China's Changing Discourse on Human Rights,
1978–2004." *Asian Perspective* 29 (3): 155–82.

Dalai Lama Bstan 'dzin rgya mtsho. 1961. *Gong sa skyabs mgon chen po mchog rgya
gar rgyal sa ldi lir chibs bsgyur bka' drin che skabs kyi mdzad deb dang / ma
'ongs pa'i bod kyi rtsa khrims snying don / dril sgrag slob gso khang nas phyogs
bsgrigs mdzad pa'i bka' slob gces bsdus dang / slob gso bcas*. Darjeeling: Freedom
Press.

Feng, Chongyi. 2009. "The Rights Defence Movement, Rights Defence Lawyers and
Prospects for Constitutional Democracy in China." *Cosmopolitan Civil Societies
Journal* 1 (3): 150–69.

Foot, Rosemary. 2000. *Rights Beyond Borders. The Global Community and the Struggle over
Human Rights in China*. London: Oxford University Press.

Garmi. 2009. "The Case for Lifeblood and Life-Force." In International Campaign for
Tibet 2009a, 99–192.

Gartse Jigme. 2009. "My Life, My Pain." In International Campaign for Tibet 2009b,
91–102.

Goldstein, Melvyn C., Dawey Sherap, and William R. Siebenschuh. 2004. *A Tibetan
Revolutionary: The Political Life and Times of Bapa Phüntso Wangye*. Berkeley: University of California Press.

Hansen, Mette Halskov. 2005. *Frontier People: Han Settlers in Minority Areas of China*.
Vancouver: UBC Press.

Hartley, Lauran R. 2003. "Contextually Speaking: Tibetan Literary Discourse and Social Change in the People's Republic of China (1980–2000)." PhD diss., Columbia
University, New York.

Institute of Language and Culture Studies, ed. 2010. *'Gro ba mi'i dbang cha dang 'brug gi rtsa khrims chen mo: Human Rights and the Constitution of Bhutan.* Thimphu: Kun gsal.

International Campaign for Tibet, ed. 2009a. *A Great Mountain Burned by Fire: China's Crackdown in Tibet.* Washington: International Campaign for Tibet.

——, ed. 2009b. *Like Gold That Fears No Fire: New Writings from Tibet.* Washington: International Campaign for Tibet. www.savetibet.org/wp-content/uploads/2013/05/Like-Gold.pdf.

Jagou, Fabienne. 2010. "Les traductions tibétaines des discours politiques chinois de Sun Yat-sen sur 'les Trois principes du peuple' en tant qu'exemples de traductions modernes d'un texte politique." In *Edition, éditions: L'écrit au Tibet, évolution et devenir,* edited by A. Chayet, C. Scherrer-Schaub, F. Robin, and J.-L. Achard, 163–84. München: Indus.

Lünpo Nyugtog. 2009. "The Force of Truth Spreads Its Wings." In International Campaign for Tibet 2009a, 78–82.

McGranahan, Carole. 2005. "In Rapga Pandgatsang's Library." *Cahiers d'Extrême Orient* 15:253–74.

Meinert, Carmen, and Hans-Bernd Zöllner, eds. 2010. *Buddhist Approaches to Human Rights: Dissonances and Resonances.* Bielefeld: Transaction.

Nyen. 2009. "What Human Rights Do We Have over Our Bodies?" In International Campaign for Tibet 2009b, 40–42.

Rin bzang. 2008. "Nga'i pha yul dang zhi ba'i bcings grol" (My homeplace and peaceful liberation). N.p.: n.p.

Römer, Stephanie. 2010. "Human Rights and Exile-Tibetan Politics." In Meinert and Zöllner 2010, 179–94.

Schwartz, Ronald D. 1994. *Circle of Protest: Political Ritual in the Tibetan Uprising.* London: Hurst.

Sobisch, Jan-Ulrich, and Trine Brox. 2010. "Translations of Human Rights: Tibetan Contexts." In Meinert and Zöllner 2010, 159–78.

Sonpo. 2009. "That Is a Lie." In International Campaign for Tibet 2009a, 75–78.

Stoddard, Heather. 1985. *Le mendiant de l'Amdo.* Paris: Société d'ethnographie.

TCHRD. 2010. *Dissenting Voices. Targeting the Intellectual, Writers and Cultural Figures.* Dharamsala: Tibetan Center for Human Rights and Democracy.

Tuttle, Gray. 2005. *Tibetan Buddhists in the Making of Modern China.* New York: Columbia University Press.

Willock, Nicole. 2011. "Tséten Zhapdrung Jikmé Rikpé Lodrö: A Tibetan Buddhist Polymath in Modern China." PhD diss., Indiana University, Bloomington.

Woeser, Tsering. 2009. "Us, Post-2008." In International Campaign for Tibet 2009b, 8–20.

Wu Qi. 2013. "Tradition and Modernity: Cultural Continuum and Transition Among Tibetans in Amdo." PhD diss., University of Helsinki, Helsinki.

Yeh, Emily T. 2013. *Taming Tibet: Landscape Transformation and the Gift of Chinese Development.* Ithaca, NY: Cornell University Press.

*Yongs khyab gsal bsgrags 'gro ba mi'i thob thang*—*Universal Declaration of Human Rights*— *Bod dbyin yi ge shan sbyar.* Dharamsala: Dha sa bod gzhung shes rig dpar khang, 1970.

Zhogs dung. (2008) 2010. "Nang deb 'Dus rabs kyi nga' yi rtsom sgrig pa'i dri ba la dris lan btab pa." In *Rigs shes kun grol,* 246–305. Lanzhou: Kan su'u mi rigs dpe skrun khang.

——. 2009. *Gnam sa 'go 'byed* [*The Demarcation of Sky and Earth*]. N.p.: n.p.

# 4

# The Chinese Education System as a Source of Conflict in Tibetan Areas

Clémence Henry

Among the major challenges facing the People's Republic of China (PRC) today are education for all,[1] the reduction of the economic gap between urban and rural areas, and the management of restive ethnic minorities. The education system in Tibetan areas lies at the convergence of these three hot topics.[2] Significant amounts of money have been invested,[3] especially in building schools and providing subsidies for poor students. Despite these efforts at the central level, however, between 2010 and 2012 exile Tibetan media recorded many student protests, which they qualified as "peaceful," particularly in the Tibetan region of Amdo, Qinghai Province. The 2010 protests were launched against the Qinghai Province textbooks and teaching language reforms project. Since 2012, some of the protests appear much more as public demonstrations of support for self-immolators. While a significant number of self-immolators denounce what they see as the eradication of Tibetan culture, students instead demand that the Tibetan language be maintained as the official language in curricula and that Tibetan people and their culture be respected. These protests reveal a deep discontent and a divide between students' expectations and the educational options available to them.

Are all Tibetan students equally implicated in the contesting of education policies? We are facing an apparent contradiction: while the education system is supposed to be applied uniformly throughout Qinghai Province, just as in other PRC provinces, the 2010 protests varied across districts. I present in this chapter some reflections about the range of applications of the official Chinese education system in Tibetan areas and the consequences of these different applications. I first review the theory and some generalities about the public education system for ethnic Tibetan students in the PRC, and then I investigate the practical application of state education policies in two Tibetan Autonomous Prefectures (TAPs), Tsolho and Yulshul, located in the central and southwestern parts of Qinghai, respectively. I will show how parallel education systems, and private institutions and courses too, have specific characteristics that vary according to their location. Finally, I propose an explanation of the crisis that Tibetan students in the PRC are currently facing.

## Education Policies in China's Tibetan Regions

A number of preferential policies have been implemented to support education in Tibetan areas, both because these areas are economically disadvantaged and also because of their "ethnic" exception. Such policies apply in the following fields: type of schools, schooling age, textbooks, and other specific areas.

One of the main exceptions is "minority nationalities schools" (Tib. *mi rigs slob grwa*). Most such schools were built after the 1978 reforms (Gcantsha in 1979, Kluchu in 1982, Dpa' ris in 1989, etc.). In 1985 "delocalized schools" (Ch. *neidi Xizang ban*) were established for Tibet Autonomous Region (TAR) students and during the 2000s for students in Tibetan areas outside of the TAR.[4] Moreover, the "minority nationalities boarding schools" (Tib. *mi rigs bca' sdod slob grwa*) seem to have been, first, a Tibetan specialty, especially in rural areas.[5] Important also is the minimum school age exception. Usually in the PRC children attend primary school from age six to age twelve. An exception was affirmed by the 1995 "Law on Education," which allows children from areas where certain basic education conditions are not satisfied, that is most rural areas, to enter school at age seven.[6] According to Postiglione, Jiao, and Gyatso (2005), Tibetans also benefit from an extension until age eight in some circumstances. The actual minimum school age is perhaps determined mainly by local practices. However, a new trend seems to be appearing: the development of preschool education before the age of six.

With regard to textbooks, a policy concerning exceptions for Tibetan teaching materials entered its main phase in 1982 with the establishment of the Office for the Editing [of Manuals] Regarding Language in the Five [i.e., four] Provinces and [one] Region (Tib. *ljongs zhing lnga'i skad yig rtsom sgrig las tshan*, Ch. *Wu Xie Ban*) (Wang 2007, 136). The policy stipulates that Tibetan textbooks in the four provinces (Qinghai, Sichuan, Gansu, Yunnan) and one autonomous region (the TAR) must be "organized by the TAR and the four provinces' editorial offices for [Tibetan] language [material]" (Tib. *ljongs zhing lnga'i skad yig rtsom sgrig las tshan gyis bsgrigs*). The main responsibility of this office is to coordinate Tibetan language textbook publication. Its headquarters are in Xining city, Qinghai. Under this policy all middle and high school textbooks in the specified regions, with the exception of textbooks on Tibetan and Chinese language and literature, should have been translated from Chinese to Tibetan language, and other textbooks should have been declared nonconforming. However, I was unable to ascertain during fieldwork whether the policy had been properly implemented.

In addition, Tibetans in the TAR officially benefit from the "three guarantees" policy (Tib. *zas 'dug slob gsum gyi 'gro gron 'gan len*, Ch. *san bao*), which guarantees exemption from school and room-and-board fees from primary education to high school for urban poor families, farmers, and nomadic pastoralists.[7] This exemption is stated in a 1985 law for "semi-farmer and semi-nomad" areas (Tib. *zhing 'brog khul*) of the TAR. Most of the sources on education in the TAR refer to this "three guarantees" policy, but I was unable to confirm how well it is implemented in practice. The nine-year free compulsory education requirement introduced by a 1986 federal law was not implemented correctly before a 2006 amendment. Therefore, the 2006 amendment is regarded as the more important legislation and should have been further supported by the 1986 law for education in rural and poor areas.

Important also is the Chinese-Tibetan "bilingual education" policy (Tib. *skad gnyis slob gso*). Officially, "bilingual education" has been promulgated since 2007 for twenty-one ethnic minorities.[8] In many Tibetan areas, however, even though the term may not have been used at the time, the bilingual education formula has been in use since the 1980s (Bangsbo 2004, 19). Recently, "bilingual education" has been extended to preschool education (Tib. *sngon gso*).[9] In an article published on Amdotibet.cn on April 1, 2012, it was reported that the budget for bilingual preschool education in Tsolho TAP should allow 90 percent of children to get access to one year of preschool education, 83 percent to access two years, and 78 percent to access three years, in county seats, villages, and hamlets before 2015.[10]

Finally, two other laws relevant to this survey are the 1984 "Chinese Law on Regional Autonomy,"[11] concerning educational structures, and the 1995 "Chinese Law on Education." Article 37 of the 1984 law stipulates:

> The organs of self-government of national autonomous areas shall independently develop education for the nationalities by eliminating illiteracy, setting up various kinds of schools. . . . The organs of self-government of national autonomous areas may set up public primary schools and secondary schools, mainly boarding schools and schools providing subsidies, in pastoral areas and economically under developed, sparsely populated mountain areas inhabited by minority nationalities. Schools where most of the students come from minority nationalities should, whenever possible, use textbooks in their own languages and use these languages as the media of instruction. Classes for the teaching of Chinese (the Han language) shall be opened for senior grades of primary schools or for secondary schools to popularize Putonghua, the common speech based on Beijing pronunciation.

Furthermore, the 1995 "Chinese Law on Education" grants minority nationalities the option to study in their own language. Article 12, in particular, states that "schools or other educational institutions which mainly consist of students from minority nationalities may use in education the language of the respective nationality or the native language commonly adopted in that region" (*Xinhua* 1995, in Bangsbo 2004, 5).

Fischer (2009, 19–20) presents statistics on education levels and illiteracy rates in 2005, taking as variables the provinces, rural and urban areas, and the school attendance level for children aged six to fifteen. These are shown in tables 4.1 and 4.2. Official Chinese sources often mention statistics that concern the TAR only and compare illiteracy between 1950 and the present day.[12] But such figures should be read with great caution: first, it is not known whether these statistics take into account literacy in Tibetan or only in Chinese. Moreover, they rarely compare illiteracy rates between Tibetans (inside and outside the TAR) or between Tibetans and other nationalities, including Han Chinese. Tables 4.1 and 4.2 give a general idea of the disparities between rural and urban populations. Those disparities often also correspond to ethnic boundaries (Tibetans/non-Tibetans). However, one needs to exercise caution interpreting these statistics because they include the Han and Hui populations of the TAR, as well as the non-Tibetan populations in the three other provinces (Tibetans make up only 22 percent of the population in Qinghai Province, for example). Thus, they do not reflect accurately the illiteracy rates of Tibetans. It is thus necessary to conduct a more specific study in order to shed light on the actual implementation of educational policies in Tibetan areas.

**TABLE 4.1**  Comparison of Rural and Urban Education Levels of Population Aged Six+, Rural and City (2004 Survey)

|         | Rural | | | City | | |
|---------|---------|-----------|----------|---------|-----------|----------|
|         | Primary | Secondary | Tertiary | Primary | Secondary | Tertiary |
| TAR     | 64.1%   | 13.1%     | 0.4%     | 59.5%   | 22.6%     | 2.3%     |
| QINGHAI | 72.2%   | 29.5%     | 0.4%     | 94.4%   | 69.2%     | 9.3%     |
| GANSU   | 78.7%   | 37.4%     | 0.6%     | 94.6%   | 76.3%     | 18.7%    |
| SICHUAN | 87.4%   | 41.1%     | 0.5%     | 96.6%   | 73.0%     | 11.9%    |
| CHINA   | 88.2%   | 48.3%     | 0.9%     | 95.4%   | 76.3%     | 15.1%    |

*Source*: Fischer (2009).

**TABLE 4.2**  Comparison of Rural and Urban Illiteracy Rates Among Population Aged 15+ (2004 Survey)

|         | Total | Rural | Town | City | Rural/City |
|---------|-------|-------|------|------|------------|
| TAR     | 44.0% | 45.6% | —    | 47.4%| 0.9        |
| QINGHAI | 22.1% | 31.9% | 9.1% | 5.9% | 5.4        |
| GANSU   | 19.4% | 25.4% | 5.3% | 5.6% | 4.5        |
| SICHUAN | 11.5% | 14.4% | 6.9% | 3.6% | 4.0        |
| CHINA   | 10.3% | 13.7% | 7.7% | 4.8% | 2.9        |

*Source*: Fischer (2009).

## Education Policies in Tsolho and Yulshul TAPs

As with most Tibetan majority areas, Yulshul (Ch. *Yushu*) and Tsolho (Ch. *Hainan*) TAPs are overwhelmingly rural; however, there are important differences between the two. Geographically, Yulshul is Qinghai's most remote TAP.[13] It is located in the historic Tibetan area of Kham and includes seven Tibetan Autonomous Counties (TACs), among which is Kyegundo (Ch. *Yushu*), the administrative prefecture seat. After the Tibetan and Mongol Autonomous Prefecture of Tsonüp (Ch. *Haixi*), it is the largest TAP in Qinghai. Its population is 95 percent ethnic Tibetan. Tsolho TAP includes five TACs, among which is Chapcha (Ch. *Gong he*), where the administrative prefecture seat is located. Tsolho is located in the historic Tibetan region of Amdo. Tsolho TAP is much more urbanized, more populated, and more Sinicized than Yulshul TAP. There is a significant presence of Han Chinese and Hui populations, and Tibetans make up 62.7 percent of the total population. However, variations within the prefecture itself are also important. Ba TAC, in Tsolho, for example, is 90 percent Tibetan.[14] Yulshul TAP is more difficult to reach because of its high altitude and remoteness from Xining, the provincial capital, and its population density is fewer than three inhabitants per square kilometer.[15] This is also a region where pastoralist and semipastoralist communities prevail. In Tsolho[16] agriculture is much more widespread than in Yulshul, especially in Trika and Chapcha,[17] the two most populated TACs. Population density is around twelve inhabitants per square kilometer. A pastoralist economy is also widespread, however, notably in Könan and Drakkar TACs; and, generally speaking, it seems that the semifarmer-seminomadic category prevails.[18] The five TAC seats of Tsolho have efficient public bus transport to Xining and are relatively well connected. Finally, from the beginning of 2000 onward, the "Opening Up of the West" (Ch. *Xibu da kaifa*) policy began, and in both TAPs nomadic pastoralists have been deeply affected by settlement policies (Ptackova 2011; Robin 2009).

It is my hypothesis that as a result of its ethnic characteristics, its proximity to the provincial capital, and its relatively high level of urbanization compared to Yulshul, Tsolho TAP has a more successful record of implementing official education policies. I address three areas of education policies—institution grouping and restructuring, bilingual education, and education materials—and compare the differences in implementation between the two TAPs.

In the last twenty years the education institutions of Tsolho TAP have undergone profound restructuring, as demonstrated in table 4.3. Regarding textbooks used, inconsistency is also evident. Generally, the teaching language is not fixed even within one prefecture. It depends largely on the nationality of the teacher, as well as on the language in which the teacher studied the subject he or she teaches, but also on the policies and decisions of individual county or village education bureaus. In Chapcha and Trika TACs all courses except Tibetan-language courses have long been taught in Mandarin. By contrast, in Könan TAC most subjects are still taught in Tibetan. But the language used in the classroom and that used in textbooks is often different. Incongruous practices such as these reached a peak during 1983–84 in Tsolho TAP, when textbooks for the Tibetan language were published with explanations in Chinese. These textbooks were used for less than a year. During my 2012 field research I found "experimental textbooks" (Tib. *tshod lta'i slob deb*) for the whole of Tsolho TAP that were published in August 2009 and distributed across the entire TAP in March 2010.

The outcome of these education reforms, however, is not necessarily improved results in written Tibetan. Indeed, the succession of short-term reforms—reforms that sometimes contradict each other—appears to have been counterproductive for improving Tibetan literacy. The budgetary increase, especially for preschool education and the creation of new classes, is significant.[19] Despite this apparent dynamism, Tsolho, and especially Chapcha TAC, has been one of the main centers of student protest since 2010. It is noteworthy also that the first expense listed in Tsolho's education budget is "Security Offices" in schools. One may reasonably surmise that this budget increase is related to the increasing number of protests; it also problematizes the idea that increased funding supports education.

In Yulshul TAP there is no generalist regular Chinese-language-only school (Ch. *putong zhongxue*). Yulshul is more rural than Tsolho TAP; its population density is extremely low; there are almost no Han or Salar/Hui migrants; and its inhabitants are largely herders and transhumant agropastoralists.[20] Still, Yulshul students have a reputation for being better at written Chinese than at written Tibetan. This can be explained by emphasizing three aspects of public schools and the application of education

**TABLE 4.3** Restructure of Tsolho TAP Education Institutions Since the 1980s

| When | Where | What | Result |
|---|---|---|---|
| Before 1985 | Könan, Chapcha, and Trika TACs (probably also in Drakkar and Ba TACs) *Village-level*: primary schools taught Tibetan. | *County seat*: one regular Chinese-language-only primary and middle school and one "minority nationalities middle school" with a Tibetan-language curriculum. However, minority middle schools accepted only the children from villages, those who had studied in the Tibetan language for six years throughout primary school. The county's "urban" students could only enter the "Chinese" middle school. | Students from the county seat could not enroll in a Tibetan language school. |
| End of the 1980s (in 1987 for Könan) | Könan, Chapcha, Trika, and Ba TACs (probably also in Drakkar TAC) | "Minority nationalities primary schools" were built in county seats. Courses in Tibetan start from class 1. | Benefits the Tibetan language level and allows children who were not from villages to choose their language of instruction. |
| 2002–3 | Chapcha TAC *Village level*: many "minority nationalities primary schools" were closed and replaced by "minority nationalities primary boarding schools" located in the county seat. | *County level*: in the "Minority Nationalities High School," reduction of the number of students who chose Tibetan as their main language of instruction because of an unofficial policy of the Education Bureau: students in possession of an urban *hukoua* were forced to choose the Chinese language curriculum, so actually only the students officially registered as "rural" were free to choose between | End of free choice of language for education. |

| Date | Location | Description | Effect |
|---|---|---|---|
| In the 2000s (exact date unknown) | Könan, Ba, and Drakkar TACs | the Chinese and the Tibetan curriculum. (My informant stated that around 80 percent of students were registered as "urban." This figure has not been validated and seems to be excessively high.)[b] *County seat:* high school classes 10 and 11 in "minority nationalities middle schools" are moved to the prefecture seat Chapcha and to Trika TAC. As a result, Trika and Chapcha TAC "Minority Nationalities High Schools" are broadened to welcome the high school students from all Tsolho's TACs. | Chinese language broadly used as a medium of teaching in Trika and Chapcha TACs: further degradation of Tibetan language level. |
| 2009 | Chapcha and Trika TACs | *Village level:* all primary schools closed, replaced by two large "boarding minority nationalities schools" for primary and middle school children, one in Chapcha TAC, the other in Trika TAC. Reasons put forward: the possibility of recruiting better trained teachers and to have better-equipped schools; reduce the education level gap between children coming from the villages, whose education level may be lower, and thus allow more students to continue the curriculum, improving the general level for the high school entrance exam. | Diverging opinions expressed during interviews: improvement in teaching and learning environment, vs. problems entailed by children's separation from families. |
| Since 2010 | Tsolho TAP and especially Chapcha TAC | | Student protests. |

[a]Tib. *them tho,* household registration residency status.
[b]Interview in winter 2012 with the son of a school headmaster in Chapcha.

policies in Yulshul: the low quality of teaching and studying conditions, the low priority given to the Tibetan language, and the difficulty of training teachers.

In Yulshul most of the children from nomadic and seminomadic households above the age of fifteen years have never been to school. This may be explained by the fact that today's fifteen-year-olds had already exceeded the official primary school entry age at the time of the 2006 education law amendment. Thus, until quite recently, education access itself was still a problem. Minority nationalities' primary boarding schools in the villages, some of which are quite close to pastureland, do exist, but the material conditions of these schools are deficient, and access for the most remote households remains difficult. Yulshul's preschools are few and located exclusively in the county seats. Moreover they seem to be attended only by the children of local state employees.

In the county seats, class sizes are extremely large, indicating that the number of teachers and classrooms is insufficient. For example, in one of the minority nationalities' primary schools in Nangchen District, most of the classes have around seventy students, and some have as many as 120. It is likely that the nomadic households settlement policies, which were implemented locally in 2003–4, have contributed to a rapid increase in the number of children attending school. By way of comparison, the "Minority Nationalities Primary and Middle School Number 1" in Trika averages thirty to forty children per class. At the national level the primary school teacher-to-student ratio is 1 to 17.[21]

In Yulshul each TAC has at least one minority nationalities middle school, but, as far as I know, there is no regular "Chinese" middle school. This can be explained by the fact that Yulshul's population is 95 percent ethnic Tibetan, a proportion significantly higher than that of Tsolho. However, and paradoxically, in Yulshul's primary and secondary minority nationalities schools the textbooks and teaching language is Mandarin. Mandarin is taught from as early as the first year. There is only one Tibetan language course in the whole curriculum. In accordance with Yulshul Education Bureau policies from 2010 onward, mathematics courses should have been taught in Tibetan for primary school levels 1 to 3. But this has rarely been implemented in practice. Teachers and students alike explained that they do not have the necessary Tibetan vocabulary to study or teach mathematics in Tibetan. Teachers would have needed, at the very least, basic training to be able to teach this subject in Tibetan. This has not been the case. As a teacher in Dritö informed me, when the courses are not taught in an "impure language"—i.e., a mixture of Tibetan and Chinese languages—they are simply taught in Chinese, "like before."

There is only one teacher training school (Tib. *dge thon slob grwa*) in Yulshul TAP.[22] It trains primary school teachers only. In Tsolho, by contrast, there are teacher training schools for various education levels.[23] Therefore, in Yulshul most students who want to become high school teachers must undertake teacher training in Xining, Qinghai's provincial capital, where a Tibetan dialect different from their own is spoken. Given that these two dialects are not mutually intelligible, it is highly likely that Yulshul students turn to the Chinese rather than the Tibetan language teacher training there and then teach in Chinese when they return to Yulshul after completing their training. Also, because of the shortage of Tibetan-language teachers in Yulshul, a significant proportion of the teachers there come from Amdo and experience the same difficulties of comprehension between students and teachers, thus leading to poor results on written Tibetan exams.

## Private Tibetan Education Initiatives

To complete my description of the educational landscape in the two TAPs, I will turn now to private Tibetan initiatives. In Tsolho TAP, since 2011, official summer courses in all subjects have been offered by Chapcha's public schools, but private lessons exist in parallel. One such private school is organized by a Tibetan-language teacher from Chapcha Minority Nationalities Middle School during school holidays. This twenty-one-day summer course costs two hundred yuan. For this class the teacher rents a private classroom. A very basic room is also rented in the city, where children sleep and eat. Children study grammar, poetry, and religious texts. Their "textbooks" are Dungkar Lozang Trinlé's poetry book, Jé Tsongkhapa's *Jangchup Lamrim*, and Yeshe Gyatso's *sungbum* (complete works).[24] According to the teacher, these works are not officially authorized as textbooks because, in the case of the last two, they deal with religious topics. His students come from Drakkar TAC, and six out of seven of them are from nomadic pastoralist households. They are between fifteen and seventeen years old and attend Drakkar Minority Nationalities Middle School. The mother of one of the children cooks their meals and takes care of their everyday living needs. According to their teacher, their Tibetan-language level is above average, and they attend his class to further improve their skills and to acquire new knowledge in the Tibetan language.

Another example of a private initiative is Tibetan-language private instruction at students' homes by a Tibetan teacher from Chapcha School. This teacher earns a small additional income by teaching at the homes of his students during the summer holidays. One of his students chose the Chinese language curriculum at the minority nationalities middle school and studies politics as his main subject. At the behest of his parents, however, he agreed to deepen his knowledge in written Tibetan via these private classes. A traditional grammar book (*sum rtags*) is used as a textbook.

Könan TAC is more rural than Chapcha, and the population comprises mainly nomadic pastoralists. In summer monks from local monasteries teach written Tibetan to some of the children attending public schools—more often friends or family. In Nangchen and Dzatö TACs (Yulshul) such private initiatives also exist in parallel with the official education system. Unlike those in Tsolho TAP, however, most are organized by religious practitioners. The influence and importance of local *khenpos* (highly qualified religious teachers)[25] is strong in the existing parallel educational system. In Nangchen, written Tibetan lessons taught by a *khenpo* in the monastery are available to Tibetan laypeople older than fifteen years old during the winter holidays. Courses last for one or two months and cost 150 yuan per month. During the holidays almost one hundred laypeople attend. Other initiatives are implemented locally with the aim of improving written and spoken Tibetan. In 2011, for example, in Sharda (Nangchen County seat), a Tibetan language competition called "Competition for the Purity of Mother Tongue" (*pha skad gtsang ma'i 'gran sdur*) was organized. The participants were asked to name in Tibetan new objects coming from Han China that in everyday life are, consequently, often designated in Chinese (e.g., microwave, mobile phone charger, etc.). The winner was a nomad who had never been formally educated. He prepared for the competition by studying the trilingual illustrated lexica of *khenpo* Tsultrim Lodrö.[26] Nowadays, one can find this book in most Tibetan households, even nomadic ones, in Nangchen and Dzatö. Moreover, during public Buddhist teachings in Nangchen, clerics publicly encourage local Tibetans to study written Tibetan.

In Dzatö district, also, religious practitioner scholars arrange many educational initiatives. A prominent example is an orphanage primary school established by a local *khenpo*.[27] The school attracts students from the whole of Yulshul and even a few from Amdo. The diploma awarded by this school is officially recognized and allows graduating students to continue in the public education system at the middle school level. It is said that because the school is close to the county seat, the official curriculum is respected. This *khenpo* also opened a "monastery school" (Tib. *shedra*)[28] in Dzogchen monastery in Dzatö, which hosts 130 monks. Chinese is taught during the first year only.

Another private school, the "School for the Benefit of the Masses" (*Dmangs phan slob grwa*), was set up a few months after a violent earthquake caused widespread destruction in Yulshul in April 2010. Because of the destruction of local schools, most students were transferred to "inner China" (translation of the Tibetan expression "*Rgya nang*") schools for more than two years. The newly built private school has eighty-two students, five teachers, and three levels of classes. Its students are aged fourteen to twenty, and most of them come from nomadic households. The headmaster of the school is also its Tibetan-language and "ethics" (*bslab bya*) courses teacher. He describes the latter subject as Buddhist general knowledge and morals. Some non-Buddhist authors, like Confucius, are also briefly introduced in these courses. In addition to the compulsory subjects taught in Tibetan (Chinese, mathematics, Tibetan), children can choose optional traditional art (*lag rtsal*): tangka painting with natural pigments, incense production, and drawing with locally made pigments. On Saturday afternoons the students and teachers gather for question-and-answer sessions and debate, essentially on Buddhist philosophy. The headmaster, a local man from Yulshul TAP, is approximately thirty years old. He didn't have the opportunity to receive a formal education during his childhood: he went to public school for fewer than two years and then studied as a monk in a monastery for a few years. He told me his aim is to "give a chance to Nangchen and Kyegundo's children." He stressed the fact that in Yulshul the nine-year compulsory education policy was far from being correctly implemented. Tibetan-language textbooks used at the School for the Benefit of the Masses deal mainly with Buddhist philosophy. Accord-ing to the headmaster, this is done "according to the students' level," and it corresponds to an education "adapted to their needs, contrary to the education given in public schools." According to him, the main objective of this school is for students to get an education benefiting them on dif-ferent levels: getting a job after graduation is important, but in his eyes it is even more important that they "go back to their home country, on the pastureland for most of them, to benefit their community, such as opening a school, teaching, etc." The headmaster explained that it is a significant sacrifice for parents to send their children to school, particularly if their sons and daughters are already of working age.

The example of the School for the Benefit of the Masses highlights a number of characteristics shared with many of the other private education institutions in Yulshul and Tsolho TAPs:

It proposes unconditional acceptance of students (regardless of sex, age, lay, or religious status).

It is established by a charismatic person from the religious sphere.

It does not have the same aims as "classical," official teaching; that is, more emphasis is placed on moral education than on entering the job market.

It contrasts with official curricula, especially on linguistic policies and course content, placing more emphasis on religion,[29] and thereby matches the expectations of the local Tibetan people.

It focuses on written and oral Tibetan-language teaching and on the pro-tection/revitalization of Tibetan culture.[30]

There are many private schools in Yulshul. The primary reason for this is remoteness of many rural households. But Yulshul's private educational structure differs on at least one point from Tsolho's. In Tsolho TAP, courses are organized and taught largely by lay university graduates or public sys-tem teachers; in Yulshul most of the teachers follow a more religious cur-riculum.[31] The majority of educated people in Yulshul are religious practi-tioners, not laypeople. However, my research also found that in Könan, a pastoralist area of Tsolho, there were religious practitioners working pri-vately as teachers.

Nevertheless, in both TAPs the private initiatives seem to exist to compensate for the perceived shortcomings of the public system. Therefore, there would appear to be a strong demand for Tibetan courses (language, culture, and especially philosophy and literature), which are particularly neglected in Kham areas such as Yulshul TAP.

## A Mutual Distrust Between Tibetan Students and PRC Authorities

In October and November 2010 thousands of Tibetan students from different places expressed their opposition to the education reforms, leaving their classrooms and protesting on the streets. *Khabda* exile website described this move as "an uprising for (Tibetan) language" (Tib. *skad yig skor gyi gyen langs*) against the "Outline of China's National Plan for Medium and Long-Term Education Reform and Development of Qinghai Province 2010–2020."[32] The point of this reform was to restrict the use of Tibetan language to Tibetan and English classes only, thereby further marginalizing the Tibetan language. Furthermore, the reform also planned for the translation of textbooks into Chinese, with the medium of instruction to be restricted to Chinese within five years. The Qinghai provincial government launched this education policy reform in September 2010. It is not clear whether it was launched at the behest of the central or provincial government or whether it was related to similar reforms in other provinces.[33] One must remember, however, that the provincial education bureau has responsibility for the production of school-teaching materials and that the "Outline of China's National Plan for Medium and Long-Term Education Reform and Development (2010–2020)" suggested further devolution of power to the provincial level.[34] It can reasonably be assumed, therefore, that this was a provincial government initiative.

The protest movements erupted simultaneously at several schools, beginning on October 19, 2010, in Repgong and Chentsa cities (Malho TAP). Then the protests spread to Chapcha, Trika (Tsolho TAP); Temchen (Tsonüp TAP); Ngawa (Ngawa TAP); Golok (Golok TAP); and Beijing Nationality University. A popular slogan during the protests was "Equality of nationalities, freedom of language" (*mi rigs kyi 'dra mnyam, skad rigs kyi rang dbang*). But one could also hear "Protection of our language, equality of nationalities"(*skad rigs gces skyong, mi rigs 'dra mnyam*) and "I want *ka, kha, ga, nga*" (*nga la ka kha ga nga dgos*).[35] Some teachers also joined the protesters. Around twenty students were allegedly arrested.

Tibetan students (and some teachers) rose up again in various places (Repgong, Chentsa, Golok, Yulshul, Malho, Tsolho, and Sokdzong) between December 26 and December 28, 2011, to demand the application of article 4 of the PRC Constitution.[36] The protests continued in March 2012. Tragically on March 3, 2012, a nineteen-year-old female high school student from Machu, named Tsering kyi, self-immolated. Woeser (2012) saw a connection between this immolation and the change from Tibetan to Chinese language textbooks in Qinghai and Gansu provinces. From March 2012, Tibetan middle school and university student protests appeared to correlate with the self-immolation movement, thus changing in character. The reasons behind the students' apparent solidarity with self-immolators need to be examined. Tibetan self-immolators are considered by PRC authorities to be "splittists," and associating oneself with them carries risks. Students expressing solidarity with them thus have a lot to lose. Indeed, taking part in a protest or being arrested may result in a forced stoppage of their nine-year compulsory education or even in their being banned from taking their exams.

It seems that around this time the causes behind student protests began to change. For example, in Sokdzong (Malho TAP), on March 18, 2012, around two thousand protesters gathered after a self-immolation. They were joined by students who shouted their own slogans in favor of the protection of the Tibetan language in schools.

An article from the exile news website *Tibet Times*, titled "Amdo Chapcha Students Protest" ("*Mdo smad Chab char slob mas ngo rgol*"), dated November 26, 2012, states that at the Chapcha Medical School (*Gso rig slob grwa*) thousands of students protested in front of the Tsolho prefecture administration office in Chapcha city, demanding "equality of nationalities" (*mi rigs 'dra mnyam*), "freedom of nationalities" (*mi rigs rang dbang*), and "we want the reform of administration" (*srid gzhung bskyar 'dzugs*).[37] Exile media reported the intervention of armed police and military personnel and stated that some students were beaten and shots were fired into the crowd, wounding fifteen students. It seems that the protest was triggered by the distribution in several schools, by local Tsolho authorities, of a booklet titled "Ten [Right] Views on the Recent Events in Tsolho Prefecture" (*Mtsho lho khul gyi mig snga'i lta tshul 'dzin stang bcu*).[38] According to the *Tibet Times* journalist, this booklet asserted that "if only spoken and written Tibetan language were studied, there would be no future" and that "self-immolations [were] stupid acts." This document "discredited the gift of one's life for religion, politics and the Tibetan people" and "encouraged gratitude towards the Chinese Communist Party." Students burned copies of these booklets during the protest. In doing so, for the first time, students were officially associated with the "political" self-immolation movement.

On November 13, 2012, the *Tibet Times* published a petition from students and teachers from several minority nationalities universities titled "Some Tibetan Universities Teachers' and Students' Hopes and Expectations Toward the Chinese Government" (*Bod nang slob chen khag gi dge slob tshos rgya gzhung la re 'dun zhu yig*).[39] The petitioners' concerns extended beyond their immediate education interests, to broader political and social concerns—language, culture, religion, politics, way of living, and ecology. Events continued to escalate in the students' environment, which seemingly contributed to the belief by the Chinese authorities that all Tibetan students were potential self-immolators. However, from the beginning of the movement in March 2011 to February 25, 2013, only five out of a total of 106 self-immolators were students.[40] In response to these protests, the winter holidays' usual Tibetan-language classes were either placed under surveillance or completely banned in several Qinghai locations.[41]

The above accounts bring us back to our initial question: assuming that there exists a similarly strong interest in the study of Tibetan language and culture in both Yulshul and Tsolho TAPs, how can we explain why protests have been far more predominant in Amdo (Tsolho) and almost absent in the Kham (Yulshul) areas of Qinghai? I would like to pose some answers. I have demonstrated that in Yulshul TAP Chinese-language medium teaching has been dominant for the past several years, whereas in Tsolho TAP there was still the opportunity to study Tibetan, despite the reduction in Tibetan-language courses brought about by the reforms.[42] In contrast, because education in Yulshul TAP was already Sinicized, the effects of the reforms did not represent a major departure. That was not the case for Amdo students. They participate in a well-organized educational system in which the Tibetan language is increasingly neglected. Moreover, in Tsolho TAP, meetings about "Tibetan education" (Tib. *bod rigs slob gso*) and "minority nationalities education" (Tib. *mi rigs slob gso*) seem to be quite frequent.[43] Some teacher-researchers have also published articles on these subjects, which helps to explain Amdo students' sensitivity to such topics. Amdo is also the area where most of the self-immolations happened, which may partly explain why some students protest both in favor of protecting their language and culture and in support of self-immolators.[44] The PRC's response to the protests has been unequivocal. Many private Tibetan classes are banned or under surveillance, even in Yulshul.

In the PRC Tibetans are not the only minority nationality to be affected by restrictive educational policies. They even appear to obtain preferential treatment, compared with other ethnic minorities such as the Uyghurs or the Mongols, or other groups that do not have their own writing systems.

I have shown in this chapter that PRC education policies for Tibetan minority students are not implemented in the same manner everywhere: Tsolho appears "reformist," whereas Yulshul is much more static. Only after looking more closely at both the public and private education systems operating in Tibetan areas, and noting their complementary aspects, can we conclude that the demands of Tibetan students in the PRC are very similar regardless of their location.

The current education system does not satisfy Tibetans because it neither preserves nor develops their cultural and linguistic heritage. Tibetan students particularly resent three aspects of the current PRC education system as it applies to them: the subjects taught, the language of instruction, and the necessary separation from their families (particularly for those who must travel to school from remote locations), resulting in an interrupted transmission of values and "damage to cultural integrity" (Barnett 2012, 46). This collective feeling of civilizational insecurity has resulted in two types of reaction: a multiplication of private education initiatives and opposition protests, especially in Amdo-speaking areas. In response the PRC has imposed surveillance, and in some cases the banning of Tibetan-language classes. Although local reactions differ, there is widespread disagreement and dissatisfaction with official policies and the lack of dialogue.

# Appendix

A. Ten [Right] Views on the Recent Events in Tsolho Prefecture (*Mtsho lho khul gyi mig snga'i lta tshul 'dzin stang bcu*)

1. In order to improve the development of Tsolho, what should we take as a basis?
2. Hasn't Tibetan culture been protected and developed?
3. Is there any contradiction between protection of the environment and development and construction?
4. Does bilingual education weaken the oral and written language of a nationality?
5. Who has ruled us and brought to reality the equality among nationalities?
6. What is the nature of the act of self-immolation?
7. What harm is involved in illegal protests?
8. Who is responsible for fomenting separatism and chaos?
9. What is the complete and perfect meaning of the policy of freedom of religion and faith?
10. How should the development of an environment characterized by peace and unity be cherished?

B. Some Tibetan Universities Teachers' and Students' Hopes and Expectations Toward the Chinese Government (*Bod nang slob chen khag gi dge slob tshos rgya gzhung la re 'dun zhu yig*)

As the 18th Congress of the Chinese Communist Party is nearing, some Tibetan universities' teachers and students and some monasteries' monks sent this letter to the Central Government of China to express their hopes and wishes.

Some Tibetan teachers and students from the Central University for Nationalities, the North-West University for Nationalities [Lanzhou], the Qinghai Higher College for Education and some other universities of Qinghai, Tsolho's Teacher Training School, some high school teachers and students, as well as some monasteries' monks, gathered and signed this letter expressing their hopes and wishes. It contains eight points and it is presented here, with their signature.

1. Social harmony and the basis of security are: the equality of nationalities and equal consideration, political and economical freedom and an environment without oppression. Therefore, the Chinese government must consider creating an environment in which the nationalities benefit from consideration and are bereft from oppression.

2. The government should be aware that the granting of equality and the right to use the Tibetan language and script on an equal basis with the Chinese language and script in the government offices of the autonomous region, prefectures and district, is the basis of equality among nationalities.

3. The basic development of the Tibetan nationality is not only about building new houses and other apparent progress. In the nationalities universities endowed with a Tibetan language department, we must open departments with specialists in Tibetan history, politics, law, economy, science, and sociology, in order to bring up [Tibetan] specialists. The [government] must consider educating many learned persons of the Tibetan nationality, thanks to these departments. It must understand that this is the basic way for a nationality to progress and the basis for the progress and development of new knowledge.

4. In the Tibetan regions, translating into Chinese all the high schools' textbooks is a cruel policy of contempt toward the nationality. Thus, the Chinese central government must absolutely reform it.

5. The Tibetan people are not only relying on and preoccupied about the external aspects of civilization. We are a nationality that considers spiritual and material civilizations as equally important, but we prize spiritual

civilization more than the material one; [the government] needs to give freedom and rights, reflecting the situation and freedom of religion in Tibetan autonomous areas.

6. In Tibetan areas, one must foster Tibetan government employees being endowed with political power. The monasteries' religion bureaus employees must not only follow the Communist Party's desires and expectations, and one must foster Tibetan employees who would be endowed with actual political power.

7. There has been an important migration of Chinese and Muslim people in Tibetan areas. The real landowner of Tibet is becoming a minority nationality on his own land. Therefore, it is affecting the minds of Tibetan people and generates anxiety. One must think of it.

8. The law decided by the Central Government for the autonomous policies must be fully applied. The policies of exceeding extraction of mineral resources and of the transformation of nomads into villagers must undergo reforms. The Tibetan nationality, during thousands of years, has led a life that respects the gods and *nagas*, and has protected the environment in accordance with Buddhism. Therefore, harming in an unthinkable way Tibetan culture and customs is creating an unbearable pain in the Tibetans' minds. So, one must think to it.

Through those eight important points, we are expressing our hopes and wishes to the central Chinese government.

## Notes

1. Data for this chapter are from interviews with teachers, and schoolchildren and their families, during the summer of 2012, in Yulshul and Tsolho TAPs, as well as from various scientific articles about education and articles published in the Tibetan blogosphere

2. The Chinese Ministry of Education's "Outline of China's National Plan for Medium and Long-Term Education Reform and Development (2010–2020)" stresses these three aspects. See Ministry of Education (2010).

3. See http://en.tibet.cn/2010jy/zchxm/201009/t20100917_714968.html (TAR); and http://english.people.com.cn/90001/90782/90872/6626154.html (Qinghai).

4. See www.merabsarpa.com/education/making-tibetans-in-china-dislocated -secondary-education; see also the website of the Congressional-Executive Commission on China for the following report: "The Fifth Forum introduced

a new and important initiative: establishing the coordinated implementation of Party and government policies on Tibetan issues in an area that will include not just the TAR, but also Tibetan autonomous prefectures and counties located in Qinghai, Gansu, Sichuan, and Yunnan provinces. The expanded area is contiguous and approximately doubles the number of Tibetans who live within the forum policy area" (www.cecc.gov/publications/ commission-analysis/communist-party-leadership-outlines-2010-2020 -tibet-work-priorities).The Fifth Forum took place in 2010; however, at least in some areas of Qinghai, students had already been sent to *neidi ban* a few years before.

5. This system was expanded to the Uyghurs (Xinjiang Province) in 2000.
6. See www.ibe.unesco.org/fileadmin/user_upload/Publications/WDE/2010/pdf -versions/China.pdf.
7. See "China's Education Policies on Tibet (II)," Oct. 12, 2011, http://chinatibet .people.com.cn/96069/7614639.html.
8. For further details see the following UNESCO report: www.ibe.unesco.org/ fileadmin/user_upload/Publications/WDE/2010/pdf-versions/China.pdf.
9. At the end of 2011 a meeting in Khri ka Minority Nationalities School (Qinghai) gathered teachers from Xining, Mtsho lho, Yulshul, and Mgo log to discuss this topic. See "*Mtsho sngon zhing chen slob sngon slob gso'i skad gnyis dge rgan gyi khrid gzhi zab sbyong bya ba'i 'dzin grwa bsdus*," http://gdmzjx.com/news/xnxw/2011 -11-22/599.html.
10. See www.qhtb.cn/news/social/2012-04-01/9115.html.
11. See www.china.org.cn/government/laws/2007-04/13/content_1207139.htm.
12. See www.china.org.cn/english/zhuanti/tibet percent20facts/163911.htm.
13. By bus, the most popular means of transport for Tibetans, one must travel around twenty hours from Xining, Qinghai's capital (510 miles), and thirty hours from Chengdu, Sichuan's capital (750 miles). A new airport was built in 2009 in Yulshul, but the price for an air ticket from Xining is relatively high at around 1,390 yuan.
14. See http://baike.baidu.com/view/928116.htm#1.
15. Yushu Zangzu Zizhizhou Tongjiju [Yushu Tibetan Autonomous Prefecture Statistics Bureau]. 2006. *Yushu Tongjiju Nianjian 2005* [Yushu Statistical Yearbook 2005], Yushu Tibetan Autonomous Prefecture Government Publishing.
16. I will refer to Mtsho lho TAP as Mtsho lho and Yulshul TAP as Yulshul.
17. See www.qhgh.gov.cn/html/1792/206066.html.
18. In Khri ka, for example, 78,749 out of 94,290 residents are semipastoralists. This figure seems to suggest that the category of seminomads-semifarmers might include the majority of Tibetans in a number of areas. See http://baike .baidu.com/view/645151.htm?pid=baike.box.
19. See *Mtsho lho khul gyi slob gso'i las don gong du spel ba* (Mtsho lho prefecture improvement of education), Bde chen mtsho 2013/2/6, www.amdotibet.cn/ html/dt/whjy/2013-02/14093.html.

20. In 2006, of a population of 302,780 habitants, 287,641 were seminomads and semifarmers (*rong ma 'brog*). This suggests that the remaining third is composed of nomads and the district's administrative center's inhabitants. See Rin chen dbang rgyal (2008, 4–5).

21. See UNESCO Institute for Statistics (2010), http://stats.uis.unesco.org/unesco/TableViewer/document.aspx?ReportId=136&IF_Language=fra&BR_Topic=0.

22. See www.amdotibet.com/tibet/content.asp?tableName_daohang=jiaoyu&table name_fenlei=xuexiao&id=20&face_n=0.

23. The Panchen Lama's Teacher Training University in Chapcha trains teachers for secondary school and for Chapha's primary schools level Teacher Training School. Many students also go to Xining to receive training.

24. Yeshe Gyatso is a prominent religious scholar from Gcan tsha in Amdo (1917–95); see www.tibetology.ac.cn/za/2009-07-03-11-38-25/zmrj/6667?view=articl e&id=6667&catid=107.

25. The title of *mkhan po* is similar to a PhD in Buddhist philosophy and can be obtained after ten years or so of higher studies.

26. *rGya bod dbyin gsum gsar byung rgyun bkol ris 'grel ming mdzod*, published by *Si khron mi rigs dpe skrun tshogs pa* and *Si khron mi rigs dpe skrun khang*, 2007 (English title: *Chinese-Tibetan-English Visual Dictionary of New Daily Vocabulary*).

27. The existence of private schools is submitted for prior authorization by the education bureau of local or superior levels (county, province, etc.).

28. The people I was speaking to call the *bshad grwa* the Monastery School (Tib. *dgon pa'i slob grwa*) or the Tibetan school (Tib. *bod kyi / bod pa'i slob grwa*).

29. According to article 4, para. 2 of the "Law of the People's Republic of China on the Promotion of Privately-Run Schools" (2002), "privately-run schools shall implement the principle of separating education from religion. No organizations or individuals may make use of religion to conduct activities designed to interfere with the educational system of the State." See www.npc.gov.cn/englishnpc/Law/2007-12/06/content_1382110.htm.

30. At the end of 2011 the "minority nationalities school" of Ba County organized an exhibition of ethnology, showing to the students objects, clothing, housing, food, and lifestyle of Tibetan nomadic herders and farmers. A press article reveals that this exhibition was a great success among children. The goal was the transmission of cultural heritage through schools: "perpetuate Tibetan culture and . . . illustrate its vitality showing the content of Tibetan culture and its specific handicraft" (*bod kyi rig gnas rgyun 'dzin byed pa dang . . . bod kyi rig gnas nang don dang khyad chos ldan pa'i sgyu rtsal gyi gson nyams dod pomtshon gyi yod*). This experiment was preceded in 2009 by a popular-art exhibition.

31. In Nangchen, monastery schools are called "*bod pa'i slob grwa*" (lit. Tibetan schools), whereas public schools are called "*rgyal khab slob grwa*" (lit. the country's schools).

32. "*2010 nas 2020 lo'i Mtsho sngon zhin chen dus yun 'bring ring gi slob gso bcos bsgyur dang 'phel rgyas kyi 'char 'god rtsag nad*." I also found "*Mtsho sgnon zhing chen gyi*

*dus yun ring 'bring gi slob gso'i bcos sgyur dang 'phel rgyas 'char 'god rtsa don 2010 lo
nas 2020 lo bar gyi srid jus."*

33. In the TAR this situation has been operative since the beginning of the 1980s.

34. See www.ibe.unesco.org/National_Reports/ICE_2008/china_NR08.pdf; and
http://planipolis.iiep.unesco.org/upload/China/China_National_Long_Term
_Educational_Reform_Development_2010-2020_eng.pdf.

35. The Tibetan alphabet's first letters.

36. Article 4 reads (in part): "All nationalities in the People's Republic of China
are equal. The state protects the lawful rights and interests of the minority
nationalities and upholds and develops the relationship of equality, unity and
mutual assistance among all of China's nationalities. . . . The people of all nationalities have the freedom to use and develop their own spoken and written
languages, and to preserve or reform their own ways and customs."

37. The article is in Tibetan. See www.tibettimes.net/news.php?showfooter=1
&id=6958.

38. Translation A in appendix.

39. See www.tibettimes.net/news.php?showfooter=1&id=6899 (translation B in
appendix).

40. See www.savetibet.org/resource-center/maps-data-fact-sheets/self-immolation
-fact-sheet.

41. See "Increased Surveillance of Holiday Classes" (Gung seng skab szur slob
bya rgyur dam bsgrags), *Tibet Times*, Dec. 20, 2012, about Nangchen, Yulshul
TAP; "For Whom Are We Building Schools?" (Slob grwa su'i ched du btsugs pa
in), Dge 'dun Chos 'phel website, Jan. 14, 2013, about Reb gong, Rma lho TAP
(www.gdqpzhx.com/bo/html/edu/201301142166.html); and "It Is Forbidden
to Teach Tibetan" (Bod yig slob sbyong byed mi chog), Radio Free Asia, Jan. 27,
2013, about Dpa' lung County (Mtsho shar Prefecture).

42. We can also connect this information with the composition of present-day
Tibetan writers' and poets' circles: Tibetan literary activity is flourishing in
Amdo but not in Khams.

43. See "Khri ka rdzong mi rigs bca' sdod slob grwas skabs gnyis pas pha skad bgrog leng
tshogs 'du bsdus," Sept. 26, 2012, www.qhtb.cn/news/social/2012-09-26/13799
.html (this document is no longer available online); "Mang rdzong mi rigs slob
gso'i gtam gleng tshogs 'du thengs dang po'i gnas tshul bkod pa," Sept. 21, 2012,
http://blog.amdotibet.cn/lhachen/archives/68664.aspx; and "Mtsho sngon
mtsho lho khul mi rigs mtho rim slob 'bring gnyis pa'i bod skad yig gi bsdus
grwa'i slob khrid byed thabs la grub 'bras mngon gsal dod po thob pa," Oct. 31,
2012, www.tibetanms.cn/shshly/xywh/2012-10-31/14314.html.

44. On Nov. 7, 2012, in Reb gong, Mdo ba County, seven hundred students low-
ered the Chinese flag of their school and protested in front of the local
administration office after the self-immolation of a young girl, Rtam grin 'tsho
(www.tibettimes.net/news.php?showfooter=1&id=6880).

# References

Bangsbo, Ellen. 2004. *Teaching and Learning in Tibet: A Review of Research and Policy Publications*. Copenhagen: NIAS Press.

Barnett, Robert. 2012. "Restrictions and Their Anomalies: The Third Forum and the Regulation of Religion in Tibet." *Journal of Current Chinese Affairs* 4, no. 1: 45–108.

Fischer, Andrew M. 2009. "Educating for Exclusion in Western China: Structural and Institutional Foundations of Conflict in the Tibetan Areas of Qinghai." CRISE Working Paper No. 69. Oxford: Centre for Research on Inequality, Security and Ethnicity, Queen Elizabeth House, Oxford University. July. www.crise.ox.ac.uk/abstract.shtml?wp69.

Ministry of Education. 2010. "Outline of China's National Plan for Medium and Long-Term Education Reform and Development (2010–2020)." Beijing. October. www.moe.edu.cn/publicfiles/business/htmlfiles/moe/s3501/index.html.

Ptackova, Jarmila. 2011. "Sedentarisation of Tibetan Nomads in China: Implementation of the *Nomadic Settlement* Project in the Tibetan Amdo Area; Qinghai and Sichuan Provinces." *Pastoralism: Research, Policy and Practice* 1:4.

Postiglione, Gerard, Ben Jiao, and Sonam Gyatso. 2005. "Education in Rural Tibet: Development, Problems and Adaptations." *China: An International Journal* 3 (1): 1–23.

Rin chen dbang rgyal. 2008. *Khams skad las khams stod (Yulshul) gyi yul skad la dpyad pa* [A study on the dialect of upper Kham region (Yushu)]. Beijing. Mi rigs dpe skrung khang [Nationalities Press]: 4–5.

Robin, Françoise. 2009. "Les nouveaux villages socialistes." *Perspectives chinoises*, no. 3, 60–68.

Wang, Shiyong. 2007. "The Failure of Education in Preparing Tibetans for Market Participation." *Asian Ethnicity* 8 (2): 131–48.

Woeser, Tsering. 2012. "The Moat and Apartheid." July 26. www.savetibet.org/media-center/tibet-news/moat-and-apartheid.

# 5

## Lucrative Chaos

### Interethnic Conflict as a Function of the Economic "Normalization" of Southern Xinjiang

Thomas Cliff

*As the great classicist Moses Finley often liked to say, in the ancient world, all revolutionary movements had a single program: "Cancel the debts and redistribute the land."*
—DAVID GRAEBER, *DEBT: THE FIRST 5,000 YEARS*

When David Graeber draws attention to the link between economic disadvantage and popular protest, he speaks to a core theme of this chapter.[1] Even so, I do not mean to suggest that debt and land dispossession are solely responsible for the repeated incidents of Uyghur-Han violence in South Xinjiang and the ongoing interethnic tensions in the region. Restrictions on certain Uyghur religious, cultural, and educational practices appear, from reports since 2009 (CECC 2011; *Global Times* 2012; Turdush 2013), to be of at least equal importance in this respect. Nevertheless, land dispossession clearly also plays a significant role in catalyzing Uyghur protest in South Xinjiang, and Uyghur protest has led in many of the reported cases since July 2009 to interethnic violence (Watts 2011; Radio Free Asia 2012a, 2012b, 2013a, 2013b, 2013c). For its part, debt is altogether more insidious: it affects elites as much as the poor, and the consequences of various types of debt are potentially far more widespread. Moreover, debt and land dispossession are often intimately related. First, in rural areas smallholder debt can lead to land dispossession and, consequently, a cycle of indebtedness that is extremely difficult to break free of. Second, in many cases it is debt-financed capital construction projects that produce the demand for land and the smallholders' separation from it. This process, which Karl Marx termed "primitive accumulation," is still very much part of economic life in South Xinjiang—as it is in other urbanizing and industrializing parts of China and the developing world. Third, both sorts of debt, as well as land dispossession, are "normal" phenomena in central and eastern China (Chin. *Neidi*). Finally, both smallholder debt and land dispossession are examples of what I characterize as "unfavorable social inclusion."[2]

In this chapter I begin by suggesting that unfavorable social inclusion is an essential complement to the exclusionary factors put forward as explanations for social unrest by scholars who have previously examined the relationship between economic transformation and interethnic conflict in western China (Gilley 2001; Hillman 2008; Fischer 2008; Chaudhuri 2010; Zhu and Blachford 2012). Social exclusion remains, therefore, a critical factor. I illustrate the inseparability of social inclusion and social exclusion through a thick description of a particular political-economic space that became very prominent in Xinjiang in the 2010s and is both chaotic and lucrative.

Lucrative chaos in South Xinjiang is created by the interactions of (mainly Han) entrepreneurs and (mainly Han) government officials in the context of certain large-scale and highly uneven flows of capital. In this political-economic space the stakes are high, and the investment horizon is short. Opportunities appear quickly and are likely to disappear just as quickly, and one cannot take for granted that any given situation or environment will continue or be stable for any length of time. This chaos should not simply be seen as an unfortunate by-product of excessively rapid economic development. Economists and political commentators from both within and outside China increasingly see such chaos as deliberate, the result of government manipulation of the economy (Pei 2006; YouTube 2011). Why? Because instability is where the opportunity lies.

While this chaos is lucrative for some, it is threatening to others. The power to manipulate the boundaries between different fragments and the rules that apply to different fragments is the power to create and to take advantage of speculative business opportunities. Party and government officials at all levels possess degrees of this power. Massive capital investment is in this way a form of payment by the center to the lower levels of party and government; each level in turn distributes to its own clients, both within and outside official structures (Shih 2004; Dickson 2008; Chen and Dickson 2010). For many Uyghurs, however, this political economy is inclusive only in the sense that it is incursive.

Large-scale infrastructure investments, inflation, webs of private finance and indebtedness, and subsidies to the cotton industry are all incursions into economic life in Xinjiang. They are the drivers or the effects of a program of rapid, yet selective, state-led economic development—"leapfrog development." This is the context in which this chapter is set. Collectively, these incursions change the nature and extent of social inclusion and social exclusion across the ethnic divide. I argue that the change in and combination of particular types of social inclusion and social exclusion underlies interethnic tension in Xinjiang.

## Normalization, Political Economy, and (In)Stability

Ethnic peripheries of the People's Republic of China are directly affected by ideas, policies, and practices that occur in *Neidi*, the Han-dominated core.[3] Some of the influences that emanate from the core are incidental—although, as I aim to show in this chapter, they may have significant effects—while others are deliberately directed at the periphery by the core-based state. Regardless of whether *Neidi* phenomena exert influence by default or by design, it is important to pay attention to how these influences play out on China's periphery if we are to gain an understanding of social interactions, including interethnic conflict, in the region.

Arguably the most pervasive of the "by design" influences on Xinjiang is the ongoing state project to integrate this periphery into the core region. At the human level on which I focus—culture, society, and micro-economics—this form of integration might be better described as "normalization." In the Foucauldian sense normalization is a process of disciplining through the imposition of precise norms (Foucault 1977). Normalization, in this context, is the process of making Xinjiang more like *Neidi* and, in particular, making people in Xinjiang more like people in *Neidi*. Normalization includes providing bilingual education, restricting religious practice and teaching (Human Rights Watch 2005; CECC 2011), "civilizing" the populace, "remaking" history, and reshaping habits (Cliff 2013). Ethnic minorities may be seriously affected by normalization, in both intended and unintended ways, not least because they are the furthest from this "normal" to begin with. But it is important to be clear that the "targets" of this normalization are not exclusively ethnic minorities. From the perspective of the core, Han people in Xinjiang are also seen to be in need of modernization—and in some respects more urgently so because they are assumed to be the basis for the primary goals of "leapfrog development" and the "maintenance of [CCP] rule through stability" (*kuayue fazhan, changzhi jiu'an*) in Xinjiang (Bovingdon 2004; Cliff 2012b). Earmarking Han for development does not, of course, imply that they are seen as equivalent in developmental status to the ethnic minority people who are their close neighbors.

An important part of economic normalization is the fostering of local private enterprise in Xinjiang, which is itself predicated on the creation of an entrepreneurial ethos among the residents of Xinjiang. Han people are undoubtedly the primary targets in this respect: Xinjiang Han are habitually criticized (often by other Xinjiang people, especially Hui) for being economically risk-averse and for lacking the entrepreneurial drive and skill sets to succeed in business; they are seen as even more nostalgic for the "iron rice bowl" and the certainties of state employment than their compatriots in *Neidi*. State media and government-enterprise work conferences have foregrounded the fostering of private enterprise since the Xinjiang Work Meeting in May 2010 and especially since the first State Owned Enterprises (SOE) Assist Xinjiang conference in October 2011 (Wei 2011; Wang 2011; XJASS 2012). Private and local enterprise is said to be an important part of the goal of "leapfrog development"—by which Xinjiang will "catch up" to *Neidi*.

An ironic precondition of a normalized Xinjiang is that, during the process of normalization, Xinjiang is not (to be) treated normally. Xinjiang is a "special region," with regard to which "special policies" are implemented and within which "special time periods" (prescribing or proscribing certain types of behavior) regularly pass. The way that the state and Han in Xinjiang talk about Xinjiang, and policies toward Xinjiang, reveals a deepseated assumption that "you have to treat it special to normalize it." Treating Xinjiang as special, in economic terms, means massive injections of capital from the central government and "partner" provincial-level units in eastern China. The "partnering" arrangement is referred to in Chinese as *duikou* and involves pairing up provincial-level units in *Neidi* with prefectural- or subprefectural-level units in Xinjiang. Along with direct government investment and capital construction, the *Neidi* partner brokers investment by companies (mainly SOEs) from its own region, provides training for government personnel from the Xinjiang side, and extends loans for these operations through banks based in *Neidi*. Thus, with regard to most of this *duikou* money, capital *is* debt.

Most of the efforts are focused on fixed capital investment—infrastructure projects like roads, bridges, railways, and oil and gas pipelines. The predominance of fixed capital investment is illustrated by the fact that it accounted for 82 percent of Xinjiang's gross domestic product (GDP) for 2012. In a comparative scope, while Beijing registered a 32 percent increase in fixed capital investment between the beginning of 2010 and the end of 2012, fixed capital investment in Xinjiang increased 126 percent, almost four times the rate, to surpass Beijing in 2012. During the first ten years of the Great Western Development Program (GWD, *Xibudakaifa*), 2000–2009 inclusive, total investment in fixed assets in Xinjiang was almost 1.4 trillion yuan (roughly equivalent to the GDP of Beijing in 2010). But the rate of growth of fixed capital investment under the "Assist Xinjiang" program means that the total fixed capital investment of the 2000s was surpassed fewer than three years into the 2010s (All China Data Centre 2013).[4]

Publications emanating from the highest levels of the Chinese Communist Party (CCP) repeatedly stress that "development" is "the key to solving the problems concerning ethnic groups" and that this approach has been promulgated and successfully implemented by successive generations of leadership for more than sixty years. Both the foremost party journal *Qiushi* and the State Council's White Paper, *China's Ethnic Policy and Common Prosperity and Development of All Ethnic Groups*, placed particular emphasis on the need to "accelerate" the "economic and social development of minority ethnic groups and regions inhabited by ethnic minorities" (State Council 2009; Yang and Yang 2010). Coming at the time that these statements did, in the months of nervous quiet between the July 2009 riots in Urumqi and the changing of the provincial-level leadership in early 2010, they were quite clearly rallying calls for belief in the notion that economic development can outrun social instability.

But is this the case? The interethnic conflict of 2008 and 2009, in Tibet and Xinjiang respectively, prompted a number of studies that considered the question of whether rapid economic growth eases or contributes to interethnic tension. Authors put forward a variety of explanations for what appears to be the failure of state economic and social developmental policies to address the grievances and unhappiness of ethnic minority peoples living in these areas.[5] One prominent school of thought dismisses poverty per se as an explanation because average standards of living (measured in quantitative economic terms) have been rising in even the poorest parts of Xinjiang for some time now (All China Data Centre 2013).[6] Debasish Chaudhuri draws on Gurr's idea of "relative deprivation"—a gap, felt as unacceptable, between a person or group's "actual economic conditions and their expectations" (Chaudhuri 2010, 10). Expectations are, of course, formed in relation to social and economic context—hence the term *relative deprivation* and the relevance, to this volume, of discussing a political economy in which the primary agents are Han.

Zhu and Blachford (2012) focus on certain effects of the "market economy" in Xinjiang and Tibet and adopt Fischer's broadening of the concept of "social exclusion" as an analytical framework. Fischer (2008, 3) defines *social exclusion* as "structural, institutional or agentive processes of propulsion or obstruction." He claims that the concept's strength is its ability to highlight "dynamic processes" rather than focus solely on outcomes like poverty, unemployment, or relative deprivation: "The value of this definition is that it adds insight to poverty approaches, in particular with reference to rising inequality. Rising inequality matters even if absolute poverty is falling, not only due to considerations raised from the perspective of relative deprivation, but also because of the exclusionary and thereby conflictive repercussions that occur at higher social strata and that are therefore not captured by standard poverty or inequality measures" (3).

Nevertheless, Zhu and Blachford (2012) make scant use of the concept as distinct from relative deprivation because they talk throughout the paper in terms of static outcomes: "In the current analysis, this could mean that individuals and groups *fail to gain access to or benefit from* social or economic possibilities" (731; my emphasis). They find that the clearest winners of "marketization" over the first decade of the twenty-first century have been Han people, and the clearest losers have been ethnic minorities—Uyghurs and Tibetans—and conclude that this is an "inevitable" consequence of a market economy because ethnic minorities have lower levels of "skills, education and [Mandarin] language ability" than the Han (and Hui) people that they are competing against (727).[7]

Zhu and Blachford would be right to claim that Uyghurs are at a distinct disadvantage under the conditions of the economic transformation that is currently taking place in Xinjiang. However, I find certain aspects of their explanation—which is based on the higher relative importance of education and skills in a market economy—unsatisfactory. First, for entrepreneurs operating in the lucrative and chaotic fragment of Xinjiang's political economy, forming and maintaining instrumental and affective ties (guanxi) with Han officials is one of the primary skills required; therefore, ethnicity is a far more important factor of success than is education. When I asked a businessman what his work involved specifically, his friend chipped in "making guanxi with government officials." The businessman— who sells expensive medical equipment to government hospitals and need only make two sales a year to be doing well—followed up with, "Much of how I do business, I can't really tell you about." Later, discussing how to create new business opportunities, he insisted that "the first step is to get your guanxi worked out here; then go to Beijing to find an appropriate opportunity." In other words without first setting up the connections with the relevant government officials in Korla, no business can be successful.

Second, although the economy is becoming more capitalistic at all levels, there is no sign that "the market" is setting prices and determining resource allocations to a greater extent than in the past. On the contrary, the state and its agents continue to play the largest part. Four years after the GWD officially began, Victor Shih (2004, 427) argued convincingly that "instead of creating the environment and incentives for local businesses to become internationally competitive, the GWD campaign was intentionally an enormous exercise in rent distribution. Politicized bureaucrats used the campaign as a means to consolidate their hold on the party and to increase the power of the central bureaucracy."

My findings suggest that a great deal of the money transferred under the "Assist Xinjiang" plan (begun ten years later) is going in a similar direction. These stylistic similarities are in line with what we might expect, given the genealogical proximity of the ideas underlying both development plans and the fact that the very same institutions are implementing them. The idea that the state's primary motive for economic development of peripheral regions is to improve the livelihoods of "people of all ethnic groups" has also been called into question by scholars from various disciplinary backgrounds and institutional affiliations. Grewal and Ahmed's (2011) recent quantitative assessment of how GWD money was spent and what effect it had over the same period concluded that "economic growth in China's western region is positively and significantly correlated with fiscal expenditure in general and fiscal expenditure on education in particular" (179). They note, however, that precious little beneficial economic growth has taken place: "So far, it has not been possible to attract large volumes of private sector investment into the western region," and "budgetary spending on capital construction appears to have been not focused sufficiently on growth promoting activities." Instead, this money was spent on "ostentatious office buildings or urban beautification projects" (180)—one might also add "repaving perfectly good roads" (Hillman 2014b). All of these are mechanisms by which local cadres create and maintain cliental networks and improve their chances for promotion by increasing the profile and the GDP of their region. Again, we can observe the same phenomenon under the "Assist Xinjiang" program. Private investors from outside China have complained that "the platform for investment remains narrow" in even the new Special Economic Zones (SEZs) (Xinhua 2011), and urbanization in Xinjiang is centrally concerned with image and political function (Cliff 2013). Social policy analyst Wang Ning, of the Xinjiang Academy of Social Sciences, warned in a June 2011 article that "some deep structurally-related contradictions still exist, and present the major obstacle to the transformation and development [of Xinjiang's economy]" (Wang 2011, 42). Wang criticized the elite mentality toward development in Xinjiang. He argued that the "motivation" for development needs rethinking, keeping in mind that "the goal of development is not GDP, and it is not income from taxation—rather, it is to allow the people to live more happily and with greater dignity" (46).

The empirical material that I present in this chapter shows how Han entrepreneurs operate within the fragmented and dynamic economic environment referred to in the above analyses. I seek to emphasize the interrelatedness of these phenomena, to expand on some of them, and to demonstrate my argument through observed ethnographic and comparative examples. To Fischer's description above I would add that exclusionary processes at lower social strata are important to take into consideration even though the condition of these people may have already been "captured" by standard measures. The lived experience of feeling excluded regardless of objective skills, implied rights, or flexibility in accepting the terms of interethnic social engagement is something that cannot be measured in quantitative terms alone, in part because it is emotive and in part because it is ongoing and cumulative. The physical absence of Uyghurs in certain parts of Xinjiang or certain occupations is notable, but it is the invisibility of Uyghurs in places where they are not absent that, on reflection, is most striking.

During three years of living in the Han community of Xinjiang I observed that the Han attitude to Uyghurs is one of *ignoring*. The concepts of ignoring and excluding overlap considerably in the material world. Ignoring is expressed economically in the way that Han people disburse, exchange, and generate resources almost exclusively within the Han community. The way that ignoring is expressed socially, however, is more subtle and possibly more hurtful. Most of the many Han people that I know, ranging from the barely employed to the political and economic elite of Korla, rarely interact with or even talk about Uyghurs, let alone associate with them. They avoid looking at Uyghurs on the street and generally seek to quickly end any verbal interaction. Taken to an extreme, many Han treat Uyghurs in Xinjiang as invisible. I suggest that this is an underlying grievance that can be brought to life by institutionalized forms of discrimination and suppression. This seeming desire on the part of the Han populace to disengage entirely from Uyghurs coexists with a state-driven push for engagement on particular terms.

Social *inclusion*, in particular forms, is as important a factor as social exclusion to interethnic tension in contemporary Xinjiang. Uyghurs are central to the Han imagination of Xinjiang: they are included as the sociocultural Other, and they are the essential justification for the perception of instability; thus, they perform an important political-discursive role in "unifying" Han within Xinjiang and across the PRC (Cliff 2012b). In a process that is termed "convergence," the Han expectation that Uyghurs are instability-producing helps, via "stability measures," employment practices and everyday social interactions, to make them that way.[8] Furthermore, the existence of Uyghurs (and the related perception of instability) is what drives the massive capital investment. In this sense we can say that Uyghurs are the primary asset of institutional Xinjiang—including, but not limited to, the *bingtuan*, the security apparatus, and the entire governing structure. The culture of economic acceleration in Xinjiang promotes economic inequality, but inequality, per se, does not appear to be the root cause of interethnic tension and communal violence. Rather, social unrest is caused by a combination of different types of inclusion and exclusion; it is not a single vector, but multiple vectors of differentiation, that squeezes the social space of ordinary people and turns them into antagonists/protesters.

## The Vectors of Lucrative Chaos, Xinjiang 2010–2013

Across China the perceived imperative of high economic growth to maintain social stability prompts large-scale government intervention in the form of aggressive fiscal stimulus followed by tightening to control inflation. Big cycles ensue, with the economy slewing back and forth between growth and the threat of a destabilizing slowdown (Song 2013; Yu 2013). Stimulus plans make corruption even more lucrative (Hillman 2014a), and selective fiscal tightening chokes competition, further concentrating political and economic power in the hands of government officials and their close business associates. In Xinjiang, the "Assist Xinjiang" program is a magnified microcosm of the national political economy, with significant implications for ethnic relations.

### INFLATION

The large capital injections associated with economic stimulus have a direct effect on inflation, so the nationwide fiscal tightening that began in 2010 did not reduce inflation in Xinjiang over 2012, as it noticeably did across the rest of China. Instead, official figures state that inflation actually *increased* over 2012 in Xinjiang (NBS 2013a, 2013b, 2013c). Although we should not take the official figures at face value—among others, celebrity economist Lang Xianping has alleged that inflation is grossly understated—official figures can be compared against each other for an idea of the relative state of Xinjiang versus other parts of China and the country as a whole. Actual inflation in urban Xinjiang for food and housing can be put at between 25 percent and 30 percent per annum for the years 2010–12, inclusive. That is, prices doubled over the period. The wages of the lowest echelon of service staff, who were grossly underpaid up until 2009, tripled. In 2009 such staff commonly earned eight hundred to one thousand yuan per month, but in late 2012 employers were having difficulty finding staff at a rate of three thousand yuan per month. The "labor shortage"[9] is a China-wide phenomenon (Tsui 2012) and is exacerbated by the ever-more entrenched national legend that Xinjiang is unstable and unsafe for Han people.

High inflation is an underlying cause of social unrest, and for this and other reasons inflation makes the central government extremely uneasy. The central government's response is to reduce liquidity by first reining in bank lending. Entrepreneurs and farmers who depend on credit must turn to private lenders or to the shadow banking industry. These lenders are themselves financed by cash-rich investors (including, indirectly, the state banks) who are looking for places to put their money that will return more than the negative real interest rates that the banks are offering.[10] The workings and the danger of this cycle are perhaps best illustrated by the case of Wenzhou, a manufacturing center south of Shanghai that is widely considered to be the bellwether of entrepreneurial China.

## PRIVATE LOANS AND SHADOW BANKING

In October 2008, six months into the Global Financial Crisis (GFC), a Wenzhou businessman who described himself as a venture capitalist explained his method of operation: "What we do is put money into banks and let the banks lend to companies. . . . If they repay the loan in time, that's fine, but if they don't, we acquire them. We target companies that are about to go bankrupt but still have a good economic foundation—we like firms to run out of money so they become ours" (Garnaut 2008).

The economic downturn that began in early 2008 meant that a lot of factories in Wenzhou had halted production or were running at well below capacity. Then the central government turned the capital flow back on, in an attempt to stimulate the national economy and ward off the threat to social stability posed by the looming economic downturn. It was not just formal bank lending to local governments and State Owned Enterprises

(SOEs) that was loosened up as a response to the GFC. The government also attempted to bring private, or informal, lending out into the open by removing the blanket ban on such activities and establishing a process of authorization for the larger and more stable of these enterprises.

The mood began to change again in mid-2010, when the government began fiscal tightening in response to the inflation caused by the November 2008 stimulus package. Private loans became more expensive as bank loans became less available.[11] By late 2011 a great many Wenzhou businesses with high exposure to private credit were up against the wall as a result of inflation, the credit squeeze, and exponentially increasing interest payments; the *New York Times* reported that "at least 90" entrepreneurs tried to disappear, leaving their debts behind, and two committed suicide (Barboza 2011). Again, Wen Jiabao visited the city, as he had done a few months into the GFC, and announced a bailout plan. Wenzhou was too big, or too significant, to fail, and the day of reckoning that most economists agree must eventually arrive, was postponed (Fan and Oster 2011).

The mood in Xinjiang in the second half of 2009 was apprehensive, almost fearful, of the economic downturn that political and interethnic violence seemed sure to generate. Then Zhang Chunxian took over from Wang Lequan in late April 2010, and the "Assist Xinjiang" program launched. The credit squeeze of mid-2010 also applied to Xinjiang, but so much money from central and eastern China was—and still is—going into the local economy that the credit squeeze did not negatively impact capital infrastructure investment and local government spending.

The credit squeeze is selective. Loans are extended to people with unmortgaged capital assets, to people with direct connections to the bank, and to companies or individuals with direct connections to local government. A budding entrepreneur whose business has picked up markedly since early 2010 explained:

> The local government, or state-linked companies can get a loan for any amount of money, within days. The bank officer will say "How much do you want? You tell me the number, I'll give you the money." . . . Ordinarily people [private entrepreneurs without relevant connections] must go through a lengthy process of, first, negotiating the amount: "Two million? Not possible . . . All right, one million." . . . Then they must fill

out many different forms. Even then the loan will not necessarily be approved, and certainly not quickly—they may need to wait one or two months, by which time the business opportunity has already passed. . . . The official statements and policies that capital will become available for small business operators are all talk[12]—at the ground level, the reality is that capital is still difficult to come by. . . . It is no easier than three or four years ago.

This young man's assertions about the difficulty of borrowing money formally through banks were supported by all but one of my interviewees.[13] Even stronger evidence is the ubiquity of both state-authorized and unauthorized private moneylenders who charge extremely high interest rates. If bank credit was widely accessible, these businesses could not operate. Every entrepreneur that I spoke to during three and a half weeks in Xinjiang was either directly involved in high-interest moneylending and/or borrowing or strongly stated that they had never done it and did not intend to.[14] The young man went on:

That's why I'm going to start a moneylending business here in Korla. It is difficult to get authorization to start such a business these days—the government cracked down a couple of years ago, and now you need starting capital of two hundred million yuan to be able to apply for a license. So I will try to start a branch office of my friend's loan company in Urumqi. I have already given him some of my money to manage—he will pay me 20 percent per year and lend it out at 30 percent or even 40 percent per year. I want to find more creditors in Korla, so I can get more capital to lend out under his company name.

Anyone who needs a loan but cannot get one through the formal banking system must consider the opportunity cost of not having capital against the high cost of borrowing that capital through the shadow banking system or privately at rates of 30 percent per annum and higher. These people are not typically desperados trying to keep ahead of their mounting debts; they include successful private entrepreneurs who are short of operating capital and ordinary farmers in the harvest season. Often, these self-employed people do not have the luxury of deciding whether or not to take out a short-term high-interest loan; it is a case of do or die. Farmers need to employ people to harvest their crops and get those crops to market in order to recoup their initial capital outlay and their labor for the year; entrepreneurs need to keep their business running and, importantly, looking good in order to bring in future contracts. One entrepreneur who owns an advertising and exhibition design company that services the oil company and government in Korla and Urumqi put it like this: "You must spend money to make money. This is the first rule of business. If you don't have operating capital, your business is dead. You have to pay your employees. . . . Even if they are willing to stay at home for a while, you can't run an empty office. If a client comes to visit and sees that your office is empty, with no life, he will see that you are not successful and won't be willing to do business with you. He will smell the decay, and he will run away fast. Capital is the lifeblood of business."

State-extended credit, despite being roughly one-fifth of the cost of private credit, also has a predatory aspect to it. Farmers who own land can apply for, and usually get, a short-term loan at the beginning of the growing season each year, at a rate of 6 to 10 percent. They need to mortgage their land or, in rare cases, some other solid asset. If they can't pay the loan back that year, they need to borrow more against the same land in order to finance the loan. If they don't make enough money for a few years in a row, they will lose their land to the bank. The risk is therefore borne entirely by the farmers. Farmers who themselves are party to this sort of arrangement, and indeed depend on this state-provided credit line for operating capital, consequently perceive the state as a predator. In other words they see this arrangement in exactly the same terms as the Wenzhou venture capitalist quoted above, but from the opposite perspective—that of the target.

## COTTON

The economy, and thus the social stability of much of rural South Xinjiang, including both *bingtuan* and local government areas, is maintained in large part by central government support of the cotton industry. This support employs essentially the same logic as the "Assist Xinjiang" package. Until September 2014 the central government bought all domestically produced cotton at a price well above the global market price. The policy made many cotton farmers very comfortable and people who do business in cotton up until the point of sale to the state even better off.[15] The general manager of a vertically integrated cotton-milling corporation in South Xinjiang showed me around a few of the factories that he manages and explained the logistics and economics of his business: "We sell all of our cotton to the government, for the national cotton reserve, and the current selling price is 15.4 yuan [per kilogram of cotton fiber]. . . . But if the government didn't buy our cotton, we wouldn't be able to sell this off at five yuan per kilogram." The price that the mills pay the growers for seed cotton was also controlled within a range set by the state and was roughly proportional to the milled cotton price. The price of milled cotton fixed by the Chinese state varied according to the price of milled cotton on the global market but was about 84 percent higher (International Cotton Advisory Committee 2012, 10; Rong 2012).

This automatic purchase policy was scrapped nationwide in September 2014, and a new policy of direct subsidies to farmers when the price falls below a government-determined benchmark (19.8 yuan per kilogram in 2014) began testing in Xinjiang. As of November 2014, Xinjiang, which produced 55 percent of China's cotton crop in 2013, was still being treated special in this respect (Xu and Zhou 2014; Reuters 2014). As we walked back to the head office, passing Uyghurs with pitchforks picking away at fifteen-meter-high piles of raw cotton, the general manager continued: "The government does this to keep the people happy, to maintain social stability. Think about it—we employ about 350 people, and each of those people has a family of at least two other people, so you can say that we are supporting as many as twelve hundred people, just in this small county. If you consider the cotton industry in Xinjiang as a whole, the figure runs to hundreds of thousands of people."

Although the mainly Uyghur laborers of this cotton milling corporation are being paid at a current market rate (roughly three thousand yuan per month) that is well above the minimum wage, it is of course not the physical laborers who are doing best from the state-supported cotton price. The managers and administrative staff of this factory and many others like it are almost exclusively Han; Uyghurs drive the trucks, shovel the cotton, and hold a few of the low and midlevel factory manager positions.

Explaining the ethnic imbalance in workplaces like this is more complex than Uyghurs being discriminated against simply because the Han entrepreneur dislikes Uyghurs. Han entrepreneurs will tend to hire Han managers for reasons that include cultural fit, family and other network connections, Mandarin literacy, and formal education.[16] Nevertheless, since managerial positions tend to entail both formal and informal business interactions with local officials, Uyghurs' social mobility, access to capital, and business opportunities are greatly constrained.

The policy of supporting the cotton price in order to stabilize farmers' incomes and social well-being has evident flaws. First, not everybody can be a cotton farmer, and of those left over, not everybody can find work in the industries that gain support from this policy. Second, rising incomes and production costs, along with the massive infrastructure construction going on in Xinjiang, has caused the price of basic commodities like food to double and in some cases triple in the past three years; the cost of living for the poorest people in society thus goes up at almost the same rate. Since the nonstate actors who are most likely to engage directly in violent conflict are these relatively poor people, the effect of investment and agricultural subsidies on overall "stability" in Xinjiang is seriously undermined.

## Making Use of Xinjiang's Fragmented Political Economy

The people who flourish within this fragmented economy are the ones who "see through" (*kantou*) it—that is, they recognize opportunities and threats—and have the social networks and economic capital to respond in a way that benefits them. We can describe these people as both *immersed* in the political economy of this specific place and *aware* of its broader context. First, the entrepreneur needs to recognize the logic and cycles that underpin the functioning of this political economy—and there is indeed a logic to it. However, to recall Victor Shih (2004, 427), it is less a logic of development than a logic of extraction—"an enormous exercise of rent distribution." The rationale can be found, among other places, in the Xinjiang Communist Party Committee's most recent adaptation of the domino theory connecting the borderlands to the political center: "If the grassroots are stable, then the whole of Xinjiang is stable; if the whole of Xinjiang is stable, then the whole country is stable" (Zhang 2011; Cui 2012). Grassroots cadres are seen as a far more important constituency in terms of political stability than Uyghur farmers. A *Global Times* (2013) editorial boldly asserted: "These violent forces may bring pain to society, but in terms of the political situation they will eventually represent nothing more than passing annoyances." This statement also implies that the well-being of "society" is secondary to the maintenance of CCP rule. Second, the entrepreneur needs personal contact with key local decision makers and government officials. Because these officials are not necessarily in the best position to take advantage of such business opportunities, they require informal partnerships with entrepreneurs. These partnerships are formed and strengthened through eating, drinking, and "playing" together and through mutual benefit. Private entrepreneurs and local government officials thus have a sort of symbiotic relationship, based on a combination of affective and instrumental ties. Third, the entrepreneur needs access to money.

The business opportunities in South Xinjiang are direct functions of the central government's spending on capital infrastructure, restrictions on bank lending, and support of the cotton price. The general manager of the cotton factory located in rural South Xinjiang is also an entrepreneur in his own right, and he described his most recent business deals to me:

> [In late 2009] I had capital of four hundred thousand yuan from selling my former business, so I bought two cranes—twenty-five-tonne, big, really big ones! Why did I want to buy these? At that time, they were building the second rail line, and they were building the expressway that we use today. I saw a very good business opportunity. So I got these two cranes and leased them to the construction contractors for two years. I knew that they would need these cranes because the scale is very large—they certainly would not have enough cranes! I was willing to bet on that. I understood the situation: in 2008–2009 the central government was investing to stimulate internal demand. The whole country was building railways. So I did cranes for two years; two years of cranes gave me a pure profit of one million yuan. After two years the road and railway were done, and the cranes were worn out, so I sold them. I bought them for 600,000 yuan and I sold them for roughly 420,000 yuan. After I sold the cranes, I looked at the national policies—to print more renminbi. Putting money in the bank was no good; it would lose value. I needed to change my money into real things, because the price of real things was going up, and my money would only be worth half as much in a few years' time. I took all my money out immediately and invested in land and two small

commercial properties. I bought a thirty-year lease on one hundred mu of orchard land for five hundred thousand yuan, and recently leased it out to a farmer for fifteen years. I calculated it carefully: I could manage it myself and earn about two hundred thousand yuan per year, but I don't have the expertise. The farmer will pay me 100,000 per year for the first five years, 120,000 per year for the second five years, and 150,000 per year for the last five years. When the lease is up in 2028, I can probably sell the land for about two million yuan.

The crane example demonstrates the importance of connections—*guanxi*—and capital, combined with local knowledge and a broad contextual outlook. I did not press him further on how he could be so sure that the contractors would not simply buy their own cranes for the duration, so how much of his insight was entrepreneurial flair and how much was connections is impossible to tell. But we can be certain that only the latter is crucial to the deal. The high visibility of the construction project itself and the staggering profit figures—a return of 115 percent per year on the initial investment of six hundred thousand yuan—strongly imply that this was an opportunity that was both exclusive and not entirely aboveboard.

At the same time, capital is so scarce for some people that they will agree to schemes like the orchard example. The narrator of the above story expects to recoup his capital in only five years,[17] and all of the risk and hard work is shouldered by the farmer-lessee (*chengbaozhe*). Farmers often need to borrow more around harvest time, and many have little choice but to take out private finance at a high interest rate. If something goes wrong, with the crop of fruit for instance, the downward spiral into indebtedness is hastened. If long-term bank credit was easier to get, the farmer would not need to lease the land because he could buy it outright and pay it off over ten or fifteen years, as for a housing loan. Housing loans are much easier to get because every level of government is heavily invested in maintaining the high prices for residential real estate, despite supply outstripping demand in regional cities like Korla. Agricultural land, though, is finite and even shrinking in supply. Speculation, land development, and investment by nonagriculturalists is pushing up the cost of land, and thus the risk of farming it, in Uyghur-dominated rural South Xinjiang.

Business has been so good for people with capital and connections that many ranking officials have quit their secure state jobs to become full-time entrepreneurs. Among my own contacts those who have "jumped into the sea" in the past few years include a police commander, the head of a Korla city government bureau, and the deputy head of a relatively well-off *bingtuan* regiment. A small-time entrepreneur noted that "if you have the resources, you can do business better and better." The criterion that he was using for "good business" was "a quick buck"—lucrative but not necessarily sustainable. As he later explained, it has to be "a quick buck" because there is no certainty to be found in the political, legal, or economic structures.

A number of entrepreneurs, including this same young man, attributed this economy of uncertainty to "government manipulations": "They invest in concrete, not people, causing inflation. This means that the rich are getting richer and the poor are getting poorer. . . . And the government keeps grabbing the resources faster and faster—*touji!* [speculating]."[18] The medical-equipment businessman verified the extractive desperation of the local state on a separate occasion. It was late at night, and we were in the teahouse talking business. Addressing his friend, he said, "The CCP lacks money; they are more lacking than you. They are always looking for investment projects (*xiangmu*); finding projects is what they most like to do." Since GDP growth is a crucial element of local government officials' performance evaluation, and thus their chances for promotion, even "projects" from which they do not personally receive a direct cash benefit are extremely important to them.

Government exploitation and deal making are based on the selective application of "market" rules. These "market" rules apply in certain sections of the economy but not others, and to certain individual or corporate entities but not others. The *bingtuan* political economy is perhaps the archetype in this respect. The result is a formalized hierarchy of differential rights that would not be permissible under normal Chinese law (Cliff 2009). A second example is predatory bank lending as described above. Regardless of whether the farmer is able to pay back the loan, the bank officials are doing good business. In the first instance they are providing credit to farmers, as dictated by upper-level policy; should the loan turn bad, bank officials—and, in some cases, their private creditors (see the Wenzhou example)—have the opportunity to disenfranchise the population while staying comfortably within the letter of the law. A third example of government deal-making is selling rights to monopoly service sectors. The license to check and certify car emissions is one such item. In early 2013 the government was considering passing a regulation that requires all vehicles to undergo an emissions test once every year, but the regulation had not yet been publicly announced. In cases like this, aspiring contractors must know about it in advance so that they can begin informal lobbying and thus have a chance at being awarded the contract. The medical-equipment businessman and two of his friends explained:

> The government is not officially allowed to make profit out of the services it provides to the people. This exhaust checking is a service: it is an environmental protection measure that is mandatory for all car owners. But they also plan to charge for it—six hundred yuan! So, if the government officials want to make money from this, they must subcontract it to a nominally private company. The private company is allowed to make a profit, and the government will grant a monopoly to keep the price high. The profits will be very big: Korla has at least two hundred thousand private cars and growing; each car is six hundred yuan, and most of it is profit once you have paid the capital cost of the emissions-checking machines. That is turnover of at least one hundred million, every year, guaranteed!

The consumers of this service—vehicle owners—would pay a premium that is equivalent to the difference between the cost of providing the service and the price charged. However, this money would not be channeled back into public coffers; it would be skimmed off by the government officials who authorized the deal and the private entrepreneur operating it.

## THE STATE-CENTERED VIEW

Even as people in all of the political economies that I outline here perceive the state as a predator, most also relate to the state as the provider of opportunities and the ultimate decider of destinies: that which giveth and that which taketh away. It is clear how and why this perception prevails within the government work unit or SOE. Outside the state system the survivors of these few years of economic turmoil in Xinjiang look to the state for their next profit-making opportunity, while the losers blame the state for their current and expected-future poverty. The medical-equipment businessman gestured to his farmer friend and said, "He and I both await opportunities." The businessman waits for a government procurement order to be announced, then makes a bid in a tender process or Dutch auction to supply the required machinery. Again, essential to the success of such a bid is close connections with the relevant government officials.[19] The farmer waits for government agricultural sector policies that promote certain techniques or crops or for opportunities to buy the usage rights for large areas of marginal or underdeveloped rural land that he can develop into better-producing land. Growing and selling agricultural produce pays wages, but land development and government subsidies are where the real profits are made. Other non-*bingtuan* farmers have told me the same.[20] In other words most significant threats and opportunities arise from state action or lack thereof: "reading the market" means "reading the state." Uyghurs are ill-positioned to read the state in this way. But they are not unaffected by the changes in Xinjiang's economic structure. They are largely excluded from the lucrative but very much included in the chaos.

## Identity and Indebtedness

The lack of access that Uyghurs in general have to the lucrative-chaotic political economy of Han entrepreneurs is important because it demonstrates that "you [Uyghurs] cannot be like us [Han]." One glaring contradiction here is that the implicit promise of Han-style cultural and economic modernization appears to be that "you *only* have to be like us in order to enjoy that which we enjoy." Uyghurs could make a legitimate complaint that "you won't let us be like us, and you won't let us be like you." This resonates with Duara's (2001, 106) formulation that "the desire is not (simply) to conquer the other, but to be desired by the other."[21] The logical conclusion is that the Chinese state wants to change Uyghurs into something that is neither the Uyghur of today nor the Han of today but rather a modified and completely imaginary Uyghur *zhonghuaminzu*.[22]

In other words Uyghurs are likely to feel that they have little living space left and that not only do they have nothing, but they also owe a great deal. State-linked discourses repeatedly emphasize what the CCP and the Han have *done for* the ethnic minorities and minority areas—a discourse of

minority indebtedness.[23] The whole premise of "Assist Xinjiang" is indebtedness. This indebtedness is both financial and moral, and the debtors and
the creditors are specifically identified. Xinjiang is in debt to *Neidi*; Xinjiang people (both Han and Uyghur) are collectively indebted to their *Neidi*
"compatriots." Of course, it is not stated like that. "Assist Xinjiang" is posed
as an act of selfless giving by the more developed eastern Chinese people to
the poorer and more backward western Chinese people. The gift is simultaneously an act of inclusiveness and of differentiation. But a gift is a debt
(Mauss 1966), and both work in similar ways to tie the giver and receiver
together. And "Assist Xinjiang" is just one aspect of an ongoing series of
exchanges—of people, minerals, money, even ideas—between Xinjiang and
*Neidi*. People in Xinjiang cannot but be aware of the tightening of this web
of indebtedness. On the one hand, Han people in Xinjiang shrug off the
largess of the central government as a stability measure. They do not feel
burdened by the implied debt because they know that they are also measures of stability themselves; they are doing their part. Indeed, they are in
some small but important sense *part of the gift*. Uyghurs, on the other hand,
are always being told that they are the cause of instability. Their very presence is debt-creating.

Receiving a gift that is overvalued by the giver, especially if it is a gift
that is unwanted in the first place, is an uncomfortable feeling. The useless
gift puts one in debt, for an unreasonable sum, to a creditor that is seen
from the outset as a burden. Graeber writes:

> Tell people they are inferior, they are unlikely to be pleased, but this sur-
> prisingly rarely leads to armed revolt. Tell people that they are poten-
> tial equals who have failed, and that therefore, even what they do have
> they do not deserve, that it isn't rightly theirs, and you are much more
> likely to inspire rage. . . . For thousands of years, the struggle between
> rich and poor has largely taken the form of conflicts between creditors
> and debtors—of arguments about the rights and wrongs of interest pay-
> ments, debt peonage, amnesty, repossession, restitution, the sequester-
> ing of sheep, the seizing of vineyards. . . . By the same token, for the last
> five thousand years, with remarkable regularity, popular insurrections
> have begun the same way: with the ritual destruction of the debt records.
> (2011, 8)

In Xinjiang in the early 2010s, the gift of Han-style cultural and economic normalization manifests as an unquantifiable, by definition unrepayable, moral debt. Sporadic examples of violence involving Uyghur people in rural areas of South Xinjiang can be viewed from this perspective as a rejection of the normalizing project and its manifestations in Xinjiang: a "destruction of the debt records."

## Notes

1. This chapter is based primarily on a series of eighteen semistructured interviews and many more unstructured discussions with people in Korla and Urumqi and on my observations during three and a half weeks of fieldwork in January and February 2013. My most important interlocutors included non-cadre state employees, including police (eleven); private employees (four); *bingtuan*, local government and oil company cadres (six); farmers (four); and private entrepreneurs (fifteen). These are not necessarily mutually exclusive groups. This new material builds on and supplements more than two years of fieldwork, from 2007 to 2009, in Xinjiang and accompanying in-depth research for my doctoral thesis.

2. This sort of social inclusion tends to be unfavorable to those people or groups who are *being included*; those who are *doing the including* do so, in many cases, to benefit themselves.

3. Although places like Xinjiang and Tibet have distinct characteristics that differentiate them from the core region, all the people of the periphery and the place itself are shaped in some way by events at the core, just as the periphery shapes the core. Scholars of imperialism have shown both how complex these dynamics are and how they exist, in some form, in every relationship between core and periphery, whether or not such a relationship is formally classified as a colonial one. See Sahadeo (2007); Stoler and McGranahan (2007); and Cliff (2012b).

4. See especially "Total Investment in Fixed Assets" and "Gross Domestic Products" for Beijing and Xinjiang.

5. By this I mean that they put forth explanations for the failure of the state to establish its legitimacy in the eyes of these peripheral subjects.

6. See "Basic Statistics on People's Livelihood."

7. When one considers that there are increasing numbers of university-educated Uyghurs who find themselves passed over in favor of Han who are no better qualified than they, this conclusion can at best be seen as incomplete.

8. This is exactly the way that certain ethnic identities have been produced and reinforced, and others diluted or eliminated altogether in the PRC since the Ethnic Classification Project in the 1950s. See Mullaney 2004.

9. It is only the shortage of a particular type of labor—unskilled labor with no benefits and no job security. There are hundreds of thousands of unemployed university graduates who refuse to take these low-status jobs—in part out of a reasonably well-grounded fear that these jobs will lead to a "dead end" for them because people will classify them as unskilled physical laborers, and they will be unable to get any other work, and in part out of a concern for "face" and a belief that they are "above" such work. The common critique of these university graduates, of course, concentrates only on the latter reason.

10. The real interest rate is the deposit rate minus inflation: if inflation is 16 percent and the deposit rate is 6 percent, the real return is *minus* 10 percent.

11. Chinese central bank data show that 45 percent of aggregate credit is nonbank finance. See Hamlin (2013). Wenzhou is the source of an estimated eight hundred billion yuan of this private capital, which is equivalent to 2 percent of China's total economic output; see Fan and Oster 2011.

12. In 2011 it was reported that access to business development funds has been made easier in Xinjiang, and in the same year preferential policies were announced for the top echelon of privately run Xinjiang-based businesses; see Bloomberg 2011; and Cui 2012.

13. This entrepreneur, nervous at being interviewed, professed "complete faith in the government and in the banking system" and claimed that "any entrepreneur with a good business plan would have no problem borrowing money from the state banks." He did not have any experience with borrowing money from the banks himself.

14. The latter tended to be restaurateurs and other people who ran small businesses that provided goods and services; like ordinary state enterprise and government employees they are peripheral to the chaotic-lucrative political economy.

15. Chinese spinners, however, are having it tough because the high domestic cost of cotton is not reflected in the price they can get for their cotton yarn. See International Cotton Advisory Committee (2012). This is a proagricultural, anti-industrial policy and therefore goes against most of what the Chinese central state has done in the past sixty years.

16. With regard to cultural fit I have observed on numerous occasions how the managers and staff of small and medium-sized enterprises in different parts of China not only work together but also eat up to three meals a day together and enjoy recreation time together. Uyghur prohibitions on eating food that is prepared in a Han kitchen prevent them from being part of this "corporate culture." With much of the business and work of private enterprise in China done outside of formal work hours and outside of a formal work environment, the inability to eat and drink like the Han would be a serious impediment to a Uyghur manager's career and a restriction on the nature of the work—in particular the informal but essential work of cozying up to government officials—that the manager is able to do for the company.

17. Perhaps it is no coincidence that the fifteen years of the lease are broken down into three "five-year plans," given the political and discursive context in which this is occurring.
18. This was spoken in English, apart from the final Chinese word.
19. When colluding, the businessman and the government officials can work out myriad ways to ensure that the businessman gets the contract. Examples include officials providing information to the businessman about competitors' bids in a tender process; officials providing an extremely brief window of opportunity to get the bid in or supply the machinery, combined with an early heads-up for the businessman on what machinery will be required in the future; and officials simply favoring a business partner's bid on grounds that would not stand up to thorough investigation.
20. See also Yuling 2009.
21. It is neither practicable nor desired for Uyghurs to be exactly like Han, of course: the Han need an other to define themselves, and a certain amount of perceived internal threat (instability in Xinjiang) has so far proven a much-used tool of governance, in Xinjiang and across the nation.
22. *Minzu* can be translated as "ethnic group." *Zhonghuaminzu* is the Chinese meta-*minzu*, which includes all fifty-six officially recognized ethnic groups.
23. Emily Yeh (2013) makes this point in relation to Tibet.

## References

All China Data Centre. 2013. "Total Investment in Fixed Assets." http://chinadataonline.org.rp.nla.gov.au/member/macroyr/macroyrtshow.asp.

Barboza, David. 2011. "In Cooling China, Loan Sharks Come Knocking." *New York Times*. Oct. 13. www.nytimes.com/2011/10/14/business/global/as-chinas-economy-cools-loan-sharks-come-knocking.html?_r=0.

Bovingdon, Gardner. 2004 *Autonomy in Xinjiang: Han Nationalist Imperatives and Uyghur Discontent*. Policy Studies, no. 11. Washington: East-West Center.

CECC. 2011. "Local Officials in Xinjiang Continue Curbs over Religious Practice." *Human Rights and Rule of Law*, Dec. 16. www.cecc.gov/pages/virtualAcad/index.phpd?showsingle=166663.

Chaudhuri, Debasish. 2010. "Minority Economy in Xinjiang—A Source of Uyghur Resentment." *China Report* 46 (1): 9–27.

Chen, Jie, and Bruce J. Dickson. 2010. *Allies of the State: China's Private Entrepreneurs and Democratic Change*. Cambridge, MA: Harvard University Press.

Cliff, Thomas. 2009 "Neo Oasis: The Xinjiang Bingtuan in the Twenty-First Century." *Asian Studies Review* 33 (1): 83–106.

——. 2012a. "Oil and Water: Experiences of Being Han in 21st-Century Korla, Xinjiang." PhD diss., Australian National University, Canberra.

———. 2012b. "The Partnership of Stability in Xinjiang: State-Society Interactions Following the July 2009 Unrest." *China Journal* 68 (July): 79–105.

———. 2013. "Peripheral Urbanism: Making History on China's Northwest Frontier." In "The Urbanisation of Rural China," edited by Ben Hillman and Jonathan Unger. Special issue, *China Perspectives*, no. 3, 13–23.

Cui Jia. 2012. "Xinjiang's Stability Important for Nation." ChinaDaily.com.cn, March 7. www.chinadaily.com.cn/china/2012-03/07/content_14772789.htm.

Dickson, Bruce J. 2008. *Wealth into Power: The Communist Party's Embrace of China's Private Sector*. Cambridge: Cambridge University Press.

Duara, Prasenjit. 2001. "The Discourse of Civilization and Pan-Asianism." *Journal of World History* 12 (1): 99–130.

Fan Wenxin and Shai Oster. 2011. "China Credit Squeeze Prompts Suicides amid Offer to Sever Finger." Bloomberg.com, Nov. 7. www.bloomberg.com/news/2011 -11-06/china-credit-squeeze-prompting-suicides-along-with-offer-to-sever -a-finger.html.

Fischer, Andrew Martin. 2008. "Resolving the Theoretical Ambiguities of Social Exclusion with Reference to Polarisation and Conflict." DESTIN Working Paper no. 08-90 (Jan.): 1–32.

Foucault, Michel. 1977. *Discipline and Punish: The Birth of the Prison*. London: Allen Lane.

Garnaut, John. 2008. "Can Chinese Government Spending Avert Recession? A Report from Wenzhou." *Asia-Pacific Journal*, no. 47 (Nov.): http://japanfocus.org/ -John-Garnaut/2954/article.html.

Gilley, Bruce. 2001. "Uighurs Need Not Apply." *Far Eastern Economic Review*, August 23, 26.

*Global Times*. 2012. "Religious Freedom Doesn't Trump Protection of Minors." *GlobalTimes*, June 12.

———. 2013. "Fight Against Riots in Xinjiang." *GlobalTimes*, June 30.

Graeber, David. 2011. *Debt: The First 5,000 Years*. Brooklyn, NY: Melville House.

Grewal, Bhajan S., and Abdullahi D. Ahmed. 2011. "Is China's Western Region Development Strategy on Track? An Assessment." *Journal of Contemporary China* 20 (69): 161–81.

Hamlin, Kevin. 2013. "China Poised for 2013 Rebound as Debt Risks Rise for Xi." Bloomberg.com, Jan 3. www.bloomberg.com/news/2013-01-02/china-poised -for-2013-rebound-as-debt-risks-rise-for-xi.html.

Hillman, Ben. 2008. "Rethinking China's Tibet Policy." *Asia-Pacific Journal: Japan Focus*. www.japanfocus.org/-ben-hillman/2773/article.html.

———. 2014a. *Patronage and Power: Local State Networks and Party-State Resilience in Rural China*. Stanford: Stanford University Press.

———. 2014b. "Unrest in Tibet: Interpreting the Post-2008 Wave of Protest and Conflict." *Dalny Vychod* [Far East] 4 (1): 50–60.

Human Rights Watch. 2005. *Devastating Blows: Religious Repression of Uighurs in Xinjiang*. Human Rights Watch 17 (2C). www.hrw.org/reports/2005/china0405/.

International Cotton Advisory Committee. 2012. *Cotton: Review of the World Situation* 66 (2): 1–24.

Mauss, Marcel. 1966. *The Gift: Forms and Functions of Exchange in Archaic Societies.* London: Cohen and West.

Mullaney, Thomas S. 2004. "Ethnic Classification Writ Large." *China Information* 18 (2): 207–41.

NBS. 2013a. "Consumer Price Index (CPI) by Category (2012.01)." National Bureau of Statistics of China. www.stats.gov.cn.

——. 2013b. "Consumer Price Index (CPI) by Region (2012.01)." National Bureau of Statistics of China. www.stats.gov.cn.

——. 2013c. "Consumer Price Index (CPI) by Region (2012.12)." National Bureau of Statistics of China. www.stats.gov.cn.

Orlik, Tom. 2011. "Unrest Grows as Economy Booms." *Wall Street Journal*, Sept. 26. http://online.wsj.com/article/SB10001424053111903703604576587070600504108.html.

Pei, Minxin. 2006. *China's Trapped Transition: The Limits of Developmental Autocracy.* Cambridge, MA: Harvard University Press.

Radio Free Asia. 2012a. "Herdsmen Demand Answers, Compensation." RFA.org, Feb. 9. www.rfa.org/english/news/uyghur/herdsmen-02092012185043.html.

——. 2012b. "Uyghur Petitioners Beaten." RFA.org, June 22. www.rfa.org/english/news/uyghur/petitioners-06222012160433.html.

——. 2013a. "Farmers Complain of Land Grabbing, Corruption in Xinjiang Village." RFA.org, June 3. www.rfa.org/english/news/uyghur/farm-06032013205126.html.

——. 2013b. "Three Uyghurs Held for Resisting Land Takeover." RFA.org, April 12. www.rfa.org/english/news/uyghur/dispute-04122013150515.html.

——. 2013c. "Uyghur Businessman Attacked After Demolition Complaint." RFA.org, April 19. www.rfa.org/english/news/uyghur/assault-04192013142140.html.

Reuters. 2014. "China to Give Cotton Farmers Outside Xinjiang Subsidies of 2,000 Yuan per T in 2014/15—Association." Reuters.com, Nov. 4. www.reuters.com/article/2014/11/05/china-cotton-idUSB9N0QA01520141105.

Rong Feiwen. 2012. "China's Cotton Reserves Enough to Meet Deficit for Six Years." Bloomberg.com, Nov. 2. www.bloomberg.com/news/2012-11-02/china-cotton-reserves-seen-enough-to-meet-deficit-for-six-years.html.

Sahadeo, Jeff. 2007. *Russian Colonial Society in Tashkent: 1865–1923.* Bloomington: Indiana University Press.

Shen Yuling. 2009. "The Social and Environmental Costs Associated with Water Management Practices in State Environmental Protection Projects in Xinjiang, China." *Environmental Science and Policy* 12 (7): 970–80.

Shih, Victor. 2004. "Development, the Second Time Around: The Political Logic of Developing Western China." *Journal of East Asian Studies* 4 (3): 427–51.

Song Ligang. 2013. "Unfinished Reform Threatens Chinese Growth." East Asia Forum, Jan. 27. www.eastasiaforum.org/2013/01/27/unfinished-reform-threatens -chinese-growth.

State Council. 2009. "China's Ethnic Policy and Common Prosperity and Development of All Ethnic Groups." www.china.org.cn/government/whitepaper/ node_7078073.htm.

Stoler, Ann Laura, and Carole McGranahan. 2007. "Refiguring Imperial Terrains." In *Imperial Formations*, edited by Ann Laura Stoler, Carole McGranahan, and Peter C. Perdue, 3–44. Santa Fe, NM: School for Advanced Research Press.

Tsui, Enid. 2012. "China's Labour Shortage: Getting Worse." *Financial Times*, June 18. http://blogs.ft.com/beyond-brics/2012/06/18/chinas-labour-shortage -getting-worse.

Turdush, Rukiye. 2013. "Xinjiang Raids Point to Religious Controls." RFA.org, March 10. www.eurasiareview.com/10032013-xinjiang-raids-point-to-religious -controls/.

Wang Ning. 2011. "Youhua gongye jingji jiegou: Tuijin Xinjiang xinxing gongyehua jincheng (Optimise the Industrial and Economic Structure: Propel the Progress of Xinjiang's New Industrial Structure)." *Xinjiang Shehui Kexue* (Social Sciences in Xinjiang) 6:42–46.

Wang Yong. 2011. "Guoyou qiye yao zai tuijin shehui zhuyi hexin jiazhi tixi jianshe zhong fahui biaoshuai zuoyong [SOEs Must Draw on Their Role as Models in Order to Push Forward Construction of a Core Socialist Values System]." *Qiushi Lilun*, Dec. 26. www.qstheory.cn/tbzt/sqjlz/zgtsshzywh/gcls/201112/ t20111226_131956.htm.

Watts, Jonathan. 2011. "China Police Station Attack Leaves Several Dead in Xinjiang." *Guardian*, July 18. www.guardian.co.uk/world/2011/jul/18/china-police -station-attack-xinjiang.

Wei Tian. 2011. "Xinjiang to Boost Local Businesses." ChinaDaily.com.cn, March 8. www.chinadaily.com.cn/bizchina/2011-08/03/content_13041765.htm.

Xinhua. 2011. "China Striving to Build Bustling Border Towns in Xinjiang by 2020." English.news.cn, Nov. 5. http://news.xinhuanet.com/english2010/ china/2011-11/05/c_131231229.htm.

XJASS. 2012. "Qiye chanye yuanjiang tisu xinjiang kuayueshi fazhan (Central SOEs' Industrial Assistance Speed Up Xinjiang's Leapfrog Development)." *Quyu jingji*, April 22.

Xu Hongyi and Zhou Xiang. 2014. "Xinjiang Said to Prepare Pilot Program for Cotton Pricing." Caixin Online, Oct. 9. http://english.caixin.com/2014-09 -10/100727095.html.

Yang Jing and Yang Chuantang. 2010 (updated Sept. 19, 2011). "Great Progress in Ethnic Minority Relations." *Qiushi*. english.qstheory.cn/politics/201109/ t20110924_112476.htm.

Yeh, Emily T. 2013. *Taming Tibet: Landscape Transformation and the Gift of Chinese Development*. Ithaca, NY: Cornell University Press.

YouTube. 2011. "China's Manufacturing Driven into Last Ditch." YouTube.com, Nov. 10. www.youtube.com/watch?v=GK31AZE7n_c.

Yu Yongding. 2013. "China's Groundhog Day Growth Pattern." East Asia Forum, Feb. 10. www.eastasiaforum.org/2013/02/10/chinas-groundhog-day-growth -pattern.

Zhang Xue. 2011. "Xinjiang Shixing Jiceng Ganbu Gangwei Butie, Cun Ganbu Gong-zuo Jiang Deng 4 Xiang Zhengce (Xinjiang Implements Four Policies to Support Grassroots and Village-Level Cadres)." Sept. 30. Xinhua. www.xj.xinhuanet .com/2011-10/01/content_23821825.htm.

Zhu, Yuchao, and Dongyan Blachford. 2012. "Economic Expansion, Marketization, and Their Social Impact on China's Ethnic Minorities in Xinjiang and Tibet." *Asian Survey* 52 (4): 714–33.

# 6

# Environmental Issues and Conflict in Tibet

Yonten Nyima and Emily T. Yeh

A mong the Tibetans who have self-immolated since 2009, at least one is reported to have shouted about the need to protect Tibet's environment while doing so. Both environmental destruction and the destructive effects of environmental improvement policies on pastoralist livelihoods have been cited as major grievances that have fueled the self-immolations (Fischer 2012).[1] A connection between the environment and current patterns of conflict and protest across Tibet is also suggested by the dramatic wave of pelt burnings in 2006 in response to the fourteenth Dalai Lama's Kalachakra speech about the conservation of tigers and other endangered animals, which was followed two years later by political protests across the plateau (Yeh 2012, 2013a). Moreover, among prominent Tibetan intellectuals who have been arrested in recent years, more than a few, including Tenzin Delek Rinpoche, Kunga Tsayang, Karma Samdrup, and Rinchen Samdrup, have been involved in environmental protection activities.[2]

All of this suggests the need to investigate whether and how environmental policies and problems contribute to current patterns of conflict and protest across Tibetan areas of China. We do so by analyzing different responses across different sectors and forms of environmental intervention, showing that in some cases assumed causal relationships between environmental issues and conflict are tenuous at best. This is the case for *tuimu huancao* (variously translated as "converting pastures to grasslands" or "retire livestock, restore rangeland"), a policy to fence and set aside areas in which grazing is banned for varying periods of time. Examining its implementation in Nagchu Prefecture of the Tibet Autonomous Region (TAR), we stress the importance of ordinary bureaucratic politics, particularly local officials' drive to seek rents and raise revenues, on the one hand, and be seen to fulfill development targets, on the other. These everyday politics of governance simultaneously plague *tuimu huancao* implementation but also allow herders space to maneuver to mitigate its impact on their livelihoods. While discussing both the *tuimu huancao* policy and the history of pastoralism and vulnerability to snowstorms in the region, herders in Nagchu made statements about the benevolence of the state. Exploring these statements, we suggest that the formation of rural subjectivities, inflected by an idiom of the "benevolent State," contributes to Nagchu Prefecture's relative quiescence compared to the eastern Tibetan regions in Kham and Amdo and that such orientations toward state intervention must be taken seriously in evaluating conflict and protest across Tibet more broadly.

From here the chapter turns to ecological migration in the Sanjiang-yuan area of Qinghai, which has been implemented along with *tuimu huancao* and which some observers have linked directly to self-immolation. It is difficult, however, to draw any direct link between even this much more disruptive policy and protest, in part because of political dynamics that lead to greatly exaggerated reports of policy implementation. Finally, the chapter concludes with an examination of a controversial sector that has been strongly linked to environmental damage and significant conflict: mining. In addition to material harm in the form of visible scars on grasslands, diversion of water, and water pollution leading to health impacts and livestock deaths, mining also directly influences Tibetan cultural and religious practices. Some of the most damaging alluvial gold mining across the plateau has been facilitated by rent-seeking behavior of local officials. The mobilization of state logics of countering "splittism" to support both small- and large-scale mineral exploitation driven by political economic imperatives contributes to the political destabilization of the region. That is, rent seeking by local officials appears, in the case of *tuimu huancao* implementation, to contribute to the overall maintenance of the current political structure, while it tends toward the opposite in mining.

Material about Nagchu in this chapter is based on research by Yonten Nyima undertaken between July 2009 and October 2010 in three rural counties, specifically two villages in Pelgön County, in western Nagchu; one village in Amdo County, in central Nagchu; and two villages in Drachen County, in eastern Nagchu. The ethnographic fieldwork included focus groups, oral histories, and interviews with householders, as well as national, provincial, prefectural, and township officials. It is also informed by government documents and work reports. Other parts of the chapter are based on secondary source material and data collected by Emily T. Yeh from June to September 2011 and February 2012. Given its sensitivity, firsthand research on mining is virtually impossible to obtain. Instead, we have used accounts relayed in the course of interactions with Tibetans and Chinese environmentalists, corroborating them wherever possible with sources such as newspaper articles and company websites, as well as secondary literature.

## The *Tuimu Huancao* Policy: From Beijing to the Village

Launched nationally in 2003, with the rationale of reversing grassland degradation, the *tuimu huancao* policy calls for fencing, the seeding of grass, and bans on grazing for ten years (*jinmu*), or seasonally (*xiumu*). The policy is based on three basic assumptions: that there is pervasive degradation across China, that this degradation results from overgrazing and irrational management practices, and that degraded rangeland can be restored through seeding and a grazing ban. All three assumptions are flawed. The problems of Hardin's "tragedy of the commons" thesis, as well as of assuming that the Tibetan Plateau is a pure equilibrium ecosystem, are well established. Furthermore, frequently cited statistics about overgrazing in China are derived from undocumented surveys, conducted by untrained staff, without a baseline, and have not been substantiated by more rigorous attempts to quantify degradation (Harris 2010). The many contradictions within and between official reports further call into question the credibility of claims of generalized degradation, as do place-based studies (Yundannima 2012).

In Nagchu herders contest the assessment that their grasslands are generally degraded. Moreover, they attribute what degradation does exist primarily to trampling of forage, which results from the limitations on livestock mobility imposed by the Rangeland Household Responsibility System (RHRS), a policy that *tuimu huancao* has intensified (Yundannima 2012). Though the Grassland Law allows rangeland use rights to be contracted to groups of households and villages, implementation of the RHRS in practice has focused heavily on contracting to individual households, which is widely viewed by Chinese officials as a key way to transform traditional pastoralism into a modern, scientific industry.

Despite these flaws, central government-level policy makers claim that the rationale for the implementation of *tuimu huancao* across China is to reverse widespread degradation, which in turn threatens the ecological security of the nation. Five central government-level institutions participated in the formulation, coordination, and implementation of the policy,[3] although in practice the Ministry of Agriculture is the actual policy implementer at the central government level. It sets targets for the areas to be fenced off and seeded each year, and the Ministry of Finance allocates the funding.

In most provinces pastoralists and provincial governments are responsible for 30 percent of the costs of fencing material. In the TAR, by contrast, the central government budget covers the entire cost of fencing material, including transportation costs (to the township headquarters), as well as compensation to herders. Given that it is not required to provide matching funding, the TAR government is particularly interested in the policy as a way to capture central state subsidies. Indeed, in an interview with Yonten Nyima the head of the Grassland Office of the Department of Animal Husbandry under the Ministry of Agriculture stated that the TAR was not initially a target region when *tuimu huancao* was implemented in 2003 because it had already "enjoyed special preferential policies and funding from the central government for socioeconomic development and ecological construction. But since 2004, the TAR has been included in the program because the TAR government and its pastoralists requested the program." Between 2004 and 2009 this amounted to a total central government investment of RMB 1.929 billion, of which 1 percent, or RMB 19.29 million, was allocated directly to the TAR regional Department of Agriculture and Animal Husbandry (AAH) as its operating budget.

Although the aim of *tuimu huancao* is the reversal of rangeland degradation, previous implementation of the Rangeland Household Responsibility System was made the primary prerequisite for the program by the five implementing agencies at the central level. The TAR lagged far behind Inner Mongolia and other parts of the Tibetan Plateau, where the RHRS was implemented in the 1980s and 1990s, but started to implement the RHRS widely in 2005 in order to be eligible for *tuimu huancao*.[4] The sequence of *tuimu huancao* implementation at different sites in the TAR suggests that site selection was indeed determined primarily by extent of previous implementation of RHRS to the household level rather than extent of purported or actual grassland degradation. The Nagchu Prefecture Bureau of Agriculture and Animal Husbandry (BAAH) explicitly decided that *tuimu huancao* would not be implemented anywhere that rangeland use rights had not been allocated to the household level, and two years after *tuimu huancao* was implemented nationally, the central government issued a document stating that rangeland use rights privatization was one of its key achievements.[5]

The imperative to capture central level subsidies results in perverse policy implementation by local governments. For example, the seeding component of the program was an utter failure in the first few rounds of the project in western Nagchu. Nothing grew. County AAH officials, who stated plainly that seeding "is just a total waste of money and labor," suggested not participating in future rounds or growing fodder instead. But they were pressured to report success in seeding and to continue with new phases of the project. Furthermore, a document jointly issued by the TAR Department of AAH and the TAR Development and Reform Commission calling for project implementation for the fiscal year 2005 reads, "This year, *tuimu huancao* will be implemented on a large scale in the region for the first time. Success or failure of project implementation will have an impact on state investment in the region hereafter. Prefectures and municipalities should install the fencing on a large scale and make sure that the fencing is not fragmented and that they are good for show."[6]

Indeed, as is also the case in other provinces where *tuimu huancao* has been implemented, the criteria by which its "success" has largely come to be judged in practice is the fencing itself rather than the state of the grassland the fences enclose. The Ministry of Agriculture's criteria for evaluating the implementation of *tuimu huancao* allocates thirty out of one hundred points to "task fulfillment," but this refers to whether a certain amount of rangeland has been fenced off, and to the quality of fencing

materials and installation, rather than rangeland condition.[7] The difficulty of traveling to remote areas, the time and effort required to evaluate grassland condition, and the interests of all levels of government from
the region down in keeping the subsidies flowing or passing performance
evaluations and achieving targets means that fencing is given a cursory
examination, and reports of success are submitted regardless of grassland
condition. As a former township party head in Amdo County explained:
"When we learn an evaluation team is coming, we township officials ask
the village heads to arrange for people to drive livestock out of the fenced
zones. . . . The evaluation team just assesses the quality of fencing and estimates the area of the fenced zone. . . . The evaluation team uses telescopes
to look around and make sure the fencing is installed where local pastoralists and officials tell them it has been set up."

While national level *tuimu huancao* policy makers are informed by flawed
environmental rationales, TAR regional- and county-level officials appear
to be motivated primarily by the logic of capturing state subsidies (see also
Bauer 2005), both as a form of rent seeking and because performance evaluation is based partially on their ability to generate funding. This reflects
a broader characteristic of governance in contemporary China, in which a
primary task of local governments has become the generation of revenue
(Hillman 2010; Smith 2013). With few enterprises to attract investment,
this takes the form in the TAR of what local officials call *pao xiangmu*, or
chasing after state subsidized projects. Officials tend to express consensus (*tongyi koujing*) about *tuimu huancao*, saying that pastoralists welcome
the program and that it has been very successful. In the absence of proper
measurement against stated policy goals, the combination of rent seeking
and emphasis on performance evaluation produces a situation in which
policies, as they are currently implemented and evaluated, appear most
successful in maintaining the political status quo.

In contrast, township government and AAH County Bureau officials
from local pastoral areas tend to view *tuimu huancao* as environmentally
useless and, aside from providing free fencing material and compensation
for pastoralists, of no benefit to rangeland. While the township level does
not receive implementation funding, a powerful driver at this level is the
cadre responsibility system with its performance targets. As a result township officials risk much by openly expressing views about the failures of
the policy. Moreover, some officials at the township level in Nagchu com-

plain they cannot fully participate in government discussion because Chinese language is used at the county level, precluding their comprehension of proceedings. Because of their desire to keep their jobs, pressure to not make trouble, and language barriers, officials often find themselves implementing policy with which they do not agree.

Once the decision is made to go ahead, the AAH County Bureau and township governments implement *tuimu huancao* through a combination of incentives and warnings to villagers, depending on pastoralists' desires for or against the project, which in turn depends on where and on what type of pasture the project is implemented, as discussed below. The process often begins with a seemingly "bottom-up" approach, wherein officials present the scheme to villagers and advise them that if they so request, it will be implemented. If villagers decline, officials do "thought work," which in this case consists of "educating" villagers about the benefits of the project, including compensation, and pointing out that acceptance of this project paves the way for future development projects. If this is refused, then negative consequences, such as the cessation of future government projects, are threatened. In addition villagers are told that by going against a mandatory project (in fact the scheme is not mandated at a central government level, rather regional-level governments request it in order to capture subsidies), they are in effect going against the wishes of the state and that they will bear the responsibility for any negative consequences. With the link now made between environmental policy and (negative) political consequences, implementation proceeds. The lack of consultation of individual pastoralist households for whether and where *tuimu huancao* fencing zones are implemented is summed up in the words of one pastoralist in Pelgön: "No, [we were not consulted] at all. . . . We have to do as we are told. We will eat the fencing if we are told to do so!"

The process of implementation is neatly illustrated in the case of a village in Pelgön County. A county government work team comprising a government leader and officials from the AAH County Bureau and the township government, went together to the village leadership to explain the project and ask if the village had any area that could be fenced off. The team then advised the village leadership they could request the project if they wished. The village leaders said they did not have anywhere they could ban grazing long-term (*jinmu*) and asked for a *xiumu* (seasonal) grazing ban zone. Needing to fulfill their quotas, however, the county government, through the township government, argued that the village should instead agree to a long-term grazing ban zone and promised that those who did so would receive decent compensation and future development projects. Thus, the village reluctantly accepted a long-term grazing ban. To mitigate its negative effects, they divided this into two separate areas. However, AAH County Bureau officials, worried because higher-level officials preferred larger zones, and also partly because they had originally suggested fencing sites by the village should be in only one area, ordered the two be recombined into one larger grazing-free zone. Otherwise, they threatened, the fencing would be removed, and the village would not be given future development projects. Moreover, they advised that if this resulted in any problems for the township or county as a whole, these villagers would bear the responsibility. Thus, the village leadership felt it had no choice but to agree to a large long-term grazing ban zone. The village leader opined, "Other than for the sake of compensation and for [the possibility of] future development projects, the *tuimu huancao* fencing is just useless."

## Project Implementation Sites and Villagers' Negotiations

Given the lack of meaningful consultation in the implementation of *tuimu huancao*, villagers' reactions are mixed and depend in large part on what kind of vegetation is fenced. In practice county officials determine the presence of "degradation" by rangeland type rather than the health of the vegetation. Alpine meadow pastures are the only type of pasture eligible for short-term grazing bans, whereas sandy pastures are designated for long-term grazing bans. Pastoralists in eastern and central Nagchu prefer to fence off alpine marsh meadow pastures in order to reserve forage for the lean times of late winter and early spring, for snowstorms, for calving and lambing, and for fattening livestock.[8] They welcome free fencing and compensation if they are able to use it to reserve alpine marsh meadow.

County-level officials do not approve of this use of fencing on the best quality rangelands, however, since the purpose of the program is to fence off degraded rangeland. Thus, they require fencing of alpine meadow pastures and sandy pastures, not alpine marsh meadows. Pastoralists generally view fencing of the alpine meadows and sandy pastures as useless;

their local knowledge suggests that fencing will not cause vegetation to be "restored" to a higher density; furthermore, what vegetation there is will simply be blown away by the wind in the winter if it is not grazed. Thus, they view it not only as useless but also as a waste of needed pasture.

An exception is when seeding has been implemented along with the long-term grazing ban. One elderly herder in Pelgön stated, "If the seeding of the grass works, this would be beneficial to us. I am hopeful about it as the state (rgyal khab) says it will work. However, I am not speaking from experience." Villagers at the western site were enthusiastic about the possibility of seeding when that component of the project was first implemented in 2009, but nothing came of their efforts over a period of two years. Because of the higher precipitation in the east, seeding was much more successful in Drachen, though some of the vegetation was destroyed by voles. Pastoralists there wanted to receive more seed from the government. This was not possible, however, given that quotas were allocated across different counties without regard to ecological data regarding where seeding would more likely be successful.

Where seeding has not been implemented, pastoralists have viewed long-term bans on grazing in sandy pasture as basically useless but relatively harmless, especially in light of the monetary compensation they receive. One pastoralist stated, "The only benefit from this program is compensation and free fencing. I guess the state has no idea how pastoralism works." According to another, "We would rather not have the project if we received no compensation as we would end up with no benefit. . . . As we pastoralists earn very little money, as long as there is compensation it is okay for us to fence off the sandy land for the sake of that money." Township leaders are well aware of this, stating, for example, that "the pastoralists want to have the project not because they think more vegetation will grow, but because they want the compensation. Of course, if more vegetation grew, that would be great." In the case of seasonal fencing of alpine meadow pastures, however, pastoralists try to find ways to not fully comply. In Amdo County, the AAH County Bureau decided to pay pastoralists to install the fencing in the first round because they were unwilling to do it otherwise. Even in that case, one group of villages used some of the fencing material designated for "degraded" alpine meadows to fence off alpine marsh meadow for reserve instead. In other cases pastoralists used the fencing to mark boundaries between seasonal pastures instead.

Overall, where the policy has been most detrimental, it simply has not been implemented strictly in practice, leading to minimal change in everyday grazing practices. Instead, in Nagchu *tuimu huancao* has largely been an exercise in subsidizing villagers and installing fences. Grazing has not been effectively banned. Even if it had been, and even if the ecological rationale of the program were sound, an improvement in ecological conditions would likely take some time. Nevertheless, local officials report very impressive improvements in grassland condition, and these reports, which suggest that pastoralists have lost access to far more land than is the case in practice, make their way up to the national level.

## The "Benevolent State"

In the course of discussions about pastoral production practices, herders young and old in Pelgön, Amdo, and Drachen counties in Nagchu often deployed the term *benevolent State* (*ryal khab drin can*). Here we present several examples and speculate that it is related to the relative quiescence of Nagchu compared to the eastern Tibetan regions in Kham and Amdo.[9] It has been suggested that Nagchu has been comparatively free of protests because of preemptive policing and perhaps, like other parts of the western TAR, a relative lack of access to mobile phones and other communication devices (ICT 2008). On the one hand, there is no doubt that heavy policing and mobility restrictions continue in Nagchu, but these conditions have also been in place in Ngaba, where they have arguably contributed to more, rather than fewer, protests. On the other hand, while mobile phone coverage is rapidly spreading in Nagchu, the area is indeed more remote and less well connected than in more restive areas to the east, a factor that appears also to contribute to herders' interpretation of certain aspects of state policy and presence through an idiom of benevolence or gratitude.

Nagchu herders' references to the "benevolent State" contrast significantly with the casting of the Chinese state by Labrang region elders as "Apa Gongjia" (Father State), where *Gongjia* is a Chinese loan word for public property and the party-state (Makley 2007).[10] As Makley (2007, 105) and others have argued, "understanding the process by which locals imagine their relationships to state agents, especially in the case of ethnic Others within the PRC, is essential for grasping the practical efficacy of state projects locally—despite the actually fragmentary and variable nature of state institutions and their capacities to control subjects over space and time" (see also Anagnost 1997; Mueggler 2001). The use of the term *Apa Gongjia* empties local Tibetans of agency and presents the state as an anthropo-morphized, masculinized, fearsome colonizing agent; at the same time, the term "sarcastically denie[s] CCP leaders' unspoken claims to absolute and unmarked authority" while "mock[ing] state claims to paternal benevo-lence" (Makley 2007, 107, 108).

While also marking the state as a distant and paternal authority, the "benevolent State" idiom employed by rural herders in Nagchu does not share these other effects. In discussing livestock feeding, a pastoralist in Amdo County stated, "In the past, I mean a long time ago, when we did not have much to eat, we ate livestock intestines and the like. Today, as our life is better thanks to the benevolent State, people do not like to eat sausage. So when we slaughter yaks, we process all the intestines specially to feed calves by filling them with tsampa, blood, poor quality meat and water."

This term also arose spontaneously in discussions about heavy taxes in pre-1950s Tibet. Memories of harsh taxation and the relief immediately af-terward, before the Cultural Revolution, still strongly shape the subjectivi-ties of some older rural pastoralists in Nagchu, much as was the case with the oldest generation of women factory workers studied by Rofel (1999), and early workers on Lhasa's July 1st State Farm (Yeh 2013b). When asked when the expression "the benevolent state" first started to be used, one elderly herder explained:

> As you know, *drin can* means to whom you are grateful because they have been so kind or good to you. For example, *drin can pha ma* (parents), *drin can rtsa b'ai lama* (root lama), *sman pa drin can* (doctor), and so on. In 1959, the work team that came to tell us about reform told us that from now on we did not have to pay heavy taxes because the state really cared about its people. This was the first time we heard of the term *rgyal khab*. So we, particularly very poor people, started to say *rgyal khab drin can* to express our gratitude to the state.

While the older generation uses the term *benevolent state* to reference the removal of heavy taxes in 1959, middle-aged pastoralists in Nagchu use it to mark the relief of the post-1980 period compared to the Cultural

Revolution and high socialism. Despite the ongoing restrictions on religious practice and the tightening of control since 2008, this critical post-1980 shift still apparently evokes a sense of limited gratitude. As a fifty-two-year-old woman from an average household explained: "I got married when I was twenty-one years old in 1981. . . . My husband and I got ten yaks and thirty-two sheep. . . . We were determined to work hard to escape the hunger and cold and hard life we experienced since our childhoods. Back then we often went hungry because there was not enough food to eat, let alone the tremendous variety of food available today thanks to the benevolent State." Younger herders, too, appear to be influenced by the narratives of their elders. As one younger pastoralist in the eastern county stated, "My grandpa and parents often say my generation is so lucky to be born into this best time of history . . . and we should cherish the good life today. From this I see I cannot complain."

Some herders also interpret provision of material goods from state programs through their understanding of the Buddhist principle of karma, or cause and effect (*las rgyu 'bras*). This is illustrated by an impoverished pastoralist family in eastern Nagchu, a household of three who owned only eight yaks in 2009. They lost their twenty-two-year-old daughter, the most capable herder in the family, in a severe snowstorm in 1990. They also lost many livestock in the snowstorms of 1990, 1995, and 2002. Consequently, the village leader arranged for the head of the household to become a village party leader in order for him to earn a salary. For this he and his family are grateful. In the course of an interview about relief they received after a major snowstorm in 2002, he remarked that he asked that the amount of tsampa he received be recorded as sixty *gyama*, a bit more than he estimated he had actually received. He did not want to underestimate the amount: "Please record sixty gyama of tsampa because if we report less [than we actually received] we will be punished by the law of karma as the benevolent State has been very kind to us."

The invocation of benevolence in reference to the state can also be double-edged in the context of development and the provision of material resources. For example, discussing an increasing tendency for young men not to wear traditional robes, an old pastoralist in the central site explained, "Today, young people do not wear *slog pa* because they are too heavy for them as they are spoiled by the benevolent State. So we can just cut them apart and cover the livestock with them." By describing the provision of material resources from the state as a form of "spoiling" Tibetans, this pastoralist suggests the ambiguity of state development, as something both desirable and dangerous (see Yeh 2007).

The discourse is also mobilized in making claims on development aid from the state. For example, some herders discussed how the provision of shelters has helped livestock but has also made it harder for them to survive when they move to places without shelters, because they become accustomed to the warmth. One herder explained:

> This year we did not move our goats with the sheep to the spring pasture. We were afraid once the goats left the shelter, they might die if severe weather hit just like last year. . . . It did not snow [but] . . . we had to make that decision as we cannot foresee the weather. Ideally we wish to have a shelter at each of the three seasonal camps, especially at the winter camp, which we wish, dare we suggest it, the benevolent State would fund. Alternatively, if we did not have one at all, then the goats would not be spoiled in the first place.

Like people, then, livestock are spoiled by the generosity of the state's material provisions. Embedded within the discourse of gratitude for material provisions is a sense of an emerging critique. At the same time, the relative mildness of the critique compared to the experience of the state as "Apa Gongjia" may also reflect the unevenness of experience that leads to an unevenness of protest and discontent across Tibetan areas of China.

## Ecological Migration

Andrew Fischer (2012) has recently argued that the region of concentrated self-immolations since 2011 is precisely the area that has been the focal point of pastoralist resettlement programs "due to their ecologically strategic location as part of, or adjacent to, the Three Rivers Source [Sanjiangyuan] area." He adds that "those who have immolated themselves so far have not made any explicit connection to the resettlements" but that it is nevertheless "striking the degree to which the occurrence of self-immolations has corresponded, with a few exceptions, to this zone of intensive resettlement."

But there are several reasons to be doubtful about a link between pastoralist resettlement and self-immolation protests. Most important, the "zone of intensive resettlement" does not in fact correspond very well with the places of the most intensive self-immolations. Ecological migration has, as Fischer notes, been implemented in the roughly 150,000 km² Sanjiangyuan National Nature Reserve in Qinghai.[11] This does not overlap at all with the two counties with the highest number of self-immolations, Ngaba and Rebgong, both of which are agricultural rather than pastoral counties; nor has it been implemented in the other locales with larger numbers of self-immolations, including Amchok Bora, Luchu, and Labrang in Gansu Province.

Where ecological migration has been implemented, in the Sanjiangyuan National Nature Reserve, it subsidizes herders to sell their livestock and move to resettlement areas of varying distance from their former homes for a period of ten years (Foggin 2008; Du 2012). Studies indicate that the program is disruptive and generates considerable dissatisfaction. Former pastoralists generally do not have the skills to find employment in town, and where technical training has been provided, it has nevertheless been quite difficult for factories established for former pastoralists to stay afloat and in operation. Obstacles to employment have made those resettled dependent on subsidies, which have often been insufficient. Herders comment that they did not realize the extent to which cash was necessary in town and regret having moved, particularly in the face of reduced living and health conditions and a forced change in diet (given the high cost of meat). Housing provided is of poor quality and insufficient size for growing families, and the move from skilled pastoralist to unskilled laborer or unemployment in towns has provoked identity crises for former herders. There is little question that the program creates social dislocation (Dell'Angelo 2007; Du 2012; Foggin 2008; Sonamkyid 2008; Wende 2009; Xu 2010).

Despite this, there is also evidence to suggest that, like the *tuimu huancao* grazing bans in Nagchu, the extent of ecological migration has been exaggerated. The first relocation project, which began in September 2003 for all herders in Gyaringhu Township, Maduo County, was to have involuntarily relocated eighteen hundred people in 388 households. However, strong opposition by herders led to relocation of only about half of the households and a reformulation of the policy to one of voluntary relocation combined with local government responsibility for guiding the relocation process (Du 2012). Government reports published prior to 2010 suggested that a target of one hundred thousand herders, or about 50 percent of the population in the Sanjiangyuan nature reserve, would be resettled, but after 2010, reports suggested fifty thousand to sixty thousand had been resettled, though with plans for more waves to follow. This number, too, may be inflated. Studies indicate that some herders simply abandon their settlements and move back to the pastures when they are unable to make a living in town. Others have left their livestock in the care of relatives, rather than selling them, and return to the pastures to pick yak dung for fuel or harvest caterpillar fungus (Xu 2010; Du 2012). Thus, as in the case of *tuimu huancao*, herders have been able to exercise a degree of agency in maneuvering within the policy of ecological migration. Within resettlement villages herders modify the living spaces designed for them, altering the ideologies embodied in the imposed spaces (Cencetti 2013).

One study of resettlement from Maduo found that 70 percent of those who migrated had very few if any livestock (fewer than twenty sheep per person), and 10 percent were wealthy families who wanted to move to town to pursue business opportunities. The remaining 20 percent moved in order to support their children's education (Du 2012). Another study suggests that most of those who migrated had few livestock and that a "threshold of dissatisfaction" separates those who owned more than thirty yaks prior to resettlement, who are disappointed with their new conditions, and those who had fewer, who are generally better off though still worried about future livelihood prospects (Dell'Angelo 2007). Some herders' willingness to take part in resettlement for education is in part a consequence of a national school consolidation policy to close down village (*minban*) schools and expand township schools, which has meant that young children in sparsely populated areas must now attend boarding schools far away from their parents, compelling parents to move to town to care for children (Postiglione, Jiao, and Li 2012). However, this trend of moving to town for children's education, or for business opportunities, extends far beyond the scope of ecological resettlement (Yeh and Gaerrang 2011). Thus, while the social dislocation of ecological resettlement has undoubtedly exacerbated the vulnerability of Tibetan livelihoods and deepened a crisis of identity, the relationship between resettlement and increased unrest on the Tibetan Plateau in recent years is not direct. Rather than the resettlement experience itself, it is the fact of the ecological migration project, with its powerful symbolic valences, that provides fuel for others in expressing dissatisfaction.

## Mining

Of all environmental problems confronted by Tibetans, those caused by mining are arguably the gravest. It is more severe than industrial pollution, which is minimal on the plateau, or climate change, which has localized severe effects, such as rising lake levels, and noticeable indicators, such as rising snow lines, but is thus far less prominently or directly perceivable in other parts of the plateau. Given the powerful array of interests that benefit from mineral extraction, mining is a problem that Tibetans can do very little about. Consequently, Lafitte (2013, 87) has recently argued that "objection to mining is at the heart of Tibetan grief at Chinese rule." Indeed, mining protests have been frequent, despite the harsh repression with which they are met. For example, June 2009 saw a standoff between local residents and representatives of a planned gold mine in Markham County, Chamdo, which led to the suspension of mining until August 2012. When operations resumed, police used tear gas and fired into a crowd of about one thousand Tibetan protestors, reportedly leading to six arrests and one death.[12]

Of the various forms of mining on the Tibetan Plateau to date, alluvial gold mining, generally small-scale and unregulated, has had the largest impact on people's livelihoods and land and is thus the major object of protest. This mining has been carried out primarily by Han and Hui migrants and small companies, often using cyanide or mercury (Lafitte 2013). These operations are enabled by the rent-seeking behavior of local governments, which, as we have seen, also shapes the implementation of policies such as *tuimu huancao*. When conflict occurs between miners and local Tibetans, the twin imperatives of personal and local government profit, on the one hand, and maintaining "stability," on the other, bring the force of the local state upon the Tibetans who participate.

Higher levels of government have recognized problems with artisanal mining, leading to multiple attempts to ban the practice in Qinghai and the TAR. Instead, the state promises a future of large-scale corporate or state mining, which has not to date lived up to its long-standing designation as a "pillar industry" (Lafitte 2013). China's only domestic source of chromite, a mine in the TAR, has been only halfheartedly exploited, with Chinese industry preferring to source chromium more cheaply from other parts of the world. The only other mineral being extracted on an industrial scale on the plateau is copper, including at Yulong, Gyama, and (soon to begin) Shetongmon, in the TAR, as well as several mines in Tibetan parts of Qinghai and Yunnan. These mines are made profitable by concessional rate financing and state investment in infrastructure, such as extensions to the Qinghai-Tibet railway. Otherwise, it would be cheaper for China to continue to import, as it has done for years. Ironically, Lafitte (2013, 178) argues, "the Tibetan Plateau has gone from being a treasure house in the making to being yesterday's story, without ever peaking as a source of major industrial raw materials. Its promise remains unfulfilled, yet China presses on with centrally planned mining projects big enough to despoil Tibet, yet not big enough" to be significant in terms of China's supplies or the world market. That is, the dynamics of state capitalism will combine with resource extraction as a form of state incorporation to fuel industrial scale mining in the coming years, even while from a total supply perspective, China can easily do without Tibet's minerals, with the possible exception of gold, which has rapidly become a favored means of storing wealth by China's new rich (Lafitte 2013).

Conflicts over mining have occurred because of pollution, death of livestock, and broken promises for both compensation and restoration. In several pastoral villages in Tagong, Ganzi Prefecture, Sichuan, for example, herders working with an international NGO on comanagement in the early 2000s attributed rangeland degradation to the mining of gold and tungsten between 1981 and 1999. Though both state-owned and private enterprises had a contractual obligation to restore the pastures they mined, they failed to do so. Some miners also left without paying promised compensation. This has led to erosion, mudslides, and the filling of mining pools with water during the rainy season, leading to livestock deaths. One local leader acknowledged that "there is no way to describe how bad the gold mining is," particularly for the winter pastures on which pastoralists spend most of the year.

In addition to damage to livelihood resources and issues of compensation, conflicts around mineral extraction are also very much engendered by the widespread understanding of the harm that results from removing substances that constitute the *bcud* (nutrition or essence) of the earth, of which minerals are the primary form. Loss of grassland productivity, generalized environmental degradation, and natural disasters such as earthquakes are all attributed to the removal of the *bcud*. As one elderly pastoralist in Golog put it, "Minerals have [also] been taken [a]way, taking away the bcud of the place. This has made it harder for people in this region to survive, decreasing their fortune (*bsod nams*) and hindering prosperity." According to another, "There are very few snow mountains nowadays. . . . People say it's because of mining everywhere. The rivers have become smaller, the sources of the springs have dried up, the marshes have dried up. . . . Because the minerals have been taken, the abundant grass that was here in the past can no longer be seen."[13] Thus, environmental changes that are arguably products of anthropogenic climate change, driven primarily by the emissions of industrialized countries, are also understood as the product of Chinese mining on the plateau.

Tibetans are particularly sensitive to the removal of minerals from sacred mountains, including both Buddhist sacred sites and abodes of local territorial deities. Mining on sacred mountains is widely understood to offend territorial deities, bringing misfortune, including illness and death, to human communities. A Tibetan idiom for explaining why sacred mountains are both places where minerals are abundant and places where digging is especially harmful, is the comparison between such sites and vital organs. Lodroe Phuntsok, a prominent Tibetan medical doctor and polymath from Dzongsar, Sichuan, explained: "We say that the outer and the inner worlds are the same. The brain, the heart, the lungs, the organs: if these are injured, you will die immediately. Sacred mountains are like that for the earth. If your limbs are injured, you won't die right away, but if you hurt your heart or your brain, it's over. That's why sacred mountains are important."

The seriousness of the offense of mining on sacred mountains is difficult to overestimate. One elderly pastoralist in Dzado, Qinghai, recounted in 2005 that various outsiders came every year to attempt to dig gold on their sacred mountain, Lama Norlha, often bearing official permits from the prefecture and province, but that local villagers always got together to stop them from doing so. He explained, "Digging gold from the mountain is like taking my heart out of my body. We won't let them take a single pinch of gold." Indeed, he claimed that the county government had threatened local villagers but that they had replied, "Go ahead and kill us" rather than allowing mineral extraction.

As a result, Tibetan protests against mining on sacred mountains are common, sometimes leading to standoffs between local protestors and mining operations or police. For instance, in February 2011 a Chinese mining company negotiated with local officials to open a gold mine near the village of Abin, on the western side of Khawa Karbo, one of the eight most important Buddhist sacred mountains on the plateau. Local residents were not consulted in the negotiations, and the mining would be against the wishes of farmers living nearby—and against official bans on alluvial gold mining in the TAR announced in 2005 and again in 2007. When villagers attempted to negotiate with the company, they were met with harassment, attacks, and death threats by company-hired thugs, as well as by local police. In response, villagers pushed some US$300,000 worth of mining equipment into the Nu River. Subsequently, women and children fled to other villages to escape violent retaliation. Local police arrested a village leader who tried to confront the mining company, leading to a riot by some two hundred villagers. Villagers also tried to appeal to higher levels of authority, writing an open letter to the government listing their grievances and asking for justice, but this had no effect other than targeting those involved in disseminating the letter for scrutiny by the state security apparatus. After several more confrontations the mining company boss fled, and an official ordered the mine shut down. However, the miners soon returned in force (Yan 2012), and as of the end of 2015 the matter remained unresolved.

In cases of Tibetan protests against mining, whether they take the form of petitions to higher levels of government or more direct confrontation with miners, the most common response has been for officials to label the protests "splittism," a dynamic that effectively creates and fuels interethnic and nationalist tensions where they might not otherwise have existed or been very strong. Tibetans angered by destroyed fields and grazing areas caused by mining in Lhundrub County, near Lhasa, reportedly wrote appeals to local and higher-level authorities about their livelihood concerns, as well as about problems caused for birds and other wildlife by frequent use of explosives. However, they were accused of engaging in "politically motivated" activities and threatened with serious consequences if they continued to complain.[14]

In another case local residents around the highly sacred Amnye Ma-
chen mountain range in Golog, Qinghai, are opposed to the extraction of
minerals from the Deerni open cast copper mine, which began operations
in 2004. Pastoralists state not only that mining sacred mountains leads to
diseases and disasters but also that water pollution from the mining has
caused livestock deaths and human illnesses. Local government officials
are also said to be unhappy about the mine, operated by Qinghai West Copper, a wholly owned subsidiary of Zijin Mining Group, one of the largest
gold producers in China and one of China's biggest state-owned enterprises. Zijin has developed a notorious environmental reputation after
two major pollution scandals in 2010. One, the release of more than nine
thousand meters of toxic slurry from a copper mine tailings dam in Fujian,
which killed four million fish, was not revealed to the public by the company or state media until nine days after the incident (Stanway 2013).

Local leaders in Qinghai are unable to oppose the mine given its close
association with the state. As a report about its activities in Fujian notes,
state firms like Zijin "were carved out of mining bureaus and never quite
lose their role as arms of the government. . . . For many residents [in Fu-
jian] seeking to complain about pollution, it is often difficult to see where
the company ends and the state begins" (Stanway 2013). Herders in Qinghai may not be aware of Zijin's environmental record, but they do perceive
a conflation of state and enterprise, as reflected in local rumors that the
company is backed by a high-level central leader, perhaps even a relative
of Hu Jintao's. This close alignment of capital and the state was also manifest in the response to a sixteen-kilometer march in protest of the mine in
2011 by six hundred students from the local minority normal school. The
central government ordered an investigation into the protest, based on
the logic that this could not be just an environmental protection issue but
rather must have had some other ethnic motive behind it. An investigation
subsequently uncovered some papers printed with the statement, "You
must speak Tibetan," in reference to a movement that has spread across
the plateau since 2009 among Tibetans to speak pure Tibetan rather than
code switching with Chinese, as has become increasingly common. Government officials declared that telling other Tibetans that they must speak
Tibetan was destroying ethnic unity.[15] Furthermore, they declared that
this "political" act was the true cause of the demonstration, denying the
validity of local dissatisfaction with mining and its effects on water quality,
human health, and livelihoods.

This squelching of mining conflicts by branding them as political and as "splittist" activities can only exacerbate the conflicts that have increased across the region in recent years. By claiming that opposition to mining is equivalent to arguing that Tibetans should maintain the ability to speak pure Tibetan, and labeling both as antistate, state authorities in effect do the work of uniting a number of disparate sources of dissatisfaction and consolidating them as reasons to protest more generally. In other words, although the "hat" of splittism is an easy one to throw and an effective way to quickly suppress protests in order to protect powerful economic interests in mining, it also works to exacerbate the more generalized discontent and conflict that have been on the rise across Tibetan areas over the past few years.

Conflict between Tibetan villagers and Chinese miners, and between villagers and apparatuses of the state—thugs, police, or paramilitary forces called in to defend mining interests—are only likely to become more frequent and serious as the expansion of infrastructure and the acceleration of investment in mineral resources leads to the realization of long-promised, larger-scale, industrial extraction of resources. Government officials assure that these will be safer and cleaner than small-scale, alluvial mining. But even if this were the case, it would not mitigate the fundamental spiritual objections to mining—removal of the bcud of the earth and the transgression of sacred sites. Moreover, evidence to date does not suggest the achievement of promised improved environmental outcomes.

For example, industrialized, artisanal mining began in 1990 at the Gyama copper-gold mine in Meldrogunkar, near Lhasa, and has been the object of protests since at least 1991, over water pollution among other issues.[16] The Gyama Valley is the birthplace of Songtsen Gampo, the seventh-century founder of the Tibetan Empire, making it a particularly historically and culturally significant place. A study conducted between 2006 and 2008 found localized severe heavy metal contamination in the surface water and streambed in the middle and upper parts of the valley, as well as in stream sediments. The authors note that these heavy metal concentrations pose a "high risk for the environment, including local human populations and their livestock. However, no information with respect to the pollution has been provided to the public" (Huang et al. 2010, 4184).

In 2009 the processing sites were closed and the mine turned over to Huatailong, a subsidiary of the Vancouver-based China Gold International (CGI), itself a subsidiary of the state-owned enterprise China National Gold

Group Corporation. Official news agency Xinhua acknowledged previous dissatisfaction with the mine but promised that with state ownership things would be different:

> "Huatailong [will] . . . bring local residents long-lasting benefits through environmental protection and community-building efforts," said Sun Zhaoxue, general manager of CNGG. . . .
>
> To ease the hostility among local residents, Huatailong has spent more than 32 million yuan on land compensations and another 3.5 million yuan to make up for herders' livestock losses at the hands of former irresponsible miners.[17]

Indeed, the mine was hailed as the "Jiama [Gyama] model," and reports described it as "a panorama of lush green trees and grasslands, new roads and infrastructure . . . giving the local people a better life" (Wong 2013).

Nevertheless, conflict has continued since the replacement of the unregulated, artisanal enterprises by Huatailong. In 2009 a conflict between local Tibetans and Chinese mine workers reportedly occurred after the latter tried to divert irrigation water during a drought, leading to serious injuries, as well as detentions of Tibetans.[18] Mandatory resettlement of one hundred pastoral families also generated considerable resentment, particularly because state authorities presented it as being for the purpose of development, while pastoralists understood it as being for the mine. In March 2013 a major landslide at the mine buried eighty-three miners, all but two of whom were Chinese migrants. This raises serious doubts about the possibilities of an improved environmental record with future large-scale mining. Moreover, as the case of Zijin also suggests, mining by state-owned enterprises, or private corporations with significant state backing, is only likely to strengthen the current response, which is to squelch mine-related conflicts by branding them as political and potentially "splittist" activities.

---

As we have argued elsewhere, the environment can be and has been an avenue for interethnic cooperation rather than conflict. China's environmental movement in the 1990s was galvanized by several campaigns around the protection of wildlife in Tibetan areas and, in that sense, had

Tibet at its very core. Transnational and domestic Chinese interest in the potential of Tibetan culture and Tibetan Buddhist religious authority to protect biodiversity produced many instances of Chinese-Tibetan cooperation while opening up a space for the assertion of Tibetan culture and identity, in the alignment of Tibetan cultural practices around sacred lands with conservation science (Yeh 2013c, 2014). But the issue of mining on sacred sites is the limit point of this cooperation. While many Chinese environmentalists and organizations would like to support Tibetans in their opposition to mining in sacred areas, the state's politicization of all things Tibetan, and the powerful political and economic interests at stake in mining operations, discourage them from doing so for fear that they too will be tainted with charges of splittism. Faced with evidence of government-sponsored mineral exploration in core areas of nature reserves on the Tibetan Plateau, conservation organizations feel they have no choice but to throw up their hands in despair at a battle that they fear cannot be won.

Indeed, it is often the dynamics of what gets labeled politically sensitive, rather than the environmental issues themselves, that lead to an escalation of tensions that can foster protest and conflict. This label, in turn, is often driven by rent seeking and the interests of capital accumulation of officials and enterprises of or closely aligned with the state. The implementation of *tuimu huancao* in Nagchu is not seen as ideal by local residents, but they are pressured into accepting it through recourse to threats about "political responsibility." In most cases where *tuimu huancao* has been implemented, the dynamics of ordinary bureaucratic politics, which produces fences for show but not strict implementation of a grazing ban, has allowed ordinary villagers a way to tolerate it and sometimes even to benefit by capturing cash subsidies. At the same time, some herders in Nagchu retain and transmit memories that predispose them to understand these small state subsidies in a positive light.

With *tuimu huancao*, and even more so with ecological migration, herders maneuver within highly constrained circumstances. While policies are not as "voluntary" as officially claimed, neither are they as rigidly or fully implemented as state authorities claim. Thus, even in what seem to be extraordinary political times, logics other than those of ethnic harmony and state sovereignty continue to play roles in governance. Revenue imperatives, rent seeking, and the importance of measurable and visible targets in the judgment of cadre job performance contribute to the maintenance of the political system, as well as to quiescence through not only coercion but also the ways in which officials benefit and the ways in which herders, through compromise, can also benefit, if only in small ways, from environmental policies. At the same time, the very facts of these policies, particularly the deeply symbolic act of resettlement, can and do add fuel to the fire of broader discontent in other parts of the Tibetan Plateau. Mining, in particular, engenders disputes as the imperative of revenue generation leads here to the failure to respect core cultural sensitivities and to implement policies to limit harm to human and environmental health. Thus, it produces not quiescence but conflict.

## Notes

1. For example, Wande Khar called for the protection of Tibet's environment as he self-immolated in Tsoe on November 28, 2012. See www.savetibet.org/resources/fact-sheets/self-immolations-by-tibetans/. See also ICT 2012.
2. See http://tibetanplateau.blogspot.com/2010/04/drop-of-tear-nyenpo-yutses-cry-for-help.html.
3. These five institutions are the Office of the State Council Leading Group for Western China Development, the National Development and Reform Commission, the Ministry of Agriculture, the Ministry of Finance, and the State Grain Administration.
4. At the beginning of 2005 the CCP Committee and the TAR government issued "opinions on further implementation and improvement [of] the Rangeland Household Responsibility" (zhonggong xizang zizhiqu weiyuanhui xizang zizhiqu renmin zhengfu guanyu jinyibu luoshi wanshan caochang chengbao jingying zerenzhi de yijian); on Jan. 29, 2005, the CCP Committee and the TAR government endorsed "a pilot implementation plan for the RHRS" (xizang zizhiqu caochang chengbao jingying zerenzhi shidian gongzuo fan'an).
5. Material on the *tuimu huancao* program in Nagchu Prefecture (naqu diqu tian-ran caoyuan *tuimu huancao* gongcheng jiaoliu cailiao), Nagchu Prefectural Bureau of Agriculture and Animal Husbandry, March 26, 2009; and "Notice Regarding Doing a Good Job in the *Tuimu Huancao* Work in 2005" (guanyu zuohao 2005 nian *tuimu huancao* gongzuo de tongzhi), Office of the State Council Leading Group for Western China Development, the National Development and Reform Commission, Ministry of Finance, Ministry of Agriculture, State Grain Administration, April 30, 2005.
6. "Notice Regarding Preparing and Proposing Implementation Plan for the *Tuimu Huancao* Program in 2005" (guan yu zuzhi bianbao 2005 nian *tuimu huancao* xiangmu shishi fang 'an de tongzhi), May 30, 2005.

7. "Notice on Issuing Detailed Codes for Evaluating the *Tuimu Huancao* Program in the Western Region" (guanyu yinfa xibu diqu caoyuan *tuimu huancao* gongcheng xiangmu yanshou xize de tongzhi), Ministry of Agriculture, Oct. 7, 2004.

8. Alpine marsh meadows contain *Kobresia schoenoides*, which is hard, tightly rooted, and more than fifteen centimeters long. Alpine meadows are *Kobresia pygmaea*, which is soft, loosely rooted, and fewer than three centimeters long.

9. Nagchu has been more restive in recent years than other regions of the TAR, particularly Ngari, Nyingtri, Lhoka, and Shigatse. However, of the 159 protests recorded by the International Campaign for Tibet between March and August of 2008, only one took place in Nagchu. More recently, of the more than 130 Tibetan self-immolations that have taken place within the PRC to date, four have taken place in Nagchu, all by men from Driru County, in eastern Nagchu. Driru appears somewhat exceptional in Nagchu given its history of a revolt in 1969 and memories of those killed during that time. Other residents of Nagchu describe the situation in Driru with the phrase, "the chang brewed by the government is ready to drink" (*lang*, meaning "rise," is used both to indicate that the chang is ready and in the sense of "rise up"), meaning that the children of those killed in 1969 are seeking revenge in the larger context of pan-Tibetan protest. Perhaps because of this history, eastern Nagchu, and Driru in particular, has been considered a center of political instability in the TAR for a number of years.

10. In Nagchu herders generally used the term *ryal khab*, or state, to refer to the central government, whereas they used the term for "government," *srid gzhung*, to refer to other levels of government, particularly the township, county, and region (provincial-level).

11. This is distinct from the even bigger "Sanjiangyuan Area," a 363,300 km2 area (half of Qinghai) that does not have any special legal status. The Sanjiangyuan National Nature Reserve includes all of Golog and Yushu prefectures (except for the western half of Zhiduo), and two counties each in Hainan, Huangnan, and Haixi prefectures.

12. See www.rfa.org/english/news/tibet/mine-08162012000425.html.

13. From *Nature Repaying Kindness* (in Tibetan), unreleased documentary by Nyanbo Yuze Environmental Protection Association, 2011.

14. See www.rfa.org/english/news/tibet/mine-01182013161904.html. "Political" in this context names anything that state authorities interpret as being against its interests or position, which is implicitly made "truth" rather than "politics." Thanks to Gardner Bovingdon for this point.

15. Ethnic unity (*minzu tuanjie*) never refers, of course, to unity within a minzu but only to minority-Han relations. Thanks to Gardner Bovingdon for this point.

16. See http://tibetanplateau.blogspot.com/2009/10/canada-and-crime-against-tibetan-people.html.

17. See Cheng et al. 2012.
18. See Wong 2013.

# References

Anagnost, Ann. 1997. *National Past-Times: Narrative, Representation, and Power in Modern China*. Durham, NC: Duke University Press.

Bauer, Kenneth. 2005. "Development and the Enclosure Movement in Pastoral Tibet Since the 1980s." *Nomadic Peoples* 9 (1): 53–83.

Cencetti, Elisa. 2013. "New Settlements on the Tibetan Plateau in Amdo-Qinghai: Spatialized Power Devices." In *On the Fringes of the Harmonious Society: Tibetans and Uyghurs in Socialist China*, edited by Trine Brox and Ildiko Beller-Hann, 159–82. Copenhagen: NIAS Press.

Cheng Yunjie, Xu Lingui, Guo Yaru, and Li Hualing. 2012. "Multi-metal Mine with World-Class Deposits Rises in Qinghai-Tibet Plateau." Xinhuanet.com, June 29. http://news.xinhuanet.com/english/china/2012-06/29/c_131684804.htm.

Dell'Angelo, Jampel. 2007. "The Sanjiangyuan Environmental Policy and the Tibetan Nomads' Last Stand: A Critical Political Ecology Analysis." MA thesis, London School of Economics and Political Science.

Du, Fachun. 2012. "Ecological Resettlement of Tibetan Herders in the Sanjiangyuan: A Case Study in Madoi County of Qinghai." *Nomadic Peoples* 16 (1): 116–33.

Fischer, Andrew M. 2012. "The Geopolitics of Politico-Religious Protest in Eastern Tibet." *Cultural Anthropology Online*, April 8. www.culanth.org/?q=node/530.

Foggin, J. Marc. 2008. "Depopulating the Tibetan Grasslands: National Policies and Perspectives for the Future of Tibetan Herders in Qinghai Province, China." *Mountain Research and Development* 28 (1): 26–31.

Harris, R. B. 2010. "Rangeland Degradation on the Qinghai-Tibetan Plateau." *Journal of Arid Environments* 74 (1): 1–12.

Hillman, Ben. 2010. "Factions and Spoils: Examining Political Behaviour Within the Local State in China." *China Journal* 64 (July): 1–18.

Huang, X., M. Sillanpaa, E. T. Gjessing, S. Peräniemi, and R. D. Vogt. 2010. "Environmental Impact of Mining Activities on the Surface Water Quality in Tibet: Gyama Valley." *Science of the Total Environment* 19 (1): 4177–84.

ICT. 2008. *Tibet at a Turning Point: The Spring Uprising and China's New Crackdown.*" Washington: International Campaign for Tibet. www.savetibet.org/wp-content/uploads/2013/03/Tibet_at_a_Turning_Point.pdf.

——. 2012. *Storm in the Grasslands: Self-Immolations in Tibet and Chinese Policy*. Washington: International Campaign for Tibet. www.savetibet.org/wp-content/uploads/2013/06/storminthegrassland-FINAL-HR.pdf.

Lafitte, Gabriel. 2013. *Spoiling Tibet: China and Resource Nationalism on the Roof of the World*. London: Zed.

Makley, Charlene E. 2007. *The Violence of Liberation: Gender and Tibetan Buddhist Revival in Post-Mao China.* Berkeley: University of California Press.

Mueggler, Erik. 2001. *The Age of Wild Ghosts: Memory, Violence, and Place in Southwest China.* Berkeley: University of California Press.

Postiglione, Gerard, Ben Jiao, and Li Xiaoliang. 2012. "Education Change and Development in Nomadic Communities of the Tibetan Autonomous Region (TAR)." *International Journal of Chinese Education* 1 (1): 89–105.

Rofel, Lisa. 1999. *Other Modernities: Gendered Yearnings in China After Socialism.* Berkeley: University of California Press.

Smith, Graeme. 2013. "Measurement, Promotions and Patterns of Behavior in Chinese Local Government." *Journal of Peasant Studies* 40 (6): 1027–50.

Sonamkyid. 2008. "The Implementation of a Resettlement Development Project: Socio-economic Changes Accompanying the Transition from Nomadic to Town Life in Sogrima Town, Western China." MA thesis, Miriam College, Quenzon City, Philippines.

Stanway, David. 2013. China's Losing Battle Against State-Backed Polluters. Reuters.com, March 31. www.reuters.com/article/2013/03/31/us-china-environment-zijin-insight-idUSBRE92U08V20130331.

Wende, Drolma. 2009. "The Ecological Migration Project: The Case of Ca Chog, Mtsho Sngon Province, China." Unpublished paper.

Wong, Edward. 2013. "Fatal Landslide Draws Attention to the Toll of Mining on Tibet." *New York Times*, April 2. www.nytimes.com/2013/04/03/world/asia/deadly-tibetan-landslide-draws-attention-to-mining.html?_r=0.

Xu Jun. 2010. "Challenges: Resettlement of Nomads in Qinghai Province." International Association of Tibetan Studies, Vancouver. www.case.edu/affil/tibet/tibetanNomads/books.htm#X.

Yan, Katy. 2012. "Tibetan Village Stops Mining Near the Nu River." International Rivers Network. www.internationalrivers.org/blogs/246/tibetan-village-stops-mining-project-near-the-nu-river.

Yeh, Emily T. 2007. "Tropes of Indolence and the Cultural Politics of Development in Lhasa, Tibe." *Annals of the Association of American Geographers* 97 (3): 593–612.

——. 2012. "Transnational Environmentalism and Entanglements of Sovereignty: The Tiger Campaign Across the Himalayas." *Political Geography* 31:418–28.

——. 2013a. "Blazing Pelts and Burning Passions: Nationalism, Cultural Politics, and Spectacular Decommodification in Tibet." *Journal of Asian Studies* 72 (2): 319–44.

——. 2013b. *Taming Tibet: Landscape Transformation and the Gift of Chinese Development.* Ithaca, NY: Cornell University Press.

——. 2013c. "Tibet in China's Environmental Movement." In *On the Fringes of the Harmonious Society: Tibetans and Uyghurs in Socialist China*, edited by Trine Brox and Ildiko Beller-Hann, 235–62. Copenhagen: NIAS Press.

——. 2014. "The Rise and Fall of the Green Tibetan: Contingent Collaboration and the Vicissitudes of Harmony." In *Mapping Shangrila: Contested Landscapes in the*

*Sino-Tibetan Borderlands*, edited by Emily T. Yeh and Chris Coggins, 255–78. Seattle: University of Washington Press.

Yeh, Emily T., and Gaerrang. 2011. "Tibetan Pastoralism in Neoliberalising China: Continuity and Change in Gouli." *Area* 43 (2): 165–72.

Yundannima. 2012. "From 'Retire Livestock, Restore Rangeland' to the Compensation for Ecological Services: State Interventions into Rangeland Ecosystems and Pastoralism in Tibet." PhD diss., University of Colorado, Boulder.

# 7

## Fringe Existence

### Uyghur Entrepreneurs and Ethnic Relations in Urban Xinjiang

Tyler Harlan

I n the summer of 2009 tensions between Han and Uyghur residents erupted into violence on the streets of Urumqi, the capital of China's Xinjiang Uyghur Autonomous Region (Xinjiang). Analyses of this outbreak have pointed to economic inequality as a root cause of the violence (Barbour and Jones 2013; Millward 2009). In Xinjiang the cities of the industrialized North have experienced rapid urbanization in recent years as both Han and Uyghur migrants arrive seeking employment opportunities (Hopper and Webber 2009). But Uyghurs often find themselves unable to find jobs in the formal private sector and experience segregation in urban labor markets vis-à-vis Han workers (Hannum and Xie 1998; Howell and Fan 2011). In Urumqi the urban economy is dominated by state-owned enterprises and a growing private sector composed largely of Han firms, neither of which hire many Uyghurs (Gilley 2001; Maurer-Fazio 2012). This has created a surplus of Uyghur labor and has exacerbated ethnic tensions, presenting a major impediment to the improvement of ethnic relations following the 2009 violence.

This chapter demonstrates that an Urumqi "ethnic enclave" of Uyghur businesses is a primary arena of interethnic interaction, tension, and cooperation in Xinjiang. Most Uyghur entrepreneurs, I suggest, cluster in fringe industries and markets where they have a cultural advantage, and they rely almost exclusively on networks with fellow Uyghurs to obtain resources and capital. This restricts their ability to compete with Han firms and stifles long-term growth. I show, however, that the few Uyghur entrepreneurs who have managed to expand their businesses—to "break out" of the ethnic enclave—have built relationships with Han firms and government officials. These entrepreneurs view interethnic cooperation and state support as crucial to the growth of their businesses and to the development of the Uyghur private sector as a whole. They also see themselves as a modernizing force in Uyghur society by challenging "backward" practices and traditions and by providing employment for Uyghur workers. In this way successful entrepreneurs promote business development and interethnic cooperation as a path to modernization, one that is not antagonistic toward the Chinese state.

Data for this chapter were collected during fieldwork from March through June 2008 via a mix of questionnaires and qualitative interviews with Uyghur entrepreneurs. In this chapter I first review the concept of the ethnic enclave and the role of ethnic resources in the establishment of small businesses. I then describe the clustering of Uyghur enterprises in Urumqi and the ethnic resources these entrepreneurs employ. I show how some entrepreneurs interact with Han firms and local state officials in order to procure resources and technology, allowing them to "break out" of the enclave and expand their businesses. I then discuss how successful entrepreneurs promote business development and act as "agents of modernization" in the Uyghur community. I conclude by examining the implications of Uyghur business development for ethnic relations in Xinjiang.

## Ethnic Enclaves and Ethnic Entrepreneurship

The literature on ethnic entrepreneurship and "ethnic enclaves" provides a useful framework for understanding the practices of Uyghur entrepreneurs. Portes (1981, 290–91) first described an ethnic enclave as "immigrant groups, which concentrate in a distinct spatial location and organize a variety of enterprises serving their own ethnic market and/or the general population. Their basic characteristic is that a significant proportion of the immigrant labor force works in enterprises owned by other immigrants." The literature's concentration on immigrant groups stems from research in North America, but the term has been applied to urban immigrant communities in Europe (Phizacklea 1988) and ethnic minorities in Israel (Schnell et al. 1995) and more recently in China (Kim 2003).

Urban ethnic entrepreneurs tend to cluster within the ethnic enclave in similar industries and markets, such as those that serve the needs of co-ethnic customers or smaller enterprises serving other "non-ethnic" populations (Aldrich and Waldinger 1990, 114). Ethnic minority–owned businesses primarily target customers of the same ethnic group. Participation in the ethnic enclave economy is based on a series of advantages that the enclave provides over involvement in the mainstream private economy, where ethnic entrepreneurs are disadvantaged in access to labor and capital (Aldrich and Waldinger 1990). These advantages and restrictions are known respectively as "pull" factors and "push" factors (den Butter et al. 2007), a combination of which shape participation in the ethnic enclave.

Light (2004, 6–8) distinguishes two forms of "push" restrictions: *labor market disadvantage* occurs when workers cannot obtain wage or salary employment that reaches the prevailing market return on their productivity, while groups experience *resource disadvantage* by entering the labor market with fewer resources than the majority population. Cultural exclusion may also result from differing language, norms, and values from the majority population and the inability of entrepreneurs to target nonethnic customers. For groups in rural or marginal areas, distance from markets creates additional disadvantage. Schnell et al. (1995, 18) demonstrate that the location of Arab entrepreneurs in Israel outside of mainstream economic centers diminishes locational advantage and makes technology and resources (including bank loans) difficult to obtain. Razin's (1989) analysis of entrepreneurship in Tel Aviv and smaller Israeli settlements draws similar conclusions.

The ethnic enclave may also "pull" potential entrepreneurs by providing better returns on human capital through the availability of "ethnic resources" to mobilize labor and financing. Light and Rosenstein (1995, 171) define *ethnic resources* as "socio-cultural features of the whole group which co-ethnic entrepreneurs actively utilize in business or from which their business passively benefits." These can include a sense of shared culture, staff from the same ethnic group, business relations, and ethnic social networks (Heberer 2005). Ethnic resources operate to overcome disadvantages for entrepreneurs, primarily by providing access to employees and financing. Strong social ties within the ethnic community also promote successful business start-up because of reliance on personal ties for information, support, and networks to obtain resources (Boissevain et al. 1990).

As businesses attempt to grow and expand, however, these ethnic networks may restrain firms that require more highly skilled management and better technology (Heberer 2007, 150–56). Schnell et al. (1995, 78–79) write that for Arab entrepreneurs in Israel, the extended family, which in the start-up phase provides encouragement and capital for the industrial venture, becomes an impediment to growth. Chinese merchants, too, have been known to leave their home territory to conduct business elsewhere without pressure from relatives for "noneconomic" claims on the business (Granovetter 1995, 145–46). Thus, entrepreneurs who attempt to "break out" of the ethnic enclave tend to rely on relationships outside of their ethnic group (Sequeira and Rasheed 2004, 84–87). These nonethnic networks, however, are often difficult for entrepreneurs to access. This is the case for many Uyghur entrepreneurs in Urumqi.

## Ethnic Entrepreneurs in Urumqi

Although the private sector in Xinjiang is still less developed than in other parts of China, the importance of private business has steadily increased in the last decade. Urumqi serves as the regional hub of Xinjiang's private sector: in 2004 there were 8,941 private enterprises (more than eight employees) and 84,375 individual enterprises (fewer than seven employees) in Urumqi (XECY 2006, table 1.9). Most enterprises are operated by Han Chinese (approximately 75 percent of Xinjiang's population is Han Chinese) (XSY 2008, table 4.7). The majority of Uyghur-owned businesses are small and relatively new. They are also clustered in an ethnic enclave and operate in similar industries. Table 7.1 provides a profile of Uyghur businesses in Urumqi. Businesses are defined as those having at least one Uyghur owner-operator and a trademark registration with the Bureau of Commerce and Industry (gongshang ju). The most striking characteristic is their relatively short operating time: nearly 70 percent of respondents had started their business in the preceding five years. In addition most are clustered in similar industries and primarily serve Uyghur customers or provide "ethnic" products.

**TABLE 7.1** Profile of Uyghur Businesses in Urumqi

| Business Type (N = 55) | Percentage of Businesses |
| --- | --- |
| Import/Export | 21.8 |
| Food/Beverage | 20.0 |
| Commercial Services | 16.4 |
| Wholesale/Retail Trade | 14.5 |
| Design | 10.9 |
| Cosmetics | 9.1 |
| Other | 7.2 |
| Employee Number (N = 37) | |
| Fewer than 8 | 32.4 |
| 8–20 | 27.0 |
| 21–50 | 24.3 |
| More than 50 | 16.2 |
| Operating Time (N = 52) | |
| Fewer than 2 years | 21.2 |
| 2–5 years | 48.1 |
| 6–10 years | 23.1 |
| More than 10 years | 7.7 |

*Source*: Author survey (2008).

A sizable number of Uyghur businesses are involved in import/export activities and trade, capitalizing on the liberalization of cross-border trade in Xinjiang. Most international trade agencies in Urumqi source goods from eastern Chinese factories and export them to Central Asia, mainly Kazakhstan. Businesses involved in food and beverage production focus largely on Islamic products. This corroborates Vicziany and Zhang's (2004) assertion that Uyghurs are able to corner the *qingzhen* (halal) restaurant market, though they still compete with Hui Muslims. Entrepreneurs within other sectors profess that they target Uyghur customers almost exclusively.

Several Uyghur businesspeople have grown highly successful targeting Uyghur customers and providing "ethnic" and Islamic products. But concentration in a few market niches leads to stiff competition and high business failure rates within the ethnic enclave. Since so many enterprises trade in similar products (mainly foodstuffs and cosmetics) and services (trade and retail), a lack of integration or partnerships creates stiff competition and a small market share for each enterprise (Abdul 2007).

Uyghur entrepreneurs participate in the ethnic enclave for both "push" and "pull" reasons described earlier. Many complained that "finding a job in Urumqi is just too hard" and that entrepreneurship provided them with a mode of social mobility. Others chose entrepreneurship over public sector employment because of the perceived greater freedom and chance of success. But entrepreneurs are clustered within the ethnic enclave largely as a result of competition from better equipped and more experienced Han companies, which limits Uyghur companies to coethnic products and markets. Uyghur entrepreneurs claim less business experience and education than Han competitors, as well as unfamiliarity with Han culture and (often) Mandarin language.

Yet the ethnic enclave also provides pull advantages over participation in the mainstream economy, primarily in the form of ethnic resources. Uyghur entrepreneurs are able to hire staff and raise start-up capital from within the ethnic enclave. Support from within Uyghur networks is useful in the start-up phase, as companies deal with market uncertainty and business inexperience.

## Ethnic Resources: Employees and Start-up Capital

Uyghur companies overwhelmingly hire Uyghur workers, particularly at the management level. Community sentiment plays a role in these decisions, as Uyghur businesses that employ Han workers are perceived by some Uyghurs as insensitive to the issue of Uyghur unemployment. The most important reason for relying on coethnic labor, however, is the availability of Uyghur employees, who are often found through friends and family networks within the enclave. The majority of entrepreneurs use a wide range of methods to attract staff, from advertisements to attending job fairs (*zhaopinhui*). With Uyghur unemployment rising, several entrepreneurs admitted to hiring only those who send unsolicited applications, though they prefer to hire those with whom they have a more personal connection.

Hiring practices depend partly on the type of company and positions available. Tsui's (2003) study of rural-urban migration in Xinjiang found that Uyghur migrants who started small businesses hired primarily friends and family members, but there is little evidence that this model exists in the formal private sector. Familiarity certainly plays a role, however, and entrepreneurs rely primarily on coethnic employees and management staff hired from within the Urumqi enclave. Several admitted to feeling pressure from friends and family members to hire certain people, though arguably less so than other studies of minority entrepreneurship have confirmed (see Heberer 2005; Schnell et al. 1995). Other entrepreneurs argue that they hire only skilled and suitable employees and don't rely on social networks or recommendations.

These hiring practices illustrate both the benefits and constraints of operating within the Uyghur ethnic enclave. Entrepreneurs who make use of social networks to hire employees are at the same time constrained by obligations to family members and a lack of sufficient capital. Some entrepreneurs also complain that few skilled employees are available in Urumqi, though others say this is due to their inability to pay high enough salaries to attract talent. Those who claim to hire based only on skills are usually from larger enterprises that can compete with Han companies and state-owned enterprises for the best employees.

Strategies of start-up financing further illustrate these opportunities and restrictions. Personal savings and investment sourced through social networks form the bulk of start-up capital for Uyghur entrepreneurs. Reliance on financial networking is common throughout China and is not exclusive to Urumqi's Uyghurs (Vicziany and Zhang 2005; Yeung 2001); however, Uyghur entrepreneurs rely heavily on savings and loans outside of formal institutions, and even those who are successful in obtaining loans or investment rely primarily on savings. As one remarked: "I only depend on my friends and relatives; if I have economic difficulty, I go to them first, not to the government or the bank. I believe most Uyghur entrepreneurs act the same way."

Besides personal savings and loans from friends and relatives, there are few other financing avenues for Uyghur businesses. Most businesses do not qualify for government bank loans or other loan resources for reasons detailed elsewhere (Harlan and Webber 2012). In addition few Uyghur companies are able to attract domestic or international investment because of their small size. I spoke with entrepreneurs from four large companies, who all claimed to receive capital from other business organizations based in eastern China, Hong Kong, or Turkey. I originally expected to find significant foreign investment from Central Asian, Turkish, or Middle Eastern firms, but this has not materialized. Businesses in the Central Asian Republics are, like Uyghur enterprises, small, ill equipped, and have little available capital. In addition one entrepreneur remarked that the Xinjiang government is wary of investment in Uyghur companies from Muslim countries or enterprises, particularly Turkey. Some types of partnerships are allowed, but direct investment (which can be difficult for officials to track) is highly restricted. Further research would be required to confirm this claim.

## Interethnic Cooperation

The majority of Uyghur entrepreneurs depend on ethnic resources to mobilize labor and capital, but this limits their ability to break out of the enclave and grow their businesses. Some entrepreneurs stress that they do not depend on coethnic networks and instead emphasize the modernization of their firm and reliance on their own experience and abilities. At the same time, these entrepreneurs acknowledge the importance of *guanxi* in growing their business, in particular their relationships with Han-operated firms and government officials. Uyghur entrepreneurs who interact with businesses and officials outside of the enclave have better access to technology, capital (through government grants and loans), and official recognition of their brand and products. In this section I begin by describing the types of business cooperation with Han that are sought by Uyghur entrepreneurs, then examine the relationship between Uyghur firms and local government in Urumqi.

Interethnic business cooperation operates in at least one of three ways. First, Uyghur entrepreneurs cooperate with Han factory owners who manufacture goods for them. Few Uyghur companies own their own processing facilities; instead, they subcontract manufacturing to established facilities operated by Han. Uyghur companies will lease production from Han-owned factories, then transport goods to Urumqi and apply a (Uyghur language) trademark. This has become common practice among Uyghur food and drink companies, many of whom outsource to Han manufacturers in the Pearl River Delta. For Uyghur-language handheld electronics, hardware is obtained from eastern China, while software is written and encoded by employees in Xinjiang. Uyghurs also partner with Han businesses within Xinjiang, though this is less common. One Uyghur beverage company contracted a Han-owned dairy conglomerate to purchase milk, and another leased factory space to manufacture packaging for medicinal products.

Second, some Uyghur businesses will source goods or prefabricated items from Han suppliers, then assemble, repackage, and/or resell the items in Xinjiang and Central Asia. One Uyghur business that assembles and sells farm machinery procures parts from Shenzhen and then sells the finished product to buyers in Kazakhstan. Many of the larger Uyghur import/export agencies maintain contracts with Han suppliers and Central Asian buyers and effectively supervise the shuttling of goods across the border and collect agency fees. Uyghur merchants popularized this form of cross-border trade but usually cooperate with a Uyghur agent based in Guangzhou or Shenzhen rather than with the factories themselves. However, international trade agencies streamline the process by partnering directly with goods suppliers, thus eliminating the need for middlemen.

Third, Uyghur entrepreneurs partner with Han firms to procure better technology and learn management and technical skills. As one Uyghur entrepreneur stated, "To make business grow and expand, closer relationships with Chinese and foreign companies are extremely important, which help us to learn management skills and how to run a manufacturing industry." Another mentioned that to obtain new techniques, he should partner with a business in eastern China. He stated that initially he acquired technological information from books and sources in Urumqi, but now he obtains it from Han firms in Shenzhen. The owner of an Internet café implied that he must cooperate with Chinese companies because they have the capital and technical expertise that his business needs to grow. While Uyghurs prefer to hire coethnic employees and management staff, they seek out skills, expertise, and technological innovation from larger and better-established Han firms.

Uyghur entrepreneurs that seek to expand their business, often through technical innovation, tend to partner with Han firms. Even those entrepreneurs with higher levels of education, training, and expertise, or those with their own production facilities, rely on Han partnerships to expand business operations. Arman, a Uyghur supermarket chain and food manufacturer, recently partnered with a Han firm to open a flagship branch in Shanghai, becoming one of the first Uyghur-owned companies to operate in eastern China. A manufacturer of Uyghur health products receives investment and technical expertise from a Han enterprise. Both of these entrepreneurs expressed belief in their own abilities and expertise but admitted that cooperation and partnerships with established Han companies are important.

The value of Han partnerships to business success in the Urumqi private sector highlights the limited access to resources, technology, and skills training within the enclave. It is important, however, to note that some entrepreneurs also seek to cooperate with Central Asian entrepreneurs and firms. Much like Han firms in Shenzhen, enterprises in Uzbekistan, Kazakhstan, and Pakistan provide raw materials and finished goods for Uyghur companies. The Ihlas supermarket chain, Arman's main competitor, partners with the Turkish food manufacturer Ülker to supply its stores with goods from the Middle East and Central Asia. Indeed, ties to Central Asian businesses are often as important as those with Han enterprises.

Nonetheless, networks with Central Asian firms do little to promote the integration of Uyghur businesses into the Han-dominated market. Many of Uyghur entrepreneurs' Central Asian suppliers or partners are new businesses, with similar management, technology, and capital shortages. Supplier networks such as those of Ihlas and Ülker demonstrate the potential for cross-border cooperation and information sharing but are unable to provide Uyghur entrepreneurs with the means to operate within the broader Chinese private sector. Han networks allow for further business expansion through access to resources, technology, and market information, which cross-border relationships can only partially fulfill.

## Political Networks

Political networks, like those of Han entrepreneurs, function in at least one of three ways. First, government *guanxi* are helpful during business startup to obtain relevant permits and operating certificates. As one businessman confided, "There is a lot of work to do for certification, and lacking only one certificate or permit makes doing business very difficult. However, having a relationship with a government official makes it much easier. Many signatures must be obtained [to start a business], but relationships help to find the right person and move things more quickly." Another commented that "gaining business permission from the government can be difficult—more difficult than in eastern China. Money is very important to gaining permission."

Second, the right political networks and government relations provide official recognition for growing firms, an essential component in building a trusted and well-known brand. For this reason, many entrepreneurs seek out relationships with government bureaus and officials as a way to boost their business appeal and brand image. An electronics salesman I interviewed subcontracted production of videodisc players and television sets to a Chinese factory, then affixed his own trademark. He prominently displayed his (trademark) certificate along with a photograph of his meeting with officials from the commerce bureau. When I asked about the meeting, he mentioned that he contacted the government office himself, who then received him and encouraged his business. Other, larger companies display numerous awards from city, provincial and even national government offices—both as proof of their success and of their healthy government relationship.

Third, relationships can provide access to government loans and subsidies. Sautman (1997, 37–38) discusses a government program of bank loans for ethnic minority businesses in China, though this is unconfirmed in other studies (Heberer 2005; Vicziany and Zhang 2004). Most entrepreneurs I interviewed were unaware of any such preferential loan scheme, though some mentioned broader (meaning not ethnicity-specific) grants and loans available to Uyghur entrepreneurs. But access to government funding has similar prerequisites to finance via bank loans, namely collateral, a long-term strategy, and personal networks. Loan applications require information about how a business will use and invest funds over the long term, and inexperienced entrepreneurs are often unable to provide a suitable strategy, do not have enough collateral, or have not established extensive government networks. As one Uyghur entrepreneur observed, "The government supports minority businesses through preferential policies, but you need relationships to benefit from them." The headmaster of an English training school remarked: "The same [strategy] applies for government money set aside for businesses in Xinjiang. Perhaps the Labor Bureau has money set aside for businesses—but how does one obtain this funding, and what are the requirements? This kind of money is not easy to get, but it can happen if one knows the requirements and has personal networks. The government does provide assistance, but one needs experience, knowledge, and networks to take advantage of this."

In interviews, many entrepreneurs emphasized their experience and education as the primary catalysts for success. Successful entrepreneurs emphasized that personal relationships alone do not contribute to business prosperity but are a necessary mechanism to further one's business interests. They argued that younger and less experienced entrepreneurs are unable to seek out and forge proper relationships or do not understand the importance of such relationships. As one entrepreneur observed, "Talented people will know how to form *guanxi* with other businessmen and officials and thus can do things efficiently." An older businessman remarked, "When I first started this business, I did not understand the value of personal relationships with the government, but after gaining experience I now realize their importance."

Many Uyghur entrepreneurs feel discriminated against when competing with Han companies for a grant or loan because of a lack of networks. This claim aligns with similar complaints of ethnic discrimination in Xinjiang (Bachman 2004). A businesswoman in charge of a fashion company claimed that "we cannot get a loan from the bank or support from the government, but Han businesses can." Another businessman observed that "for Uyghur people, we have to depend and rely on ourselves. No one will help us, not even the government—if you want to get help from the government, it will be very difficult to work with them or get a contract. It is much easier for Han businesses to work with the government, but we [Uyghurs] have to rely on ourselves." Another entrepreneur expressed difficulty in obtaining public funds, observing that "the government has a policy to set aside funds for private businesses, but this capital is hard to get. Too many businesses are vying for the same funds." His assistant added, "It's hard for Uyghurs to get these funds."

An electronics entrepreneur that I interviewed attempted to obtain a grant from a government technological center but was unsuccessful. He explained:

Some time ago I went to the government science center and saw a list of nearly 100 companies that gained support from this center. But only two or three Uyghur companies were on that list. Now there may be 500 Uyghur companies in Urumqi, but this center only helped two to three. Every day you can see [on television] government advertisements about helping minority people, minority industry, minority businesses—but this center only helped two to three. When I went to that center I only saw a few Uyghur people, as it is hard to apply for grants and to communicate with officials. So I don't believe in the government's support. If they really want to help Uyghur companies, they should support Uyghur companies. Perhaps we don't meet the requirements or are not developed enough.

Other entrepreneurs blame inability to obtain government grants and loans on Uyghurs themselves, claiming that many are unfamiliar with policies or, as with bank loan applications, do not meet the requirements. One entrepreneur remarked that "the central government has special policies to help minority businesses, but we don't know about them or how to use them. We were never told about them." Another commented that "Han people know well of these policies and they know how to get money, but Uyghur people just rely on their own capital, and they are unclear about how government policy can help them; they still do business in the 'old way.'"

The above comments illustrate a variety of opinions among Uyghur entrepreneurs about the value of forming relationships with government officials. Furthermore, Uyghur entrepreneurs who abide by Islamic regulations are unwilling to attend banquets or dinners with local officials, where alcohol may be consumed. As one entrepreneur observed, "Sometimes, in order to have good *guanxi* with the government, one must drink alcohol with them at dinners, and Muslims may be unwilling to do this." Another entrepreneur explained: "It's difficult to build strong government relationships. If I could form a better relationship with the government education center, my products might sell better, but I haven't been able to achieve this yet. Personal relationships are important with the government, but often I have to do things that I don't want to do; for instance, if I need something from the government, they [officials] may invite me to go drinking or other things of that nature that I do not want to do. So, I depend on my friends and relatives for support."

Uyghur entrepreneurs may grow successful through experience and innovation alone, without pursuing interethnic partnerships and *guanxi* with local officials. But these cases are exceptions to the larger trend. Most Uyghur entrepreneurs who have successfully expanded their business, particularly through the use of new technologies that require high capital inputs, interact with firms and officials outside of the ethnic enclave. Those who are unable or unwilling to seek out these networks, and who continue to rely on ethnic resources only, face greater difficulty in growing their businesses and breaking out of fringe industries and markets.

Uyghur entrepreneurs in Urumqi thus operate on a continuum ranging from traditional activities within the ethnic enclave to modern firms in the mainstream private sector. The types of industries in which businesses engage, and their ability to grow and expand, rely heavily on the ability of entrepreneurs to forge ties with Han firms and government officials. These social networks, in addition, must be paired with other skills, such as a sound long-term strategy, a willingness to take risks, and a talent for management. Most important, Uyghur entrepreneurs stressed that truly modern businesspeople aren't just out to make money—this is the "traditional" mind-set. "Real" entrepreneurs, those who operate modern firms, are concerned with improving Uyghur businesses, providing quality products, and advancing community issues. In this way Uyghur entrepreneurs see themselves as a modernizing force in the private sector and in Uyghur society as a whole.

## Uyghur Entrepreneurs as Agents of Modernization

In a study of Nuoso-Yi entrepreneurship in western China, Heberer (2005, 408) notes that ethnic entrepreneurs "oscillate between their role as bearers of tradition on the one hand and their role as harbingers of modernity on the other," a statement that applies to Uyghur entrepreneurs. Traditional aspects of entrepreneurship are still in effect: the emphasis on buying and selling, reliance on coethnic personal networks, and dependence on informal financial channels. However, many Uyghur entrepreneurs argue that they strive toward modern business practices. They partner with established companies, crossing ethnic lines, and seek out closer relationships with (mostly Han) government officials. By growing their businesses, then, Uyghur entrepreneurs view themselves as "agents of modernization" in the business community and in Uyghur society at large. In this section I explore this further by looking at how Uyghur entrepreneurs improve business products and practices and serve the wider Uyghur community.

Several entrepreneurs (and many Uyghur consumers) stressed the "believability" of their products, particularly *halal* food products. As I have noted, smaller food and beverage producers tend to source products from eastern Chinese factories. These products are made in factories that also produce a range of other (non-*halal*) products, raising issues of strict adherence to *halal* regulations. An examination of more than fifty Uyghur packaged-food products in one Urumqi supermarket found that at least two-thirds were produced in the Pearl River Delta. Most Uyghur food companies operate without an approved *qingzhen* (*halal*) certificate from the Chinese Islamic Association. Their goods may indeed be *halal*, but only larger firms with their own processing facilities, such as the supermarket chains Arman and Ihlas, can provide evidence of such, including the difficult-to-obtain *qingzhen* certificate. In an interview the chairman of Ihlas claimed that "our strategy is to give consumers believable products" and that his company's factories have "opened the way to industrialization for Uyghur companies."

Many Uyghur businesses that manufacture goods in eastern China hope to eventually construct their own production facilities. A soft drink company manager stated that "if the government supports us and government policy allows us, I want to open a company in Xinjiang that has its own factory"—a view shared by many others. Other entrepreneurs, too, aspired to the modern business practices outlined above, including hiring only skilled employees, attracting investment, and taking a lead role in the development of Uyghur business. This represents a shift from traditional practices that entrepreneurs associate with merchant activity. As one entrepreneur mentioned, rather than "buying chopsticks for one *yuan* and selling them for two *yuan*," entrepreneurs should think of manufacturing products themselves and building a stable company.

These entrepreneurs see themselves as being at the forefront of the Uyghur private sector and as agents of modernization within the Uyghur community. Most respondents mentioned providing employment as a means of driving economic development. As I have noted, competition with Han for both skilled and unskilled jobs disadvantages Uyghurs in the labor market, as most employers are Han and prefer to hire Han staff (Maurer-Fazio 2012). Uyghur companies, while relying on skilled co-ethnic labor, also provide employment and training. As one entrepreneur remarked, "If one Uyghur company hires ten Uyghur graduates, then one thousand companies will employ ten thousand people and can help with reducing unemployment." Another entrepreneur commented that "many government bureaus [in Urumqi] only employ one or two Uyghurs, so many Uyghur graduates are unemployed and we play a large role in providing opportunities for them." Larger companies can serve as a catalyst for additional employment; the chairman of Arman noted his company's policy of purchasing products directly from Uyghur farmers, alleviating the peasant burden of low government procurement prices.

Larger firms act as an example in business practice, as well as social engagement. In response to the 2008 Sichuan earthquake, most of the larger Uyghur companies donated to disaster relief—both to support social causes and to demonstrate involvement in the community as a whole. Both Arman and Ihlas were consistently singled out as model companies by other entrepreneurs for donating to primary school construction in poorer areas of southern Xinjiang. Other Muslim entrepreneurs in India and the Middle East are known to invest in education as a way of giving back to the community (Osella and Osella 2007). Many Uyghur entrepreneurs expressed a desire to follow this example.

This type of "modern" Uyghur entrepreneurship is thus characterized by community engagement and interconnectedness, both among Uyghurs and between Uyghurs and Han. Business relationships with Han companies and government officials underscore this fact. As in eastern China (Dickson 2003; Goodman 1999), Uyghur enterprises function more smoothly and efficiently when embedded in the state and when operating within the Han-dominated business system rather than on its fringe. Business growth and expansion occur outside the Urumqi ethnic enclave, and entrepreneurs who seek long-term growth also strive for integration into the mainstream economy (Aldrich and Waldinger 1990; Light 2004). Uyghur businesses that develop into large companies do not do so outside the state or the Han-dominated system but rather in alliance with the state.

The development of Uyghur business depends on integration within the Han-dominated system. It does not, however, entail the modernization of business to resemble Han firms but rather encapsulates a fusion of local practices and characteristics with global business norms. In Urumqi, companies like Arman and Ihlas espouse the modernization of social practices, particularly education, but are rooted in Islam and Uyghur society. The practice of manufacturing *halal* goods within Xinjiang both promotes their authenticity and the ability of Uyghur companies to produce their own products. In a sense these entrepreneurs participate in a process of development for Uyghur society as a whole, both as drivers of economic growth and as promoters of modernization. Many entrepreneurs stressed the importance of relieving rural poverty in Xinjiang and educating the Uyghur populace, the bottom-up development of Uyghur society rather than the institutionalized top-down approach taken by state development programs.

These processes of economic and social development are bound up in social relations. As Uyghur entrepreneurs break out of fringe industries and modernize their businesses, they often seek relationships outside their ethnic group and thus greater integration within the Han-dominated private sector. Thus, business growth and modernization go hand in hand with expanded social relations and contribute to the ongoing process of ethnic identity formation and construction. In his early fieldwork in Turpan, Rudelson (1997) observed that successful merchants, rather than seeing themselves as Uyghurs, identified first as Turks and second as Chinese citizens. In a similar way Uyghur entrepreneurs promote an ethnic identity both from within the nation-state (as Chinese citizens) and as a modern, developed, cohesive Uyghur ethnic group. In an urban milieu characterized by ethnic "oasis identities" (Rudelson 1997) these entrepreneurs see themselves as the face of a modernizing Uyghur society and are thus involved in the continual production of Uyghur identity. This form of identity is not relegated to an ethnic enclave in opposition to Han firms but integrated into the mainstream economy and Chinese society at large.

---

In examining Uyghur business practices in an ethnic enclave in Xinjiang, this chapter has focused on social networks to describe how some entrepreneurs move out of fringe industries into the mainstream private sector and, in doing so, see themselves as agents of modernization. I have argued that Uyghur entrepreneurs face formidable obstacles in the Urumqi private sector, which leads them to cluster in an ethnic enclave and depend largely on other Uyghurs for support. Most Uyghur enterprises remain in the enclave on the fringe of the mainstream private sector and are unable to grow and expand. But we have seen how certain entrepreneurs use their accumulated experience and networks to "break out" and create more capital-intensive and specialized businesses. These new entrepreneurs forge social ties with Han firms and government officials to expand their resource and capital base and in the process seek out better relations with the state and the Han majority. They view themselves as "agents of modernization" by shunning traditional business practices and providing "believable" products, while also demonstrating their community leadership credentials by contributing financially to social causes. In effect, this small group of entrepreneurs represents the modernizing face of Uyghur society in partnership with the new urban middle class (Goodman 2008; Mackerras 2005)—a move toward integration within the Chinese nation-state.

The expansion of Uyghur entrepreneurship and its integration in the mainstream private sector are crucial to easing ethnic tension in Xinjiang for several reasons. First, the rising influence of the private sector and increasing urbanization in Xinjiang will compel further Uyghur participation in private business. Second, the increasing movement of Han firms to Xinjiang will reduce market niches for Uyghurs and exacerbate inter- and intraethnic competition. Third, ethnic segmentation in the urban labor market forces many Uyghurs to depend on employment in Uyghur firms (Howell and Fan 2011). A healthy Uyghur business sector would help to reduce ethnic tensions by promoting interethnic relationships between firms and creating employment opportunities for Uyghurs.

However, the policy emphasis on stability and "staged development" in Xinjiang tends to ignore the importance of private sector entrepreneurship (Bequelin 2004). State-controlled extractive industries and the *bingtuan* receive the majority of central government investment and mostly employ Han (Sautman 1997; Wiemer 2004, 174–76). Economic development initiatives sponsored by the ongoing Great Western Development Program also overlook the private sector (Shih 2004). Some consideration has been given to rural entrepreneurship in the western region in line with the CCP's Seventeenth National Congress's pledge to "encourage entrepreneurship to create more employment opportunities" (ADB 2003, 2). Although there is evidence that this pledge is taken seriously by some local governments in Tibetan areas (Hillman 2009, 2010), the initiative seems to have fallen on deaf ears in Xinjiang. Many Uyghur entrepreneurs expressed frustration over government interference in their business, usually through excessive taxation, and bemoaned an overwhelming absence of state support for Uyghur business development.

The "stable development" (*wending fazhan*) of Xinjiang is touted as the party's foremost objective in the region. Even though this clearly requires greater economic participation by the Uyghur community, policies have emphasized security over autonomy (Bequelin 2004) and failed to foster inclusion (Cliff, this volume). This chapter has shown that successful Uyghur entrepreneurs seek out, indeed require, a healthy government relationship in order to grow. Entrepreneurs thus seek engagement with the state (not separatism), as other studies of China's entrepreneurs have shown (Dickson 2003; Malik 1997). The business practices promoted by Uyghur entrepreneurs also represent the modernization of social practices and development within the context of the Chinese nation-state. Therefore, the encouragement and development of Uyghur entrepreneurship is not antagonistic toward the state but instead is a key component of regional stability and economic development in Xinjiang.

The rapid rise of Uyghur business in the past few years demonstrates that Uyghur entrepreneurs are responding to private sector opportunities. As I have shown, however, Uyghur businesses continue to face challenges in moving from the ethnic enclave to the mainstream private sector. In Urumqi, Han operate most businesses, while Uyghurs are confined to ethnic products and markets. The continuation of "imposed" development policy and Han in-migration in Xinjiang threatens to envelop the Uyghur private sector. As one food manufacturer remarked, "We must open the market by ourselves, not allow companies from inner China to open the market." In the face of limitations in the urban private sector, integration within the Han system, not segregation, defines the path out of the fringe and into the mainstream economy for Uyghur entrepreneurs in Urumqi.

# References

Abdul, Awuti. 2007. "Xinjiang shaoshu minzu minying qiye de neibu fenxi" (An analysis of ethnic minority-owned private businesses in Xinjiang). *Keji Xinxi* (Science and Technology Information) 9:127.

ADB (Asian Development Bank). 2003. *The 2020 Project: Policy Support in the People's Republic of China.*

Aldrich, Howard E., and Roger Waldinger. 1990. "Ethnicity and Entrepreneurship." *Annual Review of Sociology* 16:111–35.

Bachman, David. 2004. "Making Xinjiang Safe for the Han? Contradictions and Ironies of Chinese Governance in China's Northwest." *Governing China's Multiethnic Frontiers*, edited by Morris Rossabi, 155–85. Seattle: University of Washington Press.

Barbour, Brandon, and Reese Jones. 2013. "Criminals, Terrorists, and Outside Agitators: Representational Tropes of the 'Other' in the 5 July Xinjiang, China Riots." *Geopolitics* 18 (1): 95–114.

Bequelin, Nicholas. 2004. "Staged Development in Xinjiang." *China Quarterly* 178 (1): 358–78.

Boissevain, Jeremy, Jochen Blaschke, Hanneke Grotenbreg, Isaac Joseph, Ivan Light, Marlene Sway, Roger Waldinger, and Pnina Werbner. 1990. "Ethnic Entrepreneurs and Ethnic Strategies." In *Ethnic Entrepreneurs: Immigrant Business in Industrial Societies*, edited by Roger Waldinger et al., 131–56. Newbury Park, CA: Sage.

den Butter, Frank A. G., Enno Masurel, and Robert H. J. Mosch. 2007. "The Economics of Co-ethnic Employment: Incentives, Welfare Effects and Policy Options." In *Handbook of Research on Ethnic Minority Entrepreneurship: A Co-evolutionary View on Resource Management*, edited by Leo P. Dana, 42–60. Cheltenham, UK: Edward Elgar.

Dickson, Bruce J. 2003. *Red Capitalists in China.* Cambridge: Cambridge University Press.

Gilley, Bruce. 2001. "Uighurs Need Not Apply." *Far Eastern Economic Review* 164 (33): 26–28.

Goodman, David S. 1999. "The New Middle Class." In *The Paradox of China's Post-Mao Reforms.*, edited by Merle Goldman and Roderick MacFarquhar, 241–61. Cambridge, MA: Harvard University Press.

——. 2008. "Why China Has No New Middle Class: Cadres, Managers and Entrepreneurs." In *The New Rich in China: Future Rulers, Present Lives*, edited by David S. Goodman, 23–37. London: Routledge.

Granovetter, Mark 1995. "The Economic Sociology of Firms and Entrepreneurs." In *The Economic Sociology of Immigration: Essays on Networks, Ethnicity, and Entrepreneurship*, edited by Alejandro Portes, 128–65. New York: Sage.

Hannum, Emily, and Yu Xie. 1998. "Ethnic Stratification in Northwest China: Occupational Differences Between Han Chinese and National Minorities in Xinjiang, 1982–1990." *Demography* 35 (3): 323–33.

Harlan, Tyler, and Michael Webber. 2012. "New Corporate Uyghur Entrepreneurs in Urumqi." *Central Asian Survey* 31 (2): 175–91.

Heberer, Thomas. 2005. "Ethnic Entrepreneurship and Ethnic Identity: A Case Study Among the Liangshan Yi (Nuosu) in China." *China Quarterly* 182 (1): 407–27.

——. 2007. *Doing Business in Rural China: Liangshan's New Ethnic Entrepreneurs.* Seattle: University of Washington Press.

Hillman, Ben. 2009. "Ethnic Tourism and Ethnic Politics in Tibetan China." *Harvard Asia Pacific Review* 10 (1): 3–6.

——. 2010. "China's Many Tibets." *Asian Ethnicity* 11 (2): 269–77.

Hopper, Benjamin, and Michael Webber. 2009. "Migration, Modernisation and Ethnic Estrangement: Uyghur Migration to Urumqi, Xinjiang Uyghur Autonomous Region, PRC." *Inner Asia* 11 (2): 173–203.

Howell, Anthony, and C. Cindy Fan. 2011. "Migration and Inequality in Xinjiang: A Survey of Han and Uyghur Migrants in Urumqi." *Eurasian Geography and Economics* 52 (1): 119–39.

Kim, Harris H. 2003. "Ethnic Enclave Economy in Urban China: The Korean Immigrants in Yanbian." *Ethnic and Racial Studies* 26 (5): 802–28.

Light, Ivan. 2004. "The Ethnic Ownership Economy." In *Ethnic Entrepreneurship: Structure and Process*, edited by Curt H. Stiles and Craig S. Galbraith, 3–44. Oxford: Elsevier.

Light, Ivan, and Carolyn Rosenstein. 1995. "Expanding the Interaction Theory of Entrepreneurship." In *The Economic Sociology of Immigration: Essays on Networks, Ethnicity, and Entrepreneurship*, edited by Alejandro Portes, 166–12. New York: Basic Books.

Mackerras, Colin. 2005. "China's Ethnic Minorities and the Middle Classes: An Overview." *International Journal of Social Economics* 32 (9): 814–26.

Malik, Rashid. 1997. *Chinese Entrepreneurs in the Economic Development of China.* Westport, CT: Praeger.

Maurer-Fazio, Margaret. 2012. "Ethnic Discrimination in China's Internet Job Board Labor Market." IZA Discussion Paper No. 6903. Bonn: Institute for the Study of Labor.

Millward, James. 2009. "Introduction: Does the 2009 Urumchi Violence Mark a Turning Point?" *Central Asian Survey* 28 (4): 347–60.

Osella, Filippo, and Caroline Osella. 2007. "Muslim Entrepreneurs Between India and the Gulf." *ISIM Review* 19 (Spring): 8–9.

Phizacklea, Annie. 1988. "Entrepreneurship, Ethnicity and Gender." In *Enterprising Women*, edited by Sallie Westwood and Parminder Bhachu, 21–33. New York: Routledge.

Portes, Alejandro. 1981. "Modes of Structural Incorporation and Present Theories of Labor Immigration." In *Global Trends in Migration*, edited by M. Kritz et al., 279–97. New York: Center for Migration Studies.

Razin, Eran. 1989. "Relating Theories of Entrepreneurship Among Ethnic Groups and Entrepreneurship in Space: The Case of the Jewish Population in Israel." *Geografiska Annaler. Series B, Human Geography* 71 (3): 167–81.

Rudelson, Justin. 1997. *Oasis Identities: Uyghur Nationalism Along China's Silk Road*. New York: Columbia University Press.

Sautman, Barry. 1997. "Preferential Policies for Ethnic Minorities in China: The Case of Xinjiang." Working Papers in the Social Sciences. Hong Kong: Hong Kong University of Science and Technology.

Schnell, Izhak, et al. 1995. *Arab Industrialization in Israel: Ethnic Entrepreneurship in the Periphery*. Westport, CT: Praeger.

Sequeira, Jennifer M., and Abdul A. Rasheed. 2004. "The Role of Social and Human Capital." In *Ethnic Entrepreneurship: Structure and Process*, edited by Curt H. Stiles and Craig S. Galbraith, 77–94. Oxford: Elsevier.

Shih, Victor. 2004. "Development, the Second Time Around: The Political Logic of Developing Western China." *Journal of East Asian Studies* 4 (3): 427–51.

Tsui, Yen Hu. 2003. "Uygur Movement Within Xinjiang and Its Ethnic Identity and Cultural Implications." In *China's Minorities on the Move: Selected Case Studies*, edited by Robyn Airedale et al., 123–40. New York: M. E. Sharpe.

Vicziany, Maria, and Guibin Zhang. 2004. "The Rise of the Private Sector in Xinjiang (Western China): Han and Uygur Entrepreneurship." Paper presented at the 15th Biennial Conference of the Asian Studies Association of Australia, June 29–July 2, Canberra.

——. 2005. "Raw Entrepreneurship and the Rise of the New Private Sector in Western China: The Hope Group of Chengdu, Sichuan Province." In *China's Business Reforms: Institutional Challenges in a Globalized Economy*, edited by Russell Smyth et al., 211–26. London: RoutledgeCurzon.

Wiemer, Calla. 2004. "The Economy of Xinjiang." In *Xinjiang: China's Muslim Borderland*, edited by S. F. Starr., 163–89. Armonk, NY: M. E. Sharpe.

XECY. 2006. Xinjiang Jingji Pucha Nianjian 2004 (Xinjiang Economic Census Yearbook 2004). Beijing: China Statistics Press.

XSY. 2008. *Xinjiang tongji nianjian 2007* (Xinjiang Statistical Yearbook). Beijing: China Statistics Press.

Yeung, Godfrey. 2001. "Foreign Direct Investment and Investment Environment in Dongguan Municipality of Southern China." *Journal of Contemporary China* 10 (26): 125–54.

# 8

# Prosperity, Identity, Intra-Tibetan Violence, and Harmony in Southeast Tibet

## The Case of Gyalthang

Eric D. Mortensen

This chapter addresses the question of why Gyalthang (Tib: *rgyal thang*), and in particular *Khams* (eastern Tibet), has not experienced the types of violence seen elsewhere in Tibetan regions of the People's Republic of China (PRC) in recent years. In exploring this question, I pay attention to local Gyalthang peoples' understandings of the state and its role in conflict. I also examine new aspects of violence in their communities and consider what role regional identity might play in intra-Tibetan conflict in this prosperous and relatively "harmonious" region.[1]

*Gyalthang* is the Tibetan name for the region roughly demarcated today by the geographical area called Shangri-La County (Ch. *Xianggelila xian*) and, more expansively, the Diqing Tibetan Autonomous Prefecture (Ch. *Diqing zangzu zizhizhou*). Home to between 250,000 and 350,000 people (the population ebbs and flows seasonally), Gyalthang is at the northwestern tip of the Province of Yunnan, in southwest China.

Historically, the "idea" of Gyalthang is bordered to the southwest by the (primarily Lisu, Tibetan, Naxi, and Han) Weixi Lisu Autonomous County and by Deqin County (Ch. Deqin xian) to the northwest. The country of Myanmar and the Tibetan Autonomous Region (TAR) lie not far to the west and northwest. The (Tibetan) Ganzi County of Sichuan marks the northern boundary of Gyalthang, just beyond the Daxueshan (locally: *jiarongya*) mountain and the valley system of Dongwang township (Tib. *gter ma rong*).

The (Tibetan, Primi, and Yi) Muli Tibetan Autonomous County of Sichuan, just east of the beautiful village of Nizu (Tib. *myig zur*) is the eastern border of Gyalthang, and the (primarily Naxi) Lijiang prefecture-level city lies to the south.[2] Gyalthangpa (Tibetans of *rgyal thang*) identify as Khampas, residents of the southernmost reaches of the eastern Tibetan cultural world. Gyalthangpa speak several local Tibetic languages.

Most of Gyalthang is ostensibly Gelukpa Buddhist, although the ravaging of institutional religion over the past half-century has left the region with a precarious sense of its own Buddhist vitality, and there has been a correlative reification of local (arguably nonorthodox Buddhist or pre-Buddhist) religious practices. Gyalthang's center is Jiantang Town, generally known as Xianggelila (called Zhongdian throughout at least the second half of the twentieth century until 2002), a bourgeoning small city stretching across the entire valley between the central village of Dukezong and the historically important Geluk monastery, Ganden Sumtseling. The region has long been a Tibetan interface with neighboring peoples, primarily the Naxi, Nosuo Yi, Lisu, Malimasa, Hui, and for centuries the Han. Following a 1998 logging ban, the local economy has largely transformed into a tourist service industry, with mining also providing a massive influx of capital over the past decade. The Salween (*nu jiang*), Mekong (*lancan jiang*), and Yangtze (locally: *jinsha jiang*) Rivers all descend through Gyalthang's bio-diverse Hengduan Mountains and conifer forests en route to eastern China and Southeast Asia.

Compared to other regions of Tibet that have seen an increase in conflict with the state since 2008, Gyalthang appears relatively peaceful. Why is this the case? At the time of this writing there have been no confirmed cases of self-immolation by Gyalthang Tibetans, no recent military or police occupations of monasteries (aside from the long-standing police presence at Sumtseling and other monasteries throughout southern Khams), and only occasional reminders of overt military or police presence on the streets. Many local Tibetans are genuinely satisfied with their relationship with larger China. There is precious little sense of a Tibetan liberation movement in Gyalthang. If any such sentiment exists, it currently lies dormant.

This is not to say that everyone in Gyalthang is content with the current situation of Tibet vis-à-vis the Chinese state. However, pan-Tibetan eth-

nic sentiment is not straightforward and uniform for Gyalthangpa. The recent emphasis on "harmonious society" by the local and national authorities is appreciated and well understood by many Gyalthangpa, although
a perhaps unintended consequence of this policy is a stronger sense of
pan-Tibetan identity since 2008 among Xianggelila Gyalthangpa (see Hillman 2014). Furthermore, conflict remains—mostly between Tibetans and
other locals—and the perpetrators of violence and animosity are typically
demarcated by the twin categories of regional Tibetan identity and of life-
long resident vs. returnee (from India/Nepal). Xianggelila can be a very
rough town, especially for Tibetans who hail from other parts of the Tibetan cultural world, and doubly so for those who have spent time abroad
before resettling in Gyalthang to take advantage of the tourist economy
and relative stability of this corner of Yunnan.

In this chapter I mean to be provocative—or at least to render problematic certain assumptions—in a few ways. First, I mean to apply the formulaic query "Is this really anything new in Tibet?" to several dynamics about
the contemporary situation vis-à-vis violence on the ground in Gyalthang.
The answers to this question are rarely black and white and might even
lead one to conclude that the situation for Tibetans in Gyalthang is relatively good. But such conclusions lead to further questions, such as "relative to where, for whom, and in what ways?" These questions lead, in turn,
to questions about the degree to which regionalism or regional identity
matters to local and non-local Tibetans alike, particularly in light of ongoing violence elsewhere on the plateau. Indeed, one of my tentative conclusions is that violence in regions such as Amdo and Rngaba has led to
a diminished value being placed on regional identity by Tibetans in the
relatively nonviolent region of Gyalthang.

Second, I argue that in order to understand ethnic conflict in the region,
we must scrutinize and complicate simplistic notions of what constitutes
the "state" in Gyalthang (and in the wider region). I am not alone or original in this emphasis. Excellent studies of the role of the Chinese state have
drawn attention to the problems of historical blame and to complicity in
the enactment of state policies in local non-Han contexts.[3] It is clear that
local government actors enact policies that affect ethnic minority communities in different ways in different regions (Hillman 2014). It is also useful
to understand the construction and negotiation of ethnopolitical identity

as being as much informed by interethnic and intraethnic relationships and perceptions as it is by the hitherto prioritized (and simplistic) binary model of assessing the identity of a given minority group in relationship to the Chinese state. In other words the tensions, concerns, conflicts, and everyday grievances at the forefront of the minds of locals in Gyalthang are shaped as much by their relationships with other local minority ethnic groups (such as the Naxi, Yi, and Hui) and nonlocal Tibetans as they are by their relationships with Han Chinese or with the local and national governments.[4] Local relationships with the state are further complicated in Gyalthang when many local officials are themselves Tibetan.

The widespread discontent directed at local authorities in Tibetan regions such as Lhasa, Labrang, Rngaba, and the Amdo-Khams interface in general is not evidenced in Gyalthang. There are several possible reasons for this. First, many Gyalthangpa have enjoyed economic prosperity, particularly as a result of the recent tourism boom in the town of Xianggelila, and to some extent because of the relatively lucrative Matsutake mushroom (L. *Tricholoma matsutake*; Ch. *songrong* 松茸) and caterpillar fungus (L. *Ophiocordyceps sinensis*; Tib. *yartsa gunbu*; Ch. *dong chong xia cao* 冬虫夏草) economies in more rural areas (though recent reports indicate that these markets have peaked, and money is not as abundant as it was eight or ten years ago). The fundamental economic grievances of Tibetans in other regions are far less acute in Gyalthang.

Second, there have been no recent open hostilities perpetrated by armed authorities on local communities. Violence has not been endemic in the region. Third, the monastic establishment in Xianggelila—based at Sumtseling Monastery—has not presented a significant political or social threat to the local authorities. Simply put, local government control of Sumtseling has been a success for the state. (Sumtseling, though, remains a complex and tense institution, largely because of the divisive personage of the tantric yidam [tutelary/protection deity] Dorje Shugden.) Other monasteries in Gyalthang are much less sympathetic to Chinese authority. Fourth, the local government's record of surveilling and sometimes incarcerating (primarily) nonlocal Tibetan returnees for political crimes has frightened some into silence and inaction. Finally, many Gyalthangpa genuinely appreciate being part of China and enjoy their dual Tibetan and Chinese identities. Gyalthang is in the process of being quite "successfully" assimilated into China.

## Culpability in Lament: Shells of Monasteries

Gyalthangpa destroyed their monastery, Sumtseling, in September 1966. Over several days the monastery was dismantled primarily by local Tibetans. Local prefectural work units of Han revolutionaries were also involved in the destruction, but, importantly, Tibetans themselves were swept up in the fervor of the moment and were the vanguard of the monastery's destruction. It became common in town at that time to brag of having monastery furniture in one's home. Of course, and this should be made explicitly clear, were it not for the Chinese annexation and occupation of the region, the local Tibetans would not have been caught up in the fervor of the Cultural Revolution, and Sumtseling would not have been razed. It is important to note, however, that it was not only outsider Han Chinese, but local (Tibetan, Naxi, and Han) Red Guard factions, that spearheaded religious destruction throughout the region.[5] Ethnicity, it seems, was not as prominent a factor in Cultural Revolution actions in the region as was political ideology.

Centuries ago, Geluk hegemony in northwestern Yunnan witnessed the destruction of Karma Kagyu monasteries and temples (Schwieger 2011). The ruins of a monastic complex that was later supplanted by Ganden Sumtseling in 1679 can still be seen in the back groves of the Zhongdian Gaoshan Botanical Garden above the Napahai wetlands, and the current complex of Sumtseling was built on the foundations of its Kagyu predecessor. Kagyu monasteries in Nagara (Tib. *nags rked rag*) in Geza Township (Tib. *skad tshag*), just to the north, were likewise destroyed by Ganden Phodrang forces.[6] This should not be confused with the wave of monastic destruction in the 1860s and early 1870s in Lijiang during the end of the Hui Muslim (and Yi) Panthay Rebellion (Jackson 1979).[7] Whereas in Lijiang the late nineteenth-century destruction of Kagyu monasteries precipitated the transmutation of religious authority into what we now call Naxi *dto-mba* ritual expert systems (Mortensen 2009; McKhann 2010), in Gyalthang (and east through Muli) the seventeenth-century conquering of Kagyu monasteries was caused by and was part of the consolidation of Geluk religio-military dominance (Schwieger 2011). In Gyalthang, as elsewhere on the plateau, Tibetans have long been adept at destroying Tibetan monasteries, and 1966 was not the first time the major Buddhist monastery in Gyalthang was destroyed by Tibetans.

Ganden Sumtseling has been rebuilt over the past twenty-five years and now ostensibly houses approximately seven hundred monks. In the past decade it has become a primary tourist destination (Hillman 2003; Kolås 2008). Dozens of busloads of Han tourists arrive daily from the UNESCO World Heritage Site of Lijiang Old Town to visit Sumtseling (at a cost of RMB 115 [US$18.50] per person), the scenic Pudacuo National Park (even more expensive at around RMB 240), and the "Old Town" (Dukezong) in Xianggelila.

The monks of Ganden Sumtseling are not well respected by most residents of Xianggelila. It is widely believed that the monks are not well schooled in Buddhist philosophy or ritual performance and are typically engaged by the community merely as *mo pa* (diviners), at best. While locals still give up seats and pay for the tickets of monks on public buses, there is much grumbling about the monastery behind the monks' backs. Monks are rumored to sometimes change their robes in a building near the "flying horse racer (*fei ma*)" statue, before entering town to engage in behavior inappropriate for monks. There is at least one telephone number one can call to solicit monk "muscle" in shady business disputes in town. The widespread understanding is that you can telephone for a group of monks to come and roughly deal with your adversary, and then you make a "donation" to the appropriate place in the monastery the next day.

Inside the walls of the monastery tensions remain since a flare up of violence a decade ago.[8] Of the eight *khangtsens* (monastic colleges) of Sumtseling, five are loyal to the Chinese state, while three remain sympathetic to the Geluk authorities in exile. Much of the tension surrounds the amplified denunciation of Dorje Shugden (Tib. *rdo rje shugs ldan*) by the fourteenth Dalai Lama. There is ample evidence that many Gyalthangpa engaged in Dorje Shugden practice prior to the 1990s, particularly in the area of Xiaozhongdian, about eighteen kilometers south of town. As Sumtseling was rebuilt, the main protector *lhakhang* (temple) at the west end of the monastery was dedicated to Dorje Shugden. The *khangtsens* that refuse to adopt Dorje Shugden practice correspond to the geographic regions encompassing Jidi Valley, Nixi Valley, and the "Old Town" of Xianggelila.

Much can be gleaned about the religio-geopolitics of historical and current monastic influence by mapping the geographic base of *khangtsen* influence—the regions from which monks at particular *khangtsens* within a monastery originate—to regional tensions that mirror doctrinal or political loyalties within the monastery. For example, many residents of the Old Town thumb their little fingers[9] at Tashi Dundrupling Monastery in Xiaozhongdian, and indeed at the valley of Xiaozhongdian itself, where they say Dorje Shugden practice is strong. Geza village, just to the northeast of Xianggelila, is dominated by a half-completed chorten that is rumored to have had its construction funding cut off in part because the villagers refused to take up Dorje Shugden practice. Today, many rural Gyalthangpa have retained propitiation of *tsam ba* ritual expertise for day-to-day religious concerns. The *tsam ba* religious ritual experts—similar to Naxi *dto-mba* or Yi *bimo*—have seen their ritual efficacy "street cred" augmented in places like Nizu, Geza, and Sanzhou, with the decline of Sumtseling's reputation.

Before leaving the subject of Sumtseling, it is vital to assess the reasons for the decline of the monks' reputations. First, tantric initiations are typically forbidden at the monastery. There are few if any charismatic Buddhist teachers with any following in the region aside from practitioners of Dorje Shugden. There are *sprulskus* (incarnate lamas) in the region, and one prominently ensconced at Sumtseling, but public teachings and, importantly, tantric initiations are not available. There may be quiet exceptions to this rule, but numerous monks have informed me that there are few if any public or officially sanctioned tantric *dbang* (empowerments/tantric initiations) at Sumtseling.[10]

Throughout the Tibetan plateau we have seen, time and again, religious teachers who have a popular following shut down by the state if their religious authority is understood as distinct from or independent from that of the state (Kapstein 2004). Vajrayana might be inherently threatening in that it involves a necessary authority that may or may not be independent of the state. In the case of Sumtseling it is worth considering whether the abbot himself can be considered part of the state. Since at least the 1920s the abbots of Sumtseling have worked closely with the Chinese administration, including at times acting as the local Communist Party leader. Is it any surprise, then, that the monastery is more of a modern museum than a functioning religious institution? Locals and visiting Tibetans do visit the monastery, but they are selective about their prostrations, and the Xianggelila community's dismissal of Sumtseling monks may in part be a reflective lament for the Buddha-dharma that they revere yet about which they admittedly know little.

Although I suspect that there have long been monk mafias in Tibetan communities, and there have always been large hierarchical strata of monks for whom daily responsibilities rarely involved much Buddhist study or practice, the vacuum of ethical authority at the heart of the monastic institutional establishment does not appear to be an age-old Tibetan dynamic. Furthermore, while it is likely that for much of the past millennium many Tibetans—in some regions more so than others—knew little about the doctrinal philosophies or ritual technologies of Buddhism, this does seem to be a new chapter in Tibetan history, wherein the state simultaneously endorses a facade of Buddhist authority while ensuring the systematic suppression of Buddhist knowledge and practice.

Is this really anything new in Tibet? Certainly, in many senses, it is. When asked if he were a Buddhist, a close friend of mine answered, "Of course, I'm Tibetan." When asked what school of Buddhism, he responded, "What is that monastery over there?" Geluk. "Ok, then I'm Geluk." When asked whether he practiced Buddhism or meditated or had a personal *yidam*, he stated, "I try not to hit animals when I drive." This response is not surprising in the region nor, perhaps, in much of Tibet. Indeed, it is common for local Tibetans in Gyalthang and beyond to be unaware of Buddhist daily practice and doctrine, let alone have a sense of sectarian affiliation. If local Gyalthangpa have a strong religious proclivity, it is more often toward a charismatic lama than toward a particular sectarian doctrine (this is true throughout much of Khams).

## Returning to Shangri-La

There are more Gyalthangpa (mostly youth) returning from India than departing for India. Although the precise numbers are difficult to quantify, the economic conditions and relative freedoms in Gyalthang (compared to other Tibetan areas) are a draw for many returnees. Xianggelila town is also a magnet for Tibetans who come from elsewhere on the plateau— Ganzi, Lhasa, Litang, Rebgong, Labrang, Jyekundo, etc.—many of whom have been educated in India. Jobs in the booming tourist industry attract many, as does the relative calm for Tibetans in Yunnan. Such calm and economic stability bring many benefits, most notably job security. Unlike areas in northwestern Sichuan and Qinghai, and quite unlike central Tibet, tourism has continued uninterrupted since its inception in the 1990s. At no time since 1993 has Xianggelila been "closed" to Chinese or foreign tourists.

There are three categories of Tibetan newcomers in Xianggelila. The first includes the young Gyalthangpa who were either raised in exile or went to India for a period for education. These I call "local returnees." The second category includes migrants from other parts of the Tibetan world, mostly Khams and Amdo, who have come in the last decade or so to work (and have not spent time abroad). The third category comprises Tibetans from elsewhere in Tibet, again mostly Khams and Amdo, who returned from India or Nepal and resettled in Gyalthang. These are the "nonlocal returnees."[11] The recent migration of these three groups to Gyalthang, mostly to work in the tourism industry, has created new tensions in the area. The vast majority are men between the ages of twenty and forty years old. Xianggelila has also seen a massive influx of Han and Bai migrants in recent years. These arrivals do not appear to be the targets of local Tibetan violence. If Xianggelila is a rough place, it is owing to Tibetan-on-Tibetan violence.

Local returnees are welcomed back by everyone, including the local government. There is a touch of resentment from some local youth, however, because returnees tend to speak English and have computer skills and thus get plumb jobs. There is also social jealousy, as many of the returnee men prove attractive to local women. Migrants from other parts of Tibet were welcomed less warmly and at times with outright hostility. Some of the migrants, such as the dozens of young men from Rebgong who came to work as thangka painters, garnered reputations as fighters. Indeed, Xianggelila has seen many drunken knife fights. Whether the prevalence of such fighting is genuinely linked to these Tibetan migrants is questionable, but most locals believe that outsiders have made the town less safe.

The nonlocal returnees, however, have fared the worst. There have been several instances of nonlocal returnees being rounded up, interrogated, and charged with crimes such as sedition. Many have served time in prison. Some of these incidents have corresponded with politically sensitive events such as the 2008 uprising or the passing of the Olympic Torch through town. Others were sparked by seemingly innocuous incidents that spiraled out of control. For instance, in 2012 a nonlocal returnee Tibetan man was rear-ended in his jeep by a local in a new van. The nonlocal asked the police to enforce compensation, but the police chief, who was Tibetan, allegedly told the nonlocal that because his jeep was old, it was not worth pursuing compensation. Later, friends of both men ended up in a near-brawl at the police station. A few days later the same police officers unknowingly entered the jeep owner's restaurant. A fight ensued, knives and cleavers were wielded, and eventually, once things calmed down, a group of nonlocal returnees was rounded up, detained, and interrogated by police. Many of those questioned had no relationship to the jeep owner. Part of the threat perceived by the local authorities in nonlocal returnees had to do with potential ongoing connections with the exile community. It is notable, however, that local returnees were not (to my knowledge) incarcerated or interrogated in the aftermath of the jeep incident.

The Gyalthang Tibetan police chief is, in a direct sense, part of the "state." As with the abbot of Sumtseling Monastery, the police chief was Tibetan, complicating a straightforward analysis that pits Tibetans against the "Chinese" state. More helpful, perhaps, is a multivalent analysis that attempts to understand ethnic conflict in the region as the result of a variety of interrelated factors, including ethnic identity, regional identity, depth of local roots, the Chinese national government, Han Chinese local government officials, and Tibetan members of local institutions that are either implicitly or explicitly controlled by the government (see Hillman 2014). Added to this matrix are dynamics of apathy, activism, economic or religious prioritization, and a softly resurgent pan-Tibetan identity—something very threatening to local and national authorities.

The jeep incident is just one of many local stories that illustrates the tensions between locals and nonlocals, particularly nonlocal returnees. But things have begun to change. Even though such extreme acts as self-immolation have not occurred in Gyalthang, their effect on local tensions has been notable. In numerous recent conversations with locals, local returnees, nonlocal Tibetans, and nonlocal returnees alike, I have been told that since the self-immolations began to increase (most notably since early November 2012), Tibetans on the street have begun to see each other more as Tibetan first and foremost, with regional identity mattering less and less.

Such claims are difficult to prove, but the shift is discernible to nonlocal Tibetans in the tone of everyday conversations and interactions and in the way people look at each other. I do not know the degree to which locals and nonlocal Tibetans discuss self-immolations, although the news of such events seems ubiquitous (via cell phone communication, mostly). In June 2012, at the annual horse racing festival on the grasslands outside of town, the local military and police made quite a show of force, surrounding the festival with fire department and military vehicles. Things were more or less the same at the June 2013 horse festivals near Napahai in the northern reaches of the valley. Many pairs of orange-jumpsuit-clad firefighters with fire extinguishers patrolled the event. Such immolation-extinguishing teams have become familiar sights across Tibet in the past two years or so and have even made an appearance at Sumtseling Monastery's Losar (New Year 2013) festivities. This is particularly notable given that, to date, there have been no self-immolations in Gyalthang. Attendees of the horse racing festival were deeply uncomfortable with the show of force and the reminder of the emphasis on harmonious society. Many left early in disgust. It is likely too that the patrols of orange-clad, helmeted, fire-extinguisher-wielding uniformed men might inadvertently remind locals of the state's awareness of discontent; on many occasions at recent Gyalthang horse festivals, I witnessed people subtly discussing the fire-extinguishing teams.

Interestingly, in Gyalthang over the past few years, a group of nonlocal returnees has periodically gathered to discuss improving relationships with locals (Tibetan and Han alike). This unofficial (indeed, they have been politely asked to avoid an official name) group espouses the tenets of eschewing gambling, abiding by the law, wearing traditional Tibetan garb to regular gatherings, assisting (financially or otherwise) members in need of help, and interacting with locals in a helpful and collegial manner. Such solidarity among civic-minded Tibetans indicates an attentive reorientation among nonlocal returnees to adhere to and augment the newfound sense of pan-Tibetan solidarity following the 2008 Khampa and central Tibetan uprising resulting from dissatisfaction with Chinese rule across much of the region. Whereas in other regions of Khams people have been setting themselves on fire to protest the policies and dynamics of Chinese rule, in Gyalthang outsider Tibetans have organized to behave legally to perform their Tibetan identities in ways congruent with local dispositions and priorities.

Interestingly, returnees to the region bring with them an increased awareness of the vitality of Tibetan Buddhism as practiced by Tibetan communities in Nepal and India. A café manager in the Xianggelila Old

Town, who had recently returned after living in India since he was a small child, remarked how frustrating it was to be back. He commented that religion seemed "dead" in Gyalthang, that the monastery was "fake," and that his family knew nothing about Buddhism. He further commented that his family was tired of his talking about Buddhism and wished he would learn Chinese more quickly.

It remains to be seen the degree to which the large inflow of returnees to Gyalthang—both local and nonlocal—will have a measurable effect on local religiosity. In the absence of any change in the monastic community it is doubtful that any large-scale religious resurgence will take place anytime soon. As has been well studied and noted by mainstream scholars of China, religious practice is often tolerated as long as the center of "authority" remains the state. This is quite true for Chinese Catholics, who find themselves presented with bishops appointed by Beijing. However, although there is a vibrant religious resurgence afoot in much of China, complete with sanctioned festival gatherings,[12] in much of the far west of China the circumstances of religious revival, if one were to call it that, are notably different. Without charismatic religious leadership in Gyalthang, substantive Buddhist revival seems unlikely in the near future.[13]

## Causes of Dissatisfaction, the Age of Patterns of Conflict, and the Erosion of Agency

In a sense Gyalthang is a place torn. There are all sorts of gripes on the streets. People are dissatisfied with the state of the water and power supply, and rumors abound that the reason power goes out on weekends is that the local power company sells electricity to thirsty tourist-burdened Lijiang. There are worries about the cleanliness of water, particularly given the polluted state of Napahai wetland and the secrecy surrounding the mining boom in the surrounding mountains, notably in Geza. People worry that most Xianggelila drivers are not properly licensed, that taxi driving jobs are being taken by Sichuan Han outsiders, that there is nothing really "old" about the Old Town anymore (though few people really care), and that the town is simply growing too fast. Locals swallow anxiety about the fact that in June 2013 the "laoban" mafia boss from Sanba (a predominantly Naxi area) was murdered and cut into four pieces and that deadly retaliation ensued in Xianggelila. Villagers were understandably anxious about the summer 2013 hoof-and-mouth disease quarantines and the euthanizing of yaks and cows. Everybody is worried about money; few are worried about repression of Tibetan ethnic identity, per se.

On July 12, 2007, the "Chinese Idol" (*Haonaner*) television star Zhaxi Dunzhu (a.k.a. Tashi Dundrup) made a "homecoming" appearance in the Old Town's central square. He sang a few songs in Chinese and English to an adoring crowd. A local teenage fan almost pulling her hair out—reminiscent of Beatle-mania—screaming her adoration for the star, explained: "Tashi Dundrup, daibiao women zangzu, ta shi women zangzu de yi ge guoji pinpai, jiu xiang xianggelila shi women zangzu diqu de yi ge guoji pinpai, suoyi wo hen gaoxing Zhaxi Dunzhu hui jia le gen women biaoyan le" (Tashi Dundrup represents us Tibetans. He is an international emblem for us Tibetans, just like Xianggelila the international emblem of our Tibetan area. So, I'm very happy that Tashi Dundrup has come home to perform for us). Fervor aside, this is telling, as Tashi Dundrup was raised in Kunming and Shanghai and does not speak Tibetan (though he urged the crowd to be sure to learn Tibetan, or else they would end up like him). Such things, obviously, were not what were important to his adoring fan.

Gyalthang Tibetan language is not taught in the public schools of Gyalthang. Most locals learn to speak *rgyal thang skyad* at home. However, given the lack of literate Tibetan education and the dominance of Chinese language in media and everyday administration, it is no wonder that many locals use Chinese much more than they use their native language.[14] In addition, Tibetans from outside Gyalthang cannot understand the local Tibetic languages (and vice versa), and there is no common writing system for the local parlances (Bartee 2007). In Xianggelila many Tibetans communicate with each other in Chinese. The Tibetic languages of Gyalthang are in danger of disappearing, yet this does not seem to be a serious concern for many locals.

As Tsering Shakya has pointed out, we must make no mistake; the goal of the PRC has always been to assimilate Tibetans (Shakya and Wang 2007; Herberer 1989, esp. chaps. 2 and 7). In Gyalthang, I would argue, assimilation is going relatively smoothly. Gyalthang Tibetans use Chinese language, local state officials are mostly Tibetans (as is legally required in the Tibetan Autonomous County), and people are prospering and are thus not particularly discontent. In addition the main monastery is considered by locals to be a sad joke, and Tashi Dundrup is as perfect an example of Tibeto-Chinese success as one can be. Indeed, it appears that many locals in Gyalthang are perfectly content with the current state of affairs. Prosperity has allowed them to refurbish homes, to procure desired cell phones, to purchase vehicles, to access better healthcare, to send their children to schools, and to celebrate their friends and enjoy themselves in ways that feel most comfortable—but those ways are quintessentially Tibetan.

Geza, a series of villages about a forty-five-minute drive to the northeast of Xianggelila Town, celebrated Losar (New Year) in February 2013 in the manner typical of Tibetans across the plateau. Families propitiated their clan with juniper, milk, and water on forested hillsides overlooking the village. Neighbors and relatives were hosted and visited for countless meals; gifts were exchanged; children received *hongbao* (gifts of red envelopes containing cash); fireworks lasted all week; and the festivities culminated in dance performances, basketball competitions, and horse races. I anticipated a somewhat subdued Losar owing to a quietly discussed sense of solidarity with Tibetans suffering in other regions, but the village New Year celebration went ahead as usual—and in a markedly Tibetan manner. Of course, the people in Geza have their own worries and concerns, mostly economic and health related, but the notion of ethnic conflict was absent. Everyone enjoyed the song-and-dance performances on state-sanitized Tibetan language television.

So, we return to a question posed at the outset of this chapter. Why are the people of Gyalthang relatively content while ethnic unrest simmers in other Tibetan communities in China? My experience in Gyalthang suggests that, to some extent, people's frustrations are sublimated and that Tibetans are resigned to a sense of inevitability. If a plebiscite pole were taken asking Tibetans to vote on increased political autonomy, my best guess is that the results might surprise other Tibetans. There is a genuine sense in Gyalthang that much was lost with the destruction of institutional Buddhism in the region. Dundrupling Monastery, outside nearby Benzilan Town, is universally respected, whereas Sumtseling is looked upon with sadness. As a local friend explained, "The young people don't care much because they don't miss Buddhism. They never knew what it really was. It has been a long time." But many Gyalthangpa are honestly satisfied with being part of Yunnan and part of China. Have the provincial and local authorities done a genuinely good job of making this corner of Tibet in Yunnan a successful model for a harmonious Tibetan society (Hillman 2009), or is something more insidious at play? Lhasa is far from Gyalthang, and the mountains between are high. Gyalthang's loyalties to central Tibet have for a long time been much more cultural than political. Ethnic identity, although fundamentally cultural, becomes increasingly politicized in times of interethnic conflict.

Gyalthangpa Tibetans, like Tibetans elsewhere in China, are highly resentful of Han chauvinism and racism. The tourism industry does little to help this issue, with the commodification of Tibetan culture and religion having a significant impact on local Tibetans' sense of their relationship with Han China and Han Chinese. Chinese literature of nostalgia, coupled with the exotification and the (mostly masculine) eroticization of Tibetans on the part of Han tourists to the region, conspire to paint Tibet and the Tibetans in ways that are entrancing for many urban Han tourists (Hillman and Henfry 2006, 251–72). In the Old Town of Xianggelila there are several open-fronted shops where tourists can sit with a young woman and beat on conga (yes, African conga) drums. Why? It is the same reason the Bai silversmiths have had such success selling "Tibetan" knives and barbaric swords to Han tourists in the Old Town. It is the same reason Tibetan mastiffs have become the fashionable rage as pets for the über-rich Han of East Coast cities. Machismo, particularly primitive and dangerous Tibetan machismo, sells. Han tourists can drum to experience what it feels like to be primitive, free, virile, rural, and tough.

Racism has more practical manifestations in Gyalthang, as evidenced by restricted access to *guanxi* relationship networks and economic opportunities, as well as language insecurity. But racism in Gyalthang is not unidirectional. Gyalthang Tibetans have their own prejudices against their neighbors. Laughingly, a local Tibetan thirty-year-old friend of mine disparagingly described the Yi villages we drove past in a car as understandably poor. The Yi, she explained, are lazy and foolish when it comes to money. They are also not particularly smart and so cannot do well in school. My friend understood that what she was saying seemed to offend me, so she added: "I'm not being mean! I don't have a grudge. They are just really like that."

Han racism against Tibetans is nothing new nor is Tibetan racism against their Naxi and Yi neighbors. Grumbling about one's local government is also nothing new for Tibetans. Certain forms of religious repression in important ways are new, although the history of the violence of Buddhist hegemony across the Tibetan plateau is in need of further analysis. Granted, it is admittedly a categorical error to directly compare the Chinese occupation of Tibet and the violent suppression of religion and human dignity to periods deep in Tibetan history. After all, why would one make such comparisons? What is at stake? What can be gained from such a comparison? Why does it matter if it is "really anything new in Tibet"?

One of my main queries in this chapter has been to assess if much that seems ugly on the streets of Gyalthang is justifiably attributable to the Han Chinese state or even the "state" in general (regardless if Han or local Tibetan). I ask as a way of attempting to understand why we might frame ethnic conflict as something significantly new. We know that historically violence and conflict occurred within the Tibetan world. So, in essence, I am asking what is new about the current conflict, other than the obvious fact that China has invaded Tibet and continues to occupy and forcibly repress and assimilate its people? "Newness" does not necessarily matter, but if we are looking to understand monk mafias, corrupt police, and resource exploitation, we must accept that answers may be complicated and require understanding of historical conflict.

Assimilation can also be understood as a form of coercive violence. When the Chinese-endorsed eleventh Panchen Lama visited Gyalthang on May 20, 2006, throngs of locals came out to see him—some out of curiosity, others to receive blessings. One reason to ask if such a phenomenon of acceptance of an imposed religious leader is something new is to help place it in context. For example, the office of the Dalai Lamas was established by an outside conquering force, as was, many argue, the installment of the eleventh Panchen Lama, Gyancain Norbu. That Gyalthangpa would, over time, come to accept the eleventh Panchen Lama is, in a sense, nothing new. In Gyalthang there is a strong sense that it is basically pointless to resist the enforcement of religious or political policies. Is this resignation? In a sense it is. Is the reason that there is less ethnic conflict in Gyalthang vis-à-vis the Chinese government than in other Tibetan regions because the Gyalthangpa have been more deeply assimilated and because state control is better established than in some other regions? In part the answer is yes, but it is not the only reason. The other major reason is that

Gyalthang has witnessed genuine economic successes that have benefited Tibetans.

Gyalthang has also witnessed a long period of stability that many are reluctant to change. Many different individuals in the region have explained to me that with the coming of Chinese communist control in the 1950s, patterns of local violence—between Tibetans and Naxi, between Xiangcheng (Tib. *chatreng*) Tibetans and Yagra Tibetans, between Dongwang and Geza Tibetans, etc.—came to a complete end. Locals deeply value such peace and stability and are openly thankful to the Chinese state for it. Nevertheless, new types of violence, brought about by the involvement of the state in local life from the 1950s to the 1970s have not been forgotten. The precise ways that such memories are performed, suppressed, recomposed, or rationalized remain vexing problems.

In Gyalthang nonlocal Tibetans express that they experience increasingly less discrimination from local Tibetans, in part owing to the sense of pan-Tibetan solidarity precipitated by the recent self-immolations in nearby regions. This solidarity is, ironically for a government whose priority is "harmony," considered a threat. The intention of provincial and local government officials is to keep Gyalthang separate from the rest of the Tibetan cultural sphere. Their hope is to paint it as different and to keep it that way.

In recent years in Gyalthang most conflict and violence has been intra-ethnic. In the case of Gyalthang there is a sense of disproportionate discrimination perpetrated by Han toward Tibetans (and toward other minority nationalities such as the Hui and the Yi), and there is clearly discrimination perpetrated by the Tibetans toward the Hui, Yi, and to a lesser extent the Naxi and Lisu. There is also systematic institutional repression of Tibetan religion, language, and cultural identity by the state, but many state officials, at least locally, are themselves Tibetans. The state is seen as both local and national, and it is easier to identify national level policies with the Han majority. Is the difference related to the identity of the state? (Harrell 2007). In ethnic minority (*shaoshu minzu*) autonomous political geographical spaces in China the local government is supposed to be constructed, at least as a majority (here the "state" needs to be differentiated from the "party"), by members of the locally empowered ethnic minority community. But ethnicity is not the be-all and end-all of what makes one gravitate toward a constructed identity of being repressed or marginalized *by* the state—religiously, economically, or otherwise—particularly when the state is composed, in important ways, of members of one's own ethnicity. Following the intense violence of the 1950s to the 1970s in many regions of the Chinese borderlands (read Han periphery), the sense of who was to blame for the violence became contested, intentionally sublimated, simply traumatically repressed, erased (or smudged to illegibility) from local oral histories, or poorly digested (Mueggler 2001; Mackley 2005).

On a local level the repression of certain freedoms is not seen as simply an "ethnic" conflict. There is also a sense that Tibetans are hurting each other in the town of Xianggelila. This intraethnic violence is not normally seen as a conflict with the state or with the Han, despite the fact that it could be argued that Han (national government) policies toward Tibetans have created the conditions that lead to local violence. The cultural depression that accompanies occupation and subjugation is not widely understood to be the cause of intraethnic conflict. There are exceptions to these tendencies, and there certainly are individuals who link intra-Tibetan conflict to the larger picture of Chinese occupation, but there are plenty of people in Xianggelila Town who blame the knife fights on the character of people from Rebgong more than on the political situation. And the incarceration of nonlocal returnees is generally understood to be a case of discrimination against outsider interlopers and the workings of provincially minded police more than a case of governmental fear of the potential political activist consciousness of the nonlocal returnees.

We are left with several important questions. Is it valuable to ask whether ethnic conflict in western China is anything new? What can such wonderings tell us about the nature of the current set of conflicts, if anything? Furthermore, to what degree is it intelligible to assess ethnic conflict when one side or party to the conflict is an identifiable ethnicity and the other—for example, the local state—is not? How can we most fruitfully apply multivalent models of multiple contested identities to situations of conflict? What can the case of Gyalthang, a region of relative stability and prosperity and state suppression of religion and culture, teach us about regions of Tibet that are shimmering with violence and conflict? To what degree does the phantom of prosperity shroud an acrimonious revulsion toward state repression, or is the prosperity real and more than just economic in Shangri-la?

---

On January 11, 2014, much of the "Old Town" of Xianggelila burned to the ground in an accidental fire that destroyed well over two hundred mostly wooden buildings but thankfully resulted in no fatalities. The heart of the Old Town is now gone. Much of the research that resulted in this chapter was conducted in the complex town that no longer exists. It remains to be seen how, when, and in what manners the town will be reconstituted. Nevertheless, communities are shattered, much of historical value has been forever lost, and the local senses of priorities and even political and historical sensibilities about ideology and identity have undoubtedly been affected at their radical cores. This chapter is dedicated to the inhabitants of the former Old Town of Xianggelila and the memory of communities of kindness within its streets. It seems impossible to escape the sense that Tibet is burning.

## Notes

1. "Harmony" has been the main public objective of the Chinese government's overall nationwide policy over the past few years. Local Gyalthangpa and Han Chinese transplants to the Old Town alike enjoy making fun of this term's broad multivalence. See Schwieger (2011); Kolås (2008); and Hillman (2003, 2009).

2. Historically, Gyalthang did not include areas west of the Nixi Valley. Thus, Benzilan and Dechen fell outside of Gyalthang, as did any areas west and southwest of Tacheng. Balagedzong, just to the west of Geza township (Tib: *skad tshag*) was not part of Gyalthang, although the village of Nagara (Tib: *nags rked rag*) was. Gyalthang likely extended southwest to Sanba and Baishuitai Spring and perhaps to Haba, and south as far as the land across the river from Shigu Town, as is evidenced by the territorial demarcation inscribed on the town's famous stone drum from which the town gets its moniker.

3. Mueggler's (2001) brilliant ethnography complicates the notion of simplistic blame for devastation suffered by a community that found the Chinese state both imaginatively distant and manifest as eager members of their own

community. Harrell (2007) makes a similar point, focusing on the examples of several individuals who, despite their local ethnic identity, represented the state. Both Mueggler's and Harrell's works address Yi peoples, geographically close to but not identical with Gyalthangpa Tibetans.

4. McKhann (1998) observed and warned of this needed perspective more than fifteen years ago.

5. While the degree to which it was felt differed among individuals, coercion played an undeniable role in Tibetan complicity in the dismantling of Sumtseling, as well as in other actions motivated by the Cultural Revolution. The notion of "free will" and participatory agency is a valid and problematic query as to what transpired during Sumtseling's destruction, and at whose hands, and why. For a brilliant and (perhaps somewhat) applicable formula for the notion of coercion see Frye (1983).

6. In the telling of a story about invisible villages and local monsters in the region of Nagara, storyteller Orgyen Dorje not only described to me the local memory of the destruction of the Kagyu monastery by the Gelugpa but remarked vehemently, at the tail end of a story about a flying monster called the *sher shang du du*: "We did not pay taxes to 'Jang' [the Lijiang Mu kings]. . . . We were conquered by Dewazhong [the Ganden Phodrang Gelug government of Central Tibet]."

7. See also Jackson and Anshi (1998). For an outstanding in-depth look at the Panthay Rebellion see Atwill (2005). For details about Ganden Sumtseling prior to its destruction see Bstan-pa-rgyal-mtshan (1985).

8. For a nuanced look at the monastery a decade ago see Hillman (2005).

9. In Tibetan areas the elevation of one's smallest finger toward someone or something is a gesture of disapproval or contempt. The gesture becomes a vulgar insult when one flicks the end of the smallest finger with the thumb.

10. In the winter of 2013 I was told by a resident reincarnate lama (Tib. *sprul-sku*) from Sumtseling that indeed tantric initiations do sometimes still take place and that there is still a holdout of folks at the monastery who maintain a careful and scholarly education in Buddhist philosophy and tantric practice for select students. Nevertheless, public initiations (Tib. *dbang*) remain rare.

11. There is also a small contingent of older local returnees who came back in the 1980s. These returnees are the sons of former landlords who owned large plots of land prior to the "Democratic Reforms" of 1958. Most of this contingent of returnees are now in their fifties or sixties.

12. For a detailed and careful study of the resurgence of religion in China, detailed through the lens of the case example of Shaanbei, see Chau (2006).

13. For a superb analysis of charisma and the tensions surrounding religious revitalization in Golok fifteen years ago see Germano (1998).

14. Some local Tibetans and returnees do text each other primarily in Tibetan. Some of them tell me that some sympathetic local government censors tell

them to please text in Chinese so that nobody will pay attention to what they write.

## References

Atwill, David. 2005. *The Chinese Sultanate: Islam, Ethnicity, and the Panthay Rebellion in Southwest China, 1856–1873*. Stanford: Stanford University Press.

Bartee, Ellen. 2007. "A Grammar of Dongwang Tibetan." PhD diss., University of California, Santa Barbara.

Bstan-pa-rgyal-mtshan. 1985. *Rgyal thaṅ yul luṅ dgon gnas daṅ bcas pa'i byuṅ ba mdo tsam brjod pa blo gsal mgul pa mdzes pa'i rgyan* [A History of the Rgyal-thaṅ Dgon-pa Monastic Complex and Its Environs]. Dharamsala, India: Rgyal-thaṅ Bya-'thab, Ṅag-dbaṅ Thabs-mkhas.

Chau, Adam Yuet. 2006. *Miraculous Response: Doing Popular Religion in Contemporary China*. Stanford: Stanford University Press.

Frye, Marilyn. 1983. *The Politics of Reality: Essays in Feminist Theory*. Trumansburg, NY: Crossing Press.

Germano, David. 1998. "Re-membering the Dismembered Body of Tibet: Contemporary Tibetan Visionary Movements in the People's Republic of China." In *Buddhism in Contemporary Tibet: Religious Revival and Cultural Identity*, edited by Melvyn C. Goldstein and Matthew T. Kapstein, 53–94. Berkeley: University of California Press.

Harrell, Stevan. 2007. "L'état, c'est nous, or We Have Met the Oppressor and He Is Us: The Predicament of Minority Cadres in the PRC." In *The Chinese State at the Borders*, edited by Diana Lary, 221–39. Vancouver: University of British Columbia Press.

Herberer, Thomas. 1989. *China and Its National Minorities: Autonomy or Assimilation?* London: M. E. Sharpe.

Hillman, Ben. 2003. "Paradise Under Construction: Minorities, Myths and Modernity in Northwest Yunnan." *Asian Ethnicity* 4 (2): 175–88.

——. 2005. "Monastic Politics and the Local State in China: Authority and Autonomy in an Ethnically Tibetan Prefecture." *China Journal* 54:29–51.

——. 2009. "Ethnic Tourism and Ethnic Politics in Tibetan China." *Harvard Asia Pacific Review* 10 (1): 3–6.

——. 2014. "Unrest in Tibet: Interpreting the Post-2008 Wave of Protest and Conflict." *Dalny Vychod* 4 (1): 50–60.

Hillman, Ben, and Lee-Anne Henfry. 2006. "Macho Minority: Masculinity and Ethnicity on the Edge of Tibet." *Modern China* 32 (2): 251–72.

Jackson, Anthony. 1979. *Na-khi Religion: An Analytical Appraisal of Na-khi Ritual Texts*. The Hague: Mouton.

Jackson, Anthony, and Pan Anshi. 1998. "The Authors of Naxi Ritual Books, Index Books and Books of Divination." In *Naxi and Moso Ethnography: Kin, Rites,*

*Pictographs*, edited by Michael Oppitz and Elizabeth Hsu, 237–73. Zürich: Völkerkundemuseum der Universität Zürich.

Kapstein, Matthew. 2004. "A Thorn in the Dragon's Side: Tibetan Buddhist Culture in China." In *Governing China's Multiethnic Frontiers*, edited by Morris Rossabi, 230–84. Seattle: University of Washington Press.

Kolås, Åshild. 2008. *Tourism and Tibetan Culture in Transition: A Place Called Shangrila*. New York: Routledge.

Mackley, Charlene. 2005. "'Speaking Bitterness': Autobiography, History, and Mnemonic Politics on the Sino-Tibetan Frontier." *Comparative Studies in Society and History* 47 (1): 40–78.

McKhann, Charles. 1998. "Naxi, Rerkua, Moso, Meng: Kinship, Politics and Ritual on the Yunnan-Sichuan Frontier." In *Naxi and Moso Ethnography: Kin, Rites, Pictographs*, edited by Michael Oppitz and Elizabeth Hsu, 23–46. Zürich: Völkerkundemuseum der Universität Zürich.

——. 2010. "Naxi Religion in the Age of Tourism: Persistence and (Re)Creation." In *Faiths on Display: Religion, Tourism, and the Chinese State*, edited by Tim Oakes and Donald Sutton, 183–210. Lanham, MD: Rowman and Littlefield.

Mortensen, Eric D. 2009. "Mosuo and Naxi Nationalities." *Encyclopedia of Modern China*. Edited by David Pong. Vol. 2, 613–14. Detroit: Charles Scribner's Sons.

Mueggler, Erik. 2001. *The Age of Wild Ghosts: Memory, Violence, and Place in Southwest China*. Berkeley: University of California Press.

Schwieger, Peter. 2011. "The Long Arm of the Fifth Dalai Lama: Influence and Power of the Fifth Dalai Lama in Southeast Tibet." In *Buddhist Himalaya: Studies in Religion, History, and Culture*. Vol. 1, edited by Alex McKay and Anna Balikci-Denjongpa, 239–58. Gangtok: Namgyal Institute of Tibetology.

Shakya, Tsering, and Wang Lixiong. 2009. *The Struggle for Tibet*. London: Verso.

# 9

# Interethnic Conflict in the PRC

## Xinjiang and Tibet as Exceptions?

James Leibold

According to the Chinese Communist Party (CCP), the People's Republic of China (PRC) is a harmonious, multiethnic nation-state, with the equality of China's fifty-six officially recognized "ethnic groups" (*minzu*) enshrined in the PRC constitution.[1] "In the entire world," former Chairman of the Tibet Autonomous Region (TAR) Qiangba Puncog stated in March 2012, "it's difficult to find ethnic policies as exemplary as ours" (Chen 2012). Picture here fifty-six children in colorful ethnic costumes walking hand in hand under the protective armor of the CCP, a common image in state propaganda on the Chinese mainland.

Yet bloody episodes of interethnic violence in Lhasa (2008), Urumqi (2009), Kunming (2014), and elsewhere seem to paint a different, far more odious, picture: a rising storm of ethnic contradictions that threatens to spin out of control. While CCP officials depict these incidents as the work of "separatists" or "terrorists" and their external, anti-China allies (AFP 2009), many commentators in the West, and increasingly inside China itself, view them as examples (and harbingers) of national decay. Here, metaphors like "crisis" (Brady 2012a), "emergency" (International Campaign for Tibet 2012), "powder keg" (Abbott 2011; Hao and Liu 2012), "gathering— and breaking—storm" (Millward 2009), "collision course" (Zheng 2008), and even "ticking time bomb" (ChinaFile 2014) are sometimes employed when discussing the current state of ethnic relations in the world's most populous nation-state, highlighting the sense of "urgency" in addressing perceived problems and policy failures.

Some believe that ethnic relations in China have reached a dangerous tipping point and suggest that we can expect increased tensions and communal violence in the future (ChinaFile 2014). There is disagreement, however, on the implications. In the West these clashes are viewed as a potential threat to CCP rule and its legitimacy in the eyes of majority and minority communities alike. PRC thinkers, in contrast, view these antagonisms as a challenge to national sovereignty, tapping into collective concerns over the implications of the collapse of communism in Eastern Europe (Meisels 2013).

In a recent journal special issue titled "The Politics of Ethnicity in China," Anne-Marie Brady begins by stating: "Ethnic relations in China are at an all-time low"; she then goes on to describe ethnic contradictions as "one of the most tenuous fault lines in Chinese society" (Brady 2012a, 3, 9). For Brady and others these cleavages are a potential "litmus test" for CCP rule,[2] perhaps even the single biggest problem current CCP leaders face (Hao and Liu 2012). Similarly, some mainland-based scholars sound increasingly alarmist when speaking about the state of interethnic relations, with Beijing University professor Ma Rong (among others) calling it "China's biggest social issue" and warning that unless policies are altered, China could follow the former Soviet Union and Yugoslavia down the road of national disintegration (Ma 2012). There is now a growing body of academic literature in China focused on analyzing and preventing "ethnic mass incidents" (*minzu quntixing shijian*), where it is claimed that these incidents are "constantly increasing in frequency and number" (Jia and Hu 2012; Yang 2012). This sense of crisis, of course, helps fuel China's massive domestic security apparatuses, which now spend more money on "stability maintenance" (*weiwen*) than national defense (Chen 2013).

In the face of this perception of ethnic crisis, this chapter offers an assessment of the current state of interethnic relations across the PRC. Metaphors are notoriously weak forms of generalization, and the shear size of China necessitates the disaggregation of ethnic hostilities. Other chapters in this volume have explored specific aspects of conflict in western China and their complex dynamics and local triggers. I seek to address these issues at an aggregate, national level, as the "ethnic cauldron" thesis not only obscures divergent variables of conflict (spatial, temporal, cultural, and structural) but also shapes the discursive and policy landscape in which these problems are discussed. Rather than questioning the obvious ethnic tensions that exist in pockets of the PRC, my aim is to place these troubles within a wider, comparative perspective in order to draw us back to the big picture.

Specifically, I interrogate two interrelated assumptions: (1) that ethnic relations have significantly deteriorated over the last decade, as evidenced by an increase in interethnic conflict and violence; and (2) that these ethnic contradictions pose a significant and growing threat to the political and social stability of the PRC and could even lead to the collapse of the CCP or the disintegration of the Chinese nation-state. I will argue that the current wave of interethnic conflict in Xinjiang and Tibet is the exception rather than the norm and that at a national level ethnic relations remain relatively robust and thus pose little immediate threat to regime stability and territorial integrity. Yet this could quickly alter if the party-state initiates a new round of major reforms, atrophies further, or suddenly collapses, as weak governance and shifting policies (rather than group inequality or cultural marginality) are the chief accelerants of interethnic violence.

It is important to make clear from the start that my focus is *interethnic* hostilities, that is, antagonisms between officially designated ethnic communities (*minzu*) in the PRC rather than minority or majority animus or antipathy toward the party-state, its policies, or their place within Chinese society. As noted in this volume's introduction by Ben Hillman, "ethnic protest" and "ethnic conflict" are two related yet distinct forms of ethnic collective action (Olzak 1992), and one type does not necessarily lead to the other.[3] The sense of alienation and interethnic tensions might be on the rise in parts of China, but this does not necessarily reflect patterns of communal conflict and violence.

## The Scope of Ethnic Conflict and Its Implications

Is interethnic conflict and violence on the rise in the PRC? The short reply here is that we have no way of answering this question with any level of certainty. The sensitivity of ethnic issues in China and the closed nature of PRC society mean we lack both the methods and the empirical data to systematically determine any trend lines. If the CCP and its security apparatuses maintain statistical data on the quantity and frequency of ethnic incidents—disagreements, melees, violent attacks, riots, and other forms of violence—this information is not publically available, nor is it likely to be under CCP rule.

As a result, what we know about ethnic-imbued internecine conflict is mediated through formal and informal media channels, rendering much of this information anecdotal, secondhand, or highly speculative. Yet, that said, there does appear to be an increase in reported incidents of ethnic hostilities over the last decade in Xinjiang and Tibet, which has led Nicholas Bequelin and other astute observers to conclude that the decadelong rule of Hu Jintao and Wen Jiabao (2002–12) was marred by the "most severe" interethnic violence in decades (Bequelin 2012). The tragic events of March 15, 2008, in Lhasa and July 7, 2009, in Urumqi—with more than two hundred civilians killed in street rioting and targeted interethnic violence—shocked many, and the more recent spread of this bloodshed outside the western frontiers—in the form of terror attacks in Beijing (October 29, 2013), Kunming (March 1, 2014), Changsha (March 14, 2014), and other inland cities—certainly creates the impression of ethnic crisis and a situation spinning out of control.

In addition to these widely discussed events, we have sporadic reports of smaller-scale incidents: Han-Hui communal violence in Shandong, Henan, and other places and possibly hundreds of clashes between Uyghur and Tibetan malcontents and state security forces since 2012. China has also witnessed more than 140 Tibetan self-immolations since February 2009, which, although not acts of *interethnic violence* per se, are certainly rooted in high levels of ethnic-imbued despair among some segments of the Tibetan population and add to the perception of declining interethnic amity and rising conflict. And these are only the incidents that we know about. It is conceivable that small-scale, low-level ethnic skirmishes occur across China on a daily basis, as the on-the-ground observations of contributors to this volume suggest.[4]

Yet at present we lack systematic evidence of these sorts of daily hostilities, with serious incidents of interethnic violence (those resulting in bloodshed) being reported in bursts and pockets. As Anne-Marie Brady points out, the Chinese media is prohibited (Brady 2012b), as a general rule, from reporting on ethnic incidents, meaning that most smaller-scale clashes go unreported, and the reaction of local officials is often to cover up ethnic incidents and downplay the role of ethnicity or religion in any violence that is documented.

In today's deeply interconnected, media-rich environment it is difficult to imagine, however, that a significant or major ethnic incident could occur in China without our knowing at least something about it. In fact, it could be argued that the perception of rising ethnic conflict is more reflective of the changing media landscape in the PRC (and globally) than deteriorating social relations (Shirk 2011), with new communication technologies, commercial imperatives, citizen-journalism, increased foreign reporting, as well as other media trends, contributing to a dramatic increase in the coverage and discussion of social issues, including interethnic strife and violence. In the end one is left wondering: is there more ethnic conflict today, or do we simply know more about those incidents that do occur and now speak of them in "ethnic terms"? In short, the media plays a powerful role in shaping our impressions and categorization of communal violence, leaving the quotidian reality clouded in incongruous representations, such as "ethnic harmony" versus "ethnic discord."

The limited statistical data we do have on ethnic conflict is highly suspect. Occasionally one encounters (often undocumented) attempts to quantify these clashes in the academic and journalistic literature, such as a 10.18 percent increase in the number of ethnic "mass incidents" in Xinjiang between 2002 and 2006 (Adilijiang and Abulaiti 2012), six thousand "disputes" involving ethnic minorities in Yunnan over the 2002–9 time frame (Freeman 2012), and 190 "terrorist attacks" in Xinjiang in 2012 (AFP 2013). Yet without a comparative or national statistical framework, these figures mean little, and this problem is compounded by the dubious reliability of official Chinese statistics and the tendency of security officials to pad out conflict figures to obtain increased resources. A recent *Legal Daily* (*Fazhi Ribao*) report, for example, concluded that 8.9 percent of mass incidents in China during 2012 were caused by ethnic conflict, and 4.4 percent of them involved ethnic minorities, which could mean sixteen thousand cases of the former and eight thousand of the latter in a single year (Goldkorn 2013).[5] But "mass incident" figures are "questionable at best" (Freeman 2010)[6] owing to inconsistencies in reporting, data collection, and categories of analysis; and the lack of precision and clarity over what is being counted is the only way to explain how a mere half of the mass incidents caused by ethnic conflict in the *Legal Daily* report actually involved ethnic minorities. Were the remaining Han-on-Han ethnic conflicts?

When viewed across the last sixty years, it's hard to say with any level of certainty that current conflict is any worse (in terms of scope, intensity, or frequency) than other times in PRC history. In Xinjiang, for example, the brutality of the Urumqi riots shocked both the Chinese and international public. But it could be argued this was chiefly because of the extensive, highly graphic and disturbing imagery (both photographic and video) that spread across the globe via various media outlets (television, Internet, newspapers, etc.).[7] While this sort of imagery is new, incidents of this scale certainly are not. In the appendix of his recent book Gardner Bovingdon (2010, 105–34) painstakingly catalogues nearly 150 incidents of ethnic protest and violence in Xinjiang between 1949 and 2005, including more than thirty-five that occurred in 1998–99 alone, ranging from large-scale armed insurrections to small-scale ethnic attacks that collectively caused thousands (if not hundreds of thousands) of deaths. Furthermore, Bovingdon (174–90) argues that violent acts actually declined sharply after 2001 as the party-state increased its security controls over Xinjiang society, and Uyghurs adopted "everyday forms of resistance" rather than direct attacks on state and Han targets.[8]

In fact, interethnic violence was likely far greater during the Cultural Revolution. While much of the bloodshed that occurred in minority regions involved competing Han revolutionary factions, minority communities were also involved in both attacks on Han and state organs and more frequently as the targets of Han retaliation. Kerry Brown (2007) estimates that in Inner Mongolia as many as one hundred thousand deaths occurred among Mongol cadres and herdsmen (a number that, he argues, suggests "acts of genocide"). Even official statistics put the death toll at twenty-two thousand, with a further three hundred thousand injured, including by such gruesome acts as tongue/eye gouging and public burnings. In Tibet fifty-four people were killed, and twenty others had their limbs hacked off during a violent clash involving Tibetan and Han "revolutionaries" in Nyemo in 1969 (Goldstein, Ben, and Lhundrup 2009). When compared to the ethnic violence of the Cultural Revolution, the current situation is "a piece of cake," according to Mongol scholar Uradyn Bulag who experienced firsthand the violence of Mao's revolution (ChinaFile 2014). In the post–Cold War era there is a tendency to code social violence in "ethnic" or "national" terms, while claims of rising ethnic conflict across the globe (including in China) are both empirically and conceptually flawed according to Bruce Gilley (2004).[9]

Despite the cyclical and spatially confined nature of interethnic conflict in China, there remains a strong perception of a looming crisis. For most outside observers these contradictions are added to the long list of social problems that define the fragility of CCP rule. Yet for others, especially a group of critical intellectuals inside China, ethnic antagonisms (if left unchecked) have the potential to undermine national sovereignty and Chinese territorial integrity. In the post-Mao era ethnic and national frames (i.e., *minzu*) have replaced class as the dominant analytical paradigm, and minzu conflict (either domestic or international) is now viewed as the principal threat to China's geobody. The collapse of communism in the former Soviet Union and Eastern Europe elicited extensive soul-searching among Chinese intellectuals and policy makers, as they attempted to understand the reasons for its downfall and any lessons for China. One important focus has been ethnic relations and ethnic policy. Some have questioned the extent to which ethnic contradictions contributed to the fall of the USSR and Yugoslavia in particular; others argue that majority chauvinism and minority oppression helped to undermine party-state authority; still others point their finger at the federal political system, arguing that it provided the template and institutional framework for the breakup of these two formerly multiethnic unions.[10]

These concerns continue today, with recent interethnic violence intensifying the debate. In an influential article first published in the Hong Kong magazine *Leaders* (*Lingdaozhe*) and subsequently circulated across the Sinophone Internet, Beijing University sociologist Ma Rong argues that "the biggest challenge that China could face in the twenty-first century is the break-up of the state" (Ma 2012). Ma forcefully asserts that by uncritically inheriting the "nationality theory" (*minzu lilun*) of the former Soviet Union and its Comintern advisers, the CCP created the three "prerequisite conditions" for ethnic-based disintegration, each of which directly contributed to the collapse of the USSR and Yugoslavia: (1) the existence of strong ethnic consciousness, which leads ethnic groups to reject their inclusion within a unified nation-state; (2) the existence of separately administered territories that ethnic groups considered their homeland; and (3) the existence of an ethnic leadership, namely a group of political and cultural elites capable of initiating and leading an independence movement.

Arguments like these, which place the PRC at the abyss of national disintegration, are ubiquitous in contemporary China, and foundational assumptions for those who argue for an urgent reorientation of CCP policies (Leibold 2013b; Elliot 2015; Sautman 2010). In 2011, for example, the ethnic establishment was rocked when influential Qinghua public intellectual Hu Angang used the specter of Soviet-style collapse to argue for a "second generation of ethnic policies," a set of measures that would place less emphasis on ethnic identification and more time on promoting interethnic "contact, exchange, and fusion" (jiaowang jialiu jiaorong) (Hu and Hu 2011). Shortly thereafter, one of the CCP's leading spokesmen on ethnic policy, the then executive director of the United Front Department, Zhu Weiqun, made a similar (albeit more carefully and cautiously worded) appeal for a policy rethink (Zhu 2012).

The reasons for this shift in thinking are complex, but interethnic conflict clearly stokes long-standing fears of a Soviet-style collapse. As Wang Shaoguang has argued, "within the inner most soul of the Chinese people, there exists an extraordinary fear of state dismemberment" (Wang 2002), a phobia with deep historical and psychological roots in Chinese intellectual thought. For Dr. Sun Yat-sen the fragility of state unity was inherent in the Chinese character, what he identified as the clannish nature of the Chinese people (literally, "a sheet of loose sand"), which necessitated a strong party-state to smelt this shifting sand into a firm and solid "plate of steel": what Sun (1924) praised as the "smelting together in the same furnace."[11]

Yet, with few exceptions,[12] most Western experts think a Soviet-style implosion of PRC territory is highly unlikely. As David Shambaugh (2008) puts it, "no Chinese government could tolerate or would grant independence to peripheral provinces," and any attempts by ethnic leaders in Xinjiang or Tibet to break away from China would be swiftly met with overwhelming military force (see also Mackerras 2006; Dreyer 2000). Furthermore, important institutional and demographic factors are in play that significantly reduce the probability of ethnic-based disintegration in China. First, unlike the USSR and Yugoslavia, the early leaders of the PRC rejected a federalist model, with Premier Zhou Enlai arguing that the unique size of the Han majority and the long history of ethnic intermingling rendered federalism inappropriate for the PRC. Thus, unlike these two former unions there is no institutional or legal basis for autonomous units to secede from the PRC. In fact, the PRC Constitution and the 2005 Anti-secession Law explicitly outlaw such attempts. Second, the PRC possesses one of the world's largest ethnic majorities. Ethnic Russians made up only 45 percent of the USSR and Serbs 36 percent of Yugoslavia, whereas 91.5 percent of China's roughly 1.3 billion people officially constitute a single Han super-majority (Leibold 2007; Connor 1984). As Barry Sautman (2010, 91) has convincingly argued, the role of ethnic tensions and ethnic nationalism in the collapse of the USSR has been misconceived and overstated by Chinese scholars, and the above differences mean that "China will not collapse due to separatism; rather separation can only occur if China's central government collapses," and here I would add that any successor state (even a weak one) would continue to view territorial integrity as an enduring priority and would quickly mobilize considerable resources to counter any secessionist movement.

## The Structural Ecology of Interethnic Relations in the PRC

At present, interethnic relations in China, on the whole, are relatively healthy yet unstable. Despite intermittent and patchy violence, relations between China's officially recognized ethnic groups are generally amiable on the surface, with far more examples of interethnic cooperation across the country than conflict. Yet, that said, deep-rooted bigotry, misunderstandings, and distrust in certain segments of the minority and majority communities alike (among other problems, chiefly poor governance, heavy-handed policing, and a weak legal system) engender subterranean strains that under the right conditions can flare into open discord and even bloodshed. At present, I would argue, this "wobbling pivot" of ethnic relations rests on three interrelated conditions of minority subjectivity: (1) enhanced livelihood and ethnic consciousness; (2) ethnic-based segregation and securitization; and (3) spatial and demographic marginality, with each of these structural fulcrums holding the seeds for deterioration should the sociopolitical environment shift suddenly, especially in the form of increased marketization or the rapid decay of party-state capacities. The result is a shaky equilibrium that reflects the deeper fragility of the party-state system as identified by Susan Shirk, David Shambaugh, and others (Shirk 2007).[13]

## ENHANCED LIVELIHOOD AND ETHNIC CONSCIOUSNESS

The PRC's current policies have resulted in significant improvements in the livelihood of most Chinese minorities, with increased social and economic mobility, as well as circumscribed cultural freedoms and autonomous spaces for the development of ethnic consciousness and belonging. Since Jiang Zemin launched the Great Western Development Program in 2000, the state has pumped massive resources into developing the infrastructure and economic capacities of the ethnic frontier, as well as targeting poverty-stricken frontier communities through its ongoing Poverty Alleviation Program. The TAR, for example, has received more than US$14 billion in financial subsidies since its establishment in 1965, with around 90 percent of its annual budget coming from Beijing (Wang 2008; Li 2014). Despite some obvious shortcomings—corruption, wasted and misdirected resources, increased income inequality, top-down controls, and environmental degradation, among others (Naughton 2004; Hillman 2014)—minority residents as a whole are better fed, clothed, educated, and far healthier than their 1980s counterparts. According to government statistics, the number of impoverished people in minority areas decreased from some 40 million in 1985 to 5.59 million in 2013, although the rate of decline has slowed in recent years.[14]

Most minority regions have also seen significant growth in per capita gross domestic product (GDP) and income levels. Inner Mongolia, for example, has been China's fastest growing region over the last decade, expanding at an average of 17 percent per annum between 2001 and 2011 thanks to a mining boom and preferential state policies (*Economist* 2012). Xinjiang and Tibet are not far behind, growing at 12 percent each in 2012 and have experienced double-digit growth for more than two decades now (Yao 2013). Many of these frontier regions have benefited significantly from domestic and international tourism (Hillman 2003, 2009), with the number of tourists visiting Tibet, for example, reaching nearly thirteen million and contributing US$2.68 billion in revenue to the local economy in 2013 (Xinhua 2014b; Callick 2014). In one of China's poorest regions in southern Yunnan, to take another example, Akha (Hani in Chinese) and Dai minority farmers are now some of the wealthiest residents, benefiting greatly from state policies that facilitated tea and rubber cultivation in Xishuangbanna, with some households now earning in excess of US$80,000 per year, well above the US$4,856 average rural income in 2010 (Sturgeon 2012, 123).

State policies have also produced a cohort of minority elites, including more than 5.5 million ethnic minority party members, who not only benefit from the current system but also lend it a degree of stability. By participating in what Susan McCarthy (2009) identifies as diverse forms of self-defined "citizenship practices," many minorities (especially those in southern China) are actively contributing to national cohesion and the construction of an inclusive, multicultural China, while other co-opted minority elites act as a new "ethnic aristocracy" shoring up CCP rule in frontier regions.

Yet, at the same time, other ethnic minorities, especially those in rural and remote regions, have slipped further into poverty and marginality as they struggle to adapt to market forces and state policies that encourage bilingualism, secularism, and integration. In sharp contrast this minority underclass (a sort of *lumpen-proletariat* in Marxist terms) functions as a ready-made accelerant for ethnic conflict, especially among those who are either radicalized ideologically, forced onto the run, or move freely into urban areas in search of new opportunities that are often difficult to find. There are unconfirmed reports that the 2009 violence in Urumqi was precipitated by the arrival of rural migrants from southern Xinjiang,[15] which should not surprise us considering Uyghur farmers earn twenty times less than Han energy sector workers in Xinjiang (Liu 2010, 29). The 2008 Shaoguan riots in Guangzhou were sparked by the arrival of more than eight hundred Uyghur workers from rural Shufu County, near Kashgar (RFA 2010), while the perpetrators of the 2014 Kunming attack appear to have been among the more than one hundred Uyghurs who fled Hanerik Township (Ch. *Han'airike*), in southern Xinjiang, after a clash with security forces (*East by Southeast* 2014). Market reforms, as Zang Xiaowei (2011) and Reza Hasmath (2012) have demonstrated, segment the urban labor market along ethnic lines and thus accentuate the income disparity in the growing private sector. Uyghur workers in Urumqi, for example, were found to earn 52 percent less than Han workers in a 2005 survey, and as Tyler Harlan's chapter in this volume demonstrates, Uyghur entrepreneurs struggle to break out of niche segments of the economy and into more lucrative areas dominated by the Han majority.

Current policies, including the system of regional ethnic autonomy and minzu-based affirmative action, have reinforced ethnic boundaries. State-defined categories are not only stamped on one's personal ID card but are also increasingly part of daily life in China. As a result, cross-cultural interactions are easily "ethnicized," with a complex matrix of discursive stereotypes employed by Han when contrasting the "exotic," "docile," and "feminine" minorities of the southwest with the "barbaric," "restive," and "masculine" minorities of the formally nomadic northwest steppe (McCarthy 2009). Negative images of "knife-wielding" Tibetan and Uyghur "savages" engender fear and even hatred among many Han residents, and when minorities find themselves in coastal cities through either "labor-export" programs (laowu paichu), inland schooling (neidiban), or more spontaneous forms of migration, heightened ethnic prejudices and consciousness are inevitable and conflict predictable.

Despite admirable efforts to boost minority livelihood, state policies have been far less successful in cultivating a sense of collective, national belonging among some of China's ethnic minority communities, particularly the Uyghurs and Tibetans, and to a lesser extent the Hui and Mongols. In the case of the first three, religion is an obvious factor, with the party-state's restrictions on (and at times outright hostility toward) religious practices alienating many within these communities. Using survey data, Tang Wenfang and He Gaochao (2010) argue that most Chinese minorities (or at least those surveyed) exhibit a strong sense of national belonging and patriotism,[16] yet we are again faced with the questionable reliability of these and other attempts to survey public opinion on sensitive issues of ethnic and national identity. The full picture is clearly complex, with pockets of belonging and alienation among individuals within different minority communities, making any generalizations highly problematic. Yet the classification of ethnic communities into fifty-six distinct ethnic categories, and the larger "dual structure" (eryuan jiegou) that divides Chinese society into minority and majority segments (Ma 2012, 168–91), works against a shared sense of collective citizenship, and it increases the like-

lihood that communal tensions and violence are "ethnicized" by participants, the party-state, and outside observers (Lieberman and Singh 2012).

## SEGREGATION AND SECURITIZATION

The fragile stability of interethnic relations in the PRC is built on a complex
system of social controls, with overlapping institutional structures ensuring that ethnic groups remain both segregated and closely monitored.
The system of regional ethnic autonomy and the "household registration"
(*hukou*) system, for example, have greatly restricted mobility. The limited
contact among groups is one obvious but often overlooked deterrent to
conflict, although it also prevents the sort of daily interactions that could
foster tolerance and even acceptance of ethnocultural differences in the
long run. This is particularly evident in rural Tibet and Xinjiang but is also
a feature of urban cities and can be seen in the creation of ethnic enclaves,
as well as segregated schools and, to a lesser extent, work units.

One statistical indicator of ethnic-based residential segregation is the
"dissimilarity index" (D-Index), which measures the residential evenness
of two ethnic groups across spatial units by determining the percentage of
people from one ethnic group that would have to move to another area in
order to achieve parity. Based on the 2010 census, the average D-value for
minority groups in China was 87.00 at provincial scale, with D-values as
high as 98.60 and 88.38 for the Uyghurs and Tibetans respectively (Leibold
and Deng, forthcoming). While this represents a decline from a 97 average value in 1982, ethnic residential segregation remains extremely high
in China when compared to the 59.10 D-value for black-white segregation
and 48.50 value for Hispanic-white segregation across major US cities in
2010, or the 23.40 value for Malays in Chinese-dominated Singapore in
2000 (Logan and Stults 2006).

Furthermore, the percentage of non-Han minorities remains extremely
low in major metropolitan centers like Beijing (4.1 percent), Shanghai
(0.45 percent), Guangzhou (1.35 percent), Wuhan (0.7 percent), Chongqing
(6.3 percent), and Tianjin (2.67 percent). In frontier cities minority and
majority communities live in highly segregated neighborhoods and often
attend segregated schools. For example, a recent study found extremely
limited contact between Han and Tibetan residents of Lhasa with highly

divided residences, schools, work units, and even entertainment venues (Ma 2011, 327–56). Other studies have identified a similar pattern between Uyghur and Han residents of Urumqi and other Xinjiang cities, with Linda Tsung discovering not only ethnically segregated classes but playgrounds, cafeterias, and assemblies in a supposedly integrated, bilingual school in Aksu City (Tsung 2014). In the wake of the Lhasa and Urumqi riots, local officials attempted to seal off the two cities using military-style checkpoints, limiting entry to Han visitors/tourists and those minority migrants with proper authorization, while Uyghur and Tibetan travelers are commonly refused accommodation and even transport when they travel to China proper (Woeser 2012; Hillman 2014).

Interethnic marriage has long been an important indicator of social cohesion and national integration, and here figures for China also reveal a pattern of segregation. Although interethnic marriage is common among some smaller minority communities,[17] only 3.2 percent of PRC citizens live in a biethnic household, compared to more than 8 percent in the United States (Li 2004; Wang 2012). According to 2000 census figures, only 1.05 percent of Uyghur, 1.58 percent of Han, and 7.71 percent of Tibetan households were biethnic, whereas 15 percent of all new marriages in the United States in 2008 were interracial, as were 20.2 percent of marriages in Singapore during 2010 (Saw 2012, 117). In their 2007 survey Tang and He (2010, 31–33) found strong disapproval of interethnic and interracial marriages, especially among the poorly educated, low-income Uyghur and Kazak students they questioned. As I mentioned earlier, this low level of integration mitigates ethnic conflict in the short term while reinforcing ethnic consciousness and the potential for violent clashes in the long run.

At present, the party-state ensures that any interethnic conflict is met with overwhelming force. Over the last decade the state has committed unprecedented resources to lock down, control, and in some cases brutally crush activities that they deem harmful to ethnic harmony and social stability. In 2012 China increased its public security budget by 11.5 percent and now spends more on domestic security (US$111 billion) than it does on national defense (US$106 billion) (Reuters 2012). Furthermore, this figure, David Shambaugh (2013, 328) points out, does not include funds allocated for the People's Armed Police, Ministry of State Security, and People's Armed Militia, meaning that "China's total internal security budget could plausibly be in the neighborhood of $300 billion!" While these measures might be effective in the short term, they tend to legitimize and even encourage extrajudicial punishment and violence that Chen Xi argues could ultimately undermine CCP rule (Chen 2013).

Much of this security money finds its way into the PRC's frontier regions, where local officials have dramatically increased "stability maintenance" measures in the wake of the 2008–9 ethnic riots. Since 2009 Xinjiang's public security budget has increased by more than 300 percent (reaching US$1.6 billion in 2013), with seventeen thousand surveillance cameras installed in Urumqi alone, where security officials now claim "seamless" coverage (Li 2014). In Urumqi, Lhasa, and other frontier cities authorities are rolling out a high-tech "grid management system" (*wanggehua guanli*), which has seen the establishment of tens of thousands of street-corner policing billets, "red armband" civilian patrols, and gated residential blocks (Human Rights Watch 2013a; Wu 2012). In response to the spate of Tibetan self-immolations, security officials have increased surveillance, arbitrary detentions, collective punishment, and harsh prison sentences for abettors and their families (Wong 2013; Barnett 2012). In Aba Prefecture, one of the centers of self-immolation, public security funding increased by a whopping 619 percent between 2002 and 2009, with Human Rights Watch calculating the prefecture spent US$124 per person on public security in 2009. This figure is more than double the amount spent in the regional capital of Chengdu (Human Rights Watch 2011). It is estimated that thirteen out of every one hundred dollars in the Kashgar region is spent on public security, while the XUAR spent US$73 per person on public security in 2013 (Li 2014). Finally, nearly a quarter of a million high-level party cadres have been or are in the process of being billeted in villages and communities across Tibet and Xinjiang. During their yearlong stints, these "send-down" officials are tasked with conducting door-to-door inspections, gathering detailed personal information, carrying out political reeducation work, and nipping (so it is hoped) any potential security breeches in the bud.[18]

## SPATIAL AND DEMOGRAPHIC MARGINALITY

The spatial and demographic structure of ethnicity in the PRC also limits the scope of conflict, at least as it relates to China's officially recognized minzu groups. To the extent that one can speak of a "minzu/ethnic crisis" in the PRC today, this predicament is confined to a handful of areas, with pockets of Uyghur-Han-Hui, Hui-Han, and Tibet-Han-Hui enmity contrasting significantly with the largely amicable relations between the Han majority and the more than thirty-three million ethnic minorities in southern provinces like Yunnan and Guangxi. As Colin Mackerras (2010, 229) reminds us, "Most members of minority ethnic groups are reasonably well integrated with the Han majority and enjoy relations with them that are not necessarily any more rancorous than the Han have with one another," and as a result, "there is no crisis of legitimacy on the grounds of ethnicity in most of the ethnic areas." Past experience demonstrates that relations are likely to be most strained in areas where minority and majority communities live in close proximity and directly compete for resources, such as urban areas in Qinghai, Xinjiang, Inner Mongolia, and western Gansu and Sichuan provinces, and the ethnic-based segregation and state security posture discussed above helps to limit open conflict in many of these regions.

Despite its many important contributions, the rise of minority or ethnic studies as a distinct subdiscipline of sinology has helped to obscure the fundamental incommensurability of minority and majority communities in the PRC.[19] The size of the minority population (fewer than 120 million) not only pales in significance to the more than one billion people officially registered as Han by the party-state, but a range of other factors—such as the institutional fragmentation of ethnocultural groups (each with their own history, culture, customs, and minzu); intraethnocultural divisions along class, urban/rural, education, religion, language, and other lines; and the scattered and unequal distribution of minority communities across the PRC's geobody—impose significant limitations on the importance and influence of ethnic relations to Chinese society and politics as a whole. In the end those minorities that actively resist the current system or seek to undermine Han rule and power are extremely few and largely impotent in the face of overwhelming Han/state hegemony.

In his two massive tomes on ethnic conflict Donald Horowitz (2000, 2002) notes that interethnic violence is endemic to "severely divided societies" with poor, weak, or divided systems of governance. For all its troubles, this is clearly not one of the PRC's problems. Not surprisingly, Horowitz fails to mention China and instead draws his numerous examples from India, Nigeria, Indonesia, Malaysia, Burma, Sri Lanka, and other countries. In fact, the strong authoritarian controls exhibited by the Han-dominated party-state renders ethnic strife anomalous, and when viewed comparatively, the size of China's majority community (at least in state terms) helps to explain many aspects of its current ethnic stability.

Social scientists have employed various empirical measures of ethnic and cultural diversity, which in general attempt to quantify the probability of two randomly selected individuals belonging to the same ethnocultural group across areal units (usually the nation) (Fearon 2003; Alesina et al. 2003; Montalvo and Reynal-Querol 2005; Esteban et al. 2012). Despite some significant hurdles relating to taxonomy and categories of analysis, China exhibits a high level of relative homogeneity in each of these models. For example, the countries discussed by Horowitz exhibit significantly higher rates of "ethnic fractionalization" and "cultural diversity," and this is also the case with the former USSR and Yugoslavia (see table 9.1). In fact, based on James Fearon's (2003, 215–19) analysis, China ranks 138 out of the 160 countries analyzed for ethnocultural heterogeneity, with its fractionalization (0.154) and cultural diversity (0.154) rates well below the averages (.480 and .290) for all countries surveyed.

Yet as other researchers have pointed out (Montalvo and Reynal-Querol 2005; Fuller et al. 2000), there is no direct, one-to-one correlation between diversity and conflict, as these types of empirical models tell us little about

**TABLE 9.1**  Comparative Ethnocultural Diversity by County

| Rank | Country | Ethnic Fractionalization Index | Cultural Diversity Index |
|---|---|---|---|
| 1 | Papua New Guinea | 1.000 | — |
| 8 | South Africa | 0.880 | 0.530 |
| 17 | India | 0.811 | 0.667 |
| 18 | Nigeria | 0.805 | 0.660 |
| 19 | Yugoslavia (1943–92) | 0.801 | 0.385 |
| 24 | Indonesia | 0.766 | 0.522 |
| 37 | USSR (1922–91) | 0.711 | 0.596 |
| 59 | Malaysia | 0.596 | 0.564 |
| 75 | Burma | 0.522 | 0.419 |
| 93 | Sri Lanka | 0.428 | 0.386 |
| 138 | China | 0.154 | 0.154 |

*Source:* Fearon (2003, 215–19).

social distance, ethnic cohesion, state policies, and the larger cultural and historical context. Furthermore, shifts in the spatial scale have dramatic effects on ethnic fractionalization, with the index varying from .050 along coastal China to as high as .400 in Xinjiang and Qinghai provinces (Dincer and Wang 2011). Seeking a more integrated analytical approach for assessing "ethnic conflict potential," a team of researchers led by University of Hawaii geographer Gary Fuller and colleagues (2002) developed a model that includes a range of empirical and contextual factors. When analyzing first Southeast Asia and then China, they found in 2002 that "the potential for seriously disruptive [ethnic] violence is relatively low in China over the short time horizon," and they conclude that "our analysis probably errs on the side of being overly, rather than less, sensitive to conflict potential" (Fuller et al. 2002, 608–9). Although they identify five "ethnic fracture zones" in China, with the potential for violence identified as the most serious in Xinjiang, conflict was deemed far more likely in Indonesia and Malaysia. In fact, the Han majority conceivably represents a far greater "ethnic threat" to China than its minorities, either through their own ethnolinguistic and regional divisions or the high levels of dissatisfaction with current ethnic policies among some segments of the Han population, especially in frontier regions like Xinjiang (Mullaney et al. 2012; Leibold, 2010, Joniak-Lüthi 2013; Côté 2011).[20]

Increased media coverage and broader academic interest means that (thankfully) we know much more about ethnic relations in China today than we did in the past. Yet any too-narrow focus on interethnic conflict and violence can overshadow the robustness of most social encounters and, perhaps more important, cloud the ways in which we think about and analyze the complex sociopolitical milieu of ethnic relations in China's past and present. Managed diversity is the norm in China today. A sort of museum-style multiculturalism celebrates the country's ethnocultural diversity in carefully staged and standardized performances while regulating real-world contacts and conflicts through authoritarian controls—in other words, rendition diversity and policed uniformity.

As the chapters of this volume make perfectly clear, pockets of Xinjiang and Tibetan society are experiencing a troubling spate of interethnic violence at present, with deep-rooted mistrust and alienation marring relations between the Han majority and many Uyghur and Tibet minorities, in particular, which at times boils over into deadly ethnic clashes. The extent of this conflict is impossible to quantify, yet shifting local, national, and global conditions are altering the pattern. First, in recent years this violence has flowed out of once-isolated and remote communities and into large cities like Lhasa and Urumqi as a result of increased urbanization and migration; second, what in the past was largely a frontier problem has now spread across China and even national borders, with (at times violent) demonstrations against China's ethnic policies occurring in cities across the globe and once unthinkable terror attacks unnerving inland Chinese cities like Beijing, Kunming, and Guangzhou; and finally, the targets of ethnic-imbued violence are also shifting and now include innocent civilians gathered in public places like train stations and markets, in addition to the usual symbols of the party-state such as police stations, government buildings, and security forces. As China continues to open to global and market forces, interethnic contact and competition are inevitable and ethnic violence unavoidable. Yet at present the scale of this unrest poses little immediate threat to CCP rule or the territorial integrity of the PRC.

In her pathbreaking study on ethnic conflict and violence in turn-of-the-century America, Susan Olzak (1992) demonstrates how rapid socioeconomic change (including both economic expansion and contraction) increases ethnic intercourse, rivalry, and conflict. During heightened periods of ethnic-based migration, mobility, and contact, the salience of ethnic boundaries sharpens, which in turn can ignite spontaneous forms of ethnic strife. In explaining episodes of ethnic collective action, Olzak argues that inequality and cultural marginality are less likely to produce violent clashes than naked market competition in the absence of strong state intervention. As she convincingly demonstrates, "*ethnic conflicts and protests erupt when ethnic inequalities and racially ordered systems begin to break down*" (3). One important indicator of collapse, Donald Horowitz (2002, 326) reminds us, is policy uncertainty: "The vast majority of [ethnic] riots occur when aggressors conclude that ethnic politics is dangerously in flux, that they are likely to be able to use violence without adverse consequences to themselves, and that they are thoroughly warranted in their action."

For China this suggests that any change in the status quo—such as a new round of social and economic reforms, increased transnational ties, political liberalization, and the weakening or collapse of CCP authority—would erode existing demographic, spatial, and security controls and lead to increased ethnic conflict and violence. The implications here are sobering. In spite of widespread domestic and international criticism of current ethnic policies, efforts to either increase minority autonomy or strengthen national integration will likely heighten ethnic competition, enmity, and conflict. And while any resulting violence would unlikely tear "China" asunder, the sheer size of its ethnic communities could result in significant bloodshed and loss of life. It would seem that a strong and stable party-state is more conducive to short-term interethnic harmony than an unstable, changing, or democratizing China.

As a result the options are stark: continue with targeted ethnic repression and segregation through the state's monopoly on the legitimate use of violence, or loosen state controls and facilitate ethnic mobility and competition. The former path might keep a lid on tensions at present, but for how long? The latter path will increase ethnic violence over the short-to-medium term, with the (possibly elusive) goal of greater social cohesion and national belonging in the long term. Ironically, the relative lack of interethnic conflict today could ultimately prove detrimental to the long-term sustainability of ethnocultural diversity in China, as the current system exhibits obvious weaknesses in interethnic tolerance, trust, and understanding, as well as the long-term governance, rule of law, and conflict-management strategies necessary for a healthy pluralism.

## Notes

I would like to thank the participants of the ANU/Columbia Workshop on Ethnic Conflict in Western China, where this chapter was first presented, for their helpful feedback on my approach, material, and argument. In particular, Tom Cliff, Gardner Bovingdon, and Ben Hillman each provided helpful written comments on earlier drafts. I would also like to thank Barry Sautman, Colin Mackerras, Madlen Kobi, Agnieszka Joniak-Luthi, Tim Grose, and Enze Han for additional comments and corrections.

1. *Minzu* is a deeply polysemic term that was used to gloss a range of rather distinct concepts in English (race, nation, people, ethnic group, and nationality) throughout twentieth-century China. Many authors prefer to leave it untranslated, as I have done in the past, but for the sake of clarity in this chapter I will gloss *minzu* as "ethnicity" or "ethnic group" when it clearly refers to one of China's fifty-six officially recognized minzu groups and as "nation" when referring to the Chinese nation as a collective identity, as in the term *zhonghua minzu*. Individual minzu groups used to be referred to as "nationalities" in English but are increasingly termed ethnic groups today.

2. See also Cheng (2008). In an interesting dissenting view Louisa Greve (2013) argues that China's "troubled periphery" actually "strengthen[s] rather than weaken[s] the country's authoritarian regime" (73).

3. Olzak (1992, 8–9) defines ethnic conflict as "a confrontation between members of two or more ethnic groups" and ethnic protest as a demonstration of public grievance by an ethnic group that "has the general public or some office of government as its audience."

4. For a discussion of one of these incidents, the May 2013 Ghost Street melee in Beijing, see Leibold (2013a).

5. A summary of the report posted on the newspaper's website does not provide an absolute number of such incidents in 2012—in fact the Ministry of Public Security has not issued any official figures on mass incidents since 2005—but I have used the figure of 180,000 provided by Qinghua University professor Sun Liping for 2010 as a baseline to arrive at the number of incidents caused by ethnic conflict and involving ethnic minorities. See Pomfret (2011).

6. See also Bovingdon's (2010) discussion of the "elasticity of official numbers" as it relates to unrest in Xinjiang.

7. The Internet's unique archiving capacity also means that this imagery is preserved and can be easily recalled at anytime, with numerous videos of the Lhasa, Shaoguan, and Urumqi riots available on YouTube.com, as well as news aggregating sites like zonaeuropa.com, and to a lesser extent Chinese video sharing sites like youku.com.

8. Justin Hastings (2011) arrives at a similar conclusion while stressing the role of government policies and the political geography of Xinjiang in this decline.

9. See also Brukaker (2006).

10. For a summary of these positions see Shambaugh (2008); and Zhou (2010).

11. For a recent use of these two metaphors see Xiang (2012).

12. Ross Terrill (2003) argues, for example, that it is "quite likely" that the PRC will eventually follow the USSR in an "involuntary breakup," asserting that a totalitarian and anachronistic Chinese state is incapable of dealing with multiple crises.

13. I borrow the "wobbling pivot" metaphor from Pamela Kyle Crossley (2010), who provides a historical survey of this fragility across the nineteenth and twentieth centuries.

14. Over the last five years the number declined only from 7.7 million in 2008 to 5.59 in 2013. See Information Office of the State Council (2009); and Xinhua (2014).

15. Millward (2009, 351) writes: "Both Urumchi Uyghurs and official PRC sources also say that in the days prior to the demonstration, many Uyghurs from other parts of the region, especially southern Xinjiang, came to the city."

16. For some of the challenges associated with survey data in Xinjiang see Yee (2005).

17. Wei Xing (2007) found high rates of ethnic exogamy among the Yi (81.82 percent), Bai (72.48 percent), and Hui (50.32 percent) communities in Kunming

during the 1980s, and Wang Junmin (Tang and He 2010) found high rates of interethnic marriage among the Han (23 percent), Mongol (78 percent), Manchu (99 percent), and Hui (33 percent) citizens living in Hohhot in 1994–95.

18. A 2011–14 campaign in Tibet saw twenty thousand officials in more than five thousand work teams spend yearlong stints in local communities at a cost of US$227 million, while Xinjiang initiated a similar campaign in early 2013 that will eventually see two hundred thousand cadres embedded in local villages and communities at an estimated cost of US$692 million. "In order to achieve complete grassroot[s] coverage," Xinjiang Party Secretary Zhang Chunxian stressed when outlining the campaign's objectives and key requirements, "[we must] thoroughly enter and garrison [Xinjiang society] in order that no blank spaces are left behind." See Human Rights Watch (2013b); and *Xinjiang Daily* (2014).

19. Dreyer (1976, 3–4) was one of the first scholars to stress the strategic importance of the ethnic minorities, highlighting their distribution over 60 percent of PRC territory, much of it resource rich and strategic border regions and, more recently, important sources of domestic and international tourism. See Dreyer (2006) for her most recent articulation of this position. One can find similar statements about the ethnic minorities' "significance beyond their numbers" in the scholarship of Dru Gladney, Stevan Harrell, Colin Mackerras, and many others, including some of my own writings. Yet, when viewed comparatively, leading social scientists like Ernest Gellner, Eric Hobsbawm, Jared Diamond, and others have uniformly stressed China's unique ethnic and cultural homogeneity. This is misleading given the rich linguistic and cultural diversity among those classified as "Han," with a great deal of intra-Han conflict throughout the modern period, including intense struggles over land and other issues between the Hakka and Cantonese natives of Guangdong. But there are important aspects of Chinese society (its written language being just one important example) that engender a high level of cultural and social cohesiveness that can easily be overlooked.

20. Tom Cliff (2012) demonstrates convincingly that the removal of longtime Xinjiang party secretary Wang Lequan was due to Han discontent following the Urumqi riot and argues that the "Han problem" is a far more serious challenge to CCP rule in Xinjiang than the Uyghurs and other minorities.

## References

Abbott, Jason. 2011. "China's Ethnic Problem: Pandora's Box or Powder Keg?" *Durian*, August 1. www.thedurian.org/2011/08/chinas-ethnic-problem-pandoras-box-or.html.

Adilijiang and Abulaiti. 2012. "Shaoshu minzu diqu tufa gonggong shijian shili qianxi" (Analysis of the governing of public emergency events in the minorities concentrated area). *Heilongjiang minzu congkan* 129:27–33.

AFP. 2009. "China Denies Government Policy Reason for Ürümqi Riots." *AFP*, July 21. www.channelnewsasia.com/stories/afp_asiapacific/view/443778/1/.html.

——. 2013. "China Media: Nearly 200 'Terrorist' Attacks in Xinjiang." *Malay Mail*, Nov. 25. www.themalaymailonline.com/world/article/china-media-nearly-200-terrorist-attacks-in-xinjiang.

Alesina, Alberto, Arnaud Devleeschauwer, William Easterly, Sergio Kurlat, and Romain Wacziarg. 2003. "Fractionalization." *Journal of Economic Growth* 8: 155–94.

Barnett, Robert. 2012. "Political Self-Immolation in Tibet: Causes and Influences." *Revue d'études tibétaines* 25 (Dec.): 41–63.

Bequelin, Nicholas. 2012. "Ethnic Unrest in China: The View from Beijing." Lecture at the Weatherhead East Asian Institute, Columbia University, Sept. 12. https://itunes.apple.com/us/itunes-u/weatherhead-east-asian-institute/id534934901.

Bovingdon, Gardner. 2010. *The Uyghurs*. New York: Columbia University Press.

Brady, Anne-Marie. 2012a. "Ethnicity and the State in Contemporary China." *Journal of Current Chinese Affairs* 41 (4): 3–9.

——. 2012b. "'We Are All Part of the Same Family.'" *Journal of Current Chinese Affairs* 41 (4): 159–81.

Brown, Kerry. 2007. "The Cultural Revolution in Inner Mongolia, 1967–1969." *Asian Affairs* 38 (2): 173–87.

Brukaker, Rogers. 2006. *Ethnicity Without Groups*. Cambridge, MA: Harvard University Press.

Callick, Rowan. 2014. "China Claims to Have Tamed Tibet with a Velvet Glove, Not an Iron Fist." *Australian Magazine*, May 3. www.theaustralian.com.au/news/features/china-claims-to-have-tamed-tibet-with-a-velvet-glove-not-an-iron-fist/story-e6frg8h6-1226902472282.

Chen Fang. 2012. "Xiangba Pingcuo" (Qiangba Puncog). *Huangfeng wang*, March 28. http://news.qq.com/a/20120328/000758_4.htm.

Chen Xi. 2013. "The Rising Cost of Stability." *Journal of Democracy* 24 (1): 57–64.

Cheng Li. 2008. "Ethnic Minority Elites in China's Party-State Leadership: An Empirical Assessment." *China Leadership Monitor* 25:1–13.

ChinaFile. 2014. "Are Ethnic Tensions on the Rise in China?" *ChinaFile*, Feb. 13. www.chinafile.com/are-ethnic-tensions-rise-china.

Cliff, Thomas. 2012. "The Partnership of Stability in Xinjiang." *China Journal* 68 (July): 79–105.

Connor, Walker. 1984. *The National Question in Marxist-Leninist Theory and Strategy*. Princeton, NJ: Princeton University Press.

Côté, Isabelle. 2011. "Political Mobilization of a Regional Minority: Han Chinese Settlers in Xinjiang." *Ethnic and Racial Studies* 34 (11): 1–19.

Crossley, Pamela Kyle. 2010. *The Wobbling Pivot*. London: Wiley-Blackwell.

Dincer, Oguzhan, and Fan Wang. 2011. "Ethnic Diversity and Economic Growth in China." *Journal of Policy Reform* 14 (1): 1–10.

Dreyer, June Teufel. 1976. *China's Forty Millions: Minority Nationalities and National Integration in the People's Republic of China.* Cambridge, MA: Harvard University Press.

——. 2000. "The Potential for Instability in Minority Regions." In *Is China Unstable?* edited by David Shambaugh, 125–42. Armonk, NY: M. E. Sharpe.

——. 2006. "Ethnic Minorities and National Integration." In *China's Political System: Modernization and Tradition.* 5th edition. New York: Pearson Longman.

*East by Southeast.* 2014. "The Kunming Train Station Attack: A Hypothesis." *East by Southeast,* March 9. www.eastbysoutheast.com/kunming-train-station-attack-hypothesis/.

*Economist.* 2012. "Inner Mongolia: Little Hu and the Mining of the Grasslands." *Economist,* July 14. www.economist.com/node/21558605.

Elliott, Mark. 2015. "The Case of the Missing Indigene." *China Journal* 73 (Feb.): 1–28.

Esteban, Joan, Laura Mayoral, and Debraj Ray. 2012. "Ethnicity and Conflict: Theory and Facts." *Science* 336:858–65.

Fearon, James. 2003. "Ethnic and Cultural Diversity by Country." *Journal of Economic Growth* 8:195–219.

Freeman, Carla. 2012. "From 'Blood Transfusion' to 'Harmonious Development.'" *Journal of Current Chinese Affairs* 41 (4): 11–44.

Freeman, Will. 2010. "The Accuracy of China's 'Mass Incidents.'" *Financial Times,* March 2. www.ft.com/cms/s/0/9ee6fa64-25b5-11df-9bd3-00144feab49a.html.

Fuller, Gary, Alexander Murphy, Mark Ridgley, and Richard Ulack. 2000. "Measuring Potential Ethnic Conflict in Southeast Asia." *Growth and Change* 31 (2): 305–31.

Fuller, Gary, Rebecca Morrison, Alexander Murphy, and Mark Ridgley. 2002. "Potential for Ethnic Conflict in China." *Eurasian Geography and Economics* 43 (8): 583–609.

Gilley, Bruce. 2004. "Against the Concept of Ethnic Conflict." *Third World Quarterly* 25 (6): 1155–66.

Goldkorn, Jeremy. 2013. "Legal Daily Report on Mass Incidents in China in 2012." *Danwei,* Jan. 6. www.danwei.com/a-report-on-mass-incidents-in-china-in-2012.

Goldstein, Melvyn, Ben Jiao, and Tanzen Lhundrup. 2009. *On the Cultural Revolution in Tibet: The Nyemo Incident of 1969.* Berkeley: University of California Press.

Greve, Louisa. 2013. "The Troubled Periphery." *Journal of Democracy* 24 (1): 73–78.

Hao Yufan and Liu Weihua. 2012. "Xinjiang: Increasing Pain in the Heart of China's Borderland." *Journal of Contemporary China* 21 (74): 205–25.

Hasmath, Reza. 2012. "Migration, Labour and the Rise of Ethno-religious Consciousness Among Uyghurs in Urban Xinjiang." *Journal of Sociology* 49:1–15.

Hastings, Justin. 2011. "Charting the Course of Uyghur Unrest." *China Quarterly* 208 (Dec.): 893–912.

Hillman, Ben. 2003. "Paradise under Construction: Minorities, Myths and Modernity in Northwest Yunnan." *Asian Ethnicity* 4 (2): 177–90.

——. 2009. "Ethnic Tourism and Ethnic Politics in Tibetan China." *Harvard Asia Pacific Review* 10 (1): 3–6.

——. 2014. *Patronage and Power: Local State Networks and Party-State Resilience in Rural China*. Stanford: Stanford University Press.

Horowitz, Donald. 2000. *Ethnic Groups in Conflict*. 2nd edition. Berkeley: University of California Press.

——. 2002. *The Deadly Ethnic Riot*. Berkeley: University of California Press.

Hu Angang and Hu Lianhe. 2011. "Dierdai minzu zhengce" (Second generation of ethnic policies). *Xinjiang shifan daxue xuebao (zhexue shehui kexue bao)* 32 (5): 1–13.

Human Rights Watch. 2011. "China: End Crackdown on Tibetan Monasteries." Oct. 12. www.hrw.org/news/2011/10/12/china-end-crackdown-tibetan-monasteries.

——. 2013a. "China: Alarming New Surveillance, Security in Tibet." March 20. www hrw.org/news/2013/03/20/china-alarming-new-surveillance-security-tibet.

——. 2013b. "China: 'Benefit the Masses' Campaign Surveilling Tibetans." June 19. www.hrw.org/news/2013/06/18/china-benefit-masses-campaign-surveilling -tibetans.

Information Office of the State Council. 2009. *China's Ethnic Policy and Common Prosperity and Development of All Ethnic Groups*. www.china.org.cn/government/ whitepaper/node_7078073.htm.

International Campaign for Tibet. 2012. *Storm in the Grasslands: Self-Immolations in Tibet and Chinese Policy*. www.savetibet.org/resource-center/ict-publications/ reports/storm-grasslands-self-immolations-tibet-and-chinese-policy.

Jia Yujiao and Hu Jingbin. 2012. "Woguo minzu diqu qunti xing shijian de guiluxing renshi ji duice jianyi" (Understanding the nature and policy suggestions for mass incidents in minority areas of China). *Guizhou minzu yanjiu* 4:10–16.

Joniak-Lüthi, Agnieszka. 2013. "The Han Minzu, Fragmented Identities, and Ethnicity." *Journal of Asian Studies* 72 (4): 849–71.

Leibold, James. 2007. *Reconfiguring Chinese Nationalism*. New York: Palgrave Macmillan.

——. 2010. "More Than a Category." *China Quarterly* 203:539–59.

——. 2013a. "China's Museum-Style Multiculturalism." *Inside Story*, May 23. http:// inside.org.au/chinas-museum-style-multiculturalism/.

——. 2013b. *Ethnic Policy in the PRC: Is Reform Inevitable?* Honolulu: East-West Center.

Leibold, James, and Danielle Deng. Forthcoming. "Uyghur Residential Segregation and Its Implication in Xinjiang, China." In *Inside Xinjiang: Space, Place and Power in China's Muslim Far Northwest*, edited by Anna Hayes and Michael Clarke. London: Routledge.

Lieberman, Evan, and Prerna Singh. 2012. "The Institutional Origins of Ethnic Violence." *Comparative Politics* 45 (1): 1–24.

Liu Yong. 2010. "An Economic Band-Aid." *China Security* 6 (2): 27–40.

Li Weiao. 2014. "Gonggong anquan, Xinjiang yao hua duoshao qian" (Public security: How much does Xinjiang spend?). *Nanfang zhoumo*, Aug. 28. www.infzm.com/ content/103612.

Li Xiaoxia. 2004. "Zhongguo ge minzu jian zuji hunyin de xianzhuang fenxi" (Analysis of the current state of interethnic marriage among different Chinese ethnic groups). *Renkou yanjiu* 3. www.xjass.com/shx/content/2008-07/30/content_25784.htm.

Logan, John, and Brian Stults. 2010. "The Persistence of Segregation in the Metropolis." *US 2010 Project.* www.s4.brown.edu/us2010/Data/Report/report2.pdf.

Ma Rong. 2011. *Population and Society in Contemporary Tibet.* Hong Kong: Hong Kong University Press.

——. 2012. *Zuqun, minzu yu guojia goujian: Dangdai Zhongguo minzu wenti* (Ethnicity, nationality and nation-building: Ethnic issues in contemporary China). Beijing: Shehui kexue wenxian chubanshe.

Mackerras, Colin. 2006. "Ethnic Minorities." In *Critical Issues in Contemporary China,* edited by Czeslaw Tubilewicz, 167–91. New York: Routledge.

——. 2010. "Tibetans, Uyghurs, and Multinational 'China.'" In *Chinese Politics: State, Society and the Market,* edited by Peter Hays Gries and Stanley Rosen, 222–42. London: Routledge.

McCarthy, Susan K. 2009. *Communist Multiculturalism.* Seattle: University of Washington Press.

Meisels, Greer. 2013. "Lessons Learned in China from the Collapse of the Soviet Union." *China Studies Centre Policy Paper Series* 3. http://sydney.edu.au/china_studies_centre/en/policy-papers/2013/lessons-learned-in-china-from-the-collapse-of-the-soviet-union.shtml.

Millward, James. 2009. "Introduction: Does the 2009 Urumchi Violence Mark a Turning Point?" *Central Asian Survey* 28 (4): 347–60.

Montalvo, Jose, and Marta Reynal-Querol. 2005. "Polarization, Potential Conflict, and Civil Wars." *American Economic Review* 95 (3): 796–816.

Mullaney, Thomas, James Leibold, Stéphane Gros, and Eric Vanden Bussche. 2012. *Critical Han Studies.* Berkeley: University of California Press.

Naughton, Barry. 2004. "Western Development Program." In *Holding China Together,* edited by Barry Naughton and Dali Yang, 253–96. Cambridge: Cambridge University Press.

Olzak, Susan. 1992. *The Dynamics of Ethnic Competition and Conflict.* Stanford: Stanford University Press.

Pomfret, James. 2011. "Tension Simmers in Blockaded China Village After Land Protest." Reuters, Dec. 14. www.reuters.com/article/2011/12/14/us-china-unrest-idUSTRE7BD14U20111214.

Reuters. 2012. "China Domestic Security Spending Rises to $111 Billion." Reuters, March 5. www.reuters.com/article/2012/03/05/us-china-parliament-security-idUSTRE82403J20120305.

RFA. 2010. "Shaoguan, One Year On." *Radio Free Asia,* June 29. www.rfa.org/english/news/uyghur/shaoguan-06292010110913.html.

Sautman, Barry. 2010. "Scaling Back Minority Rights?" *Stanford Journal of International Law* 46:51–120.

Saw Swee-Hock. 2012. *The Population of Singapore.* 3rd ed. Singapore: ISEAS.

Shambaugh, David. 2008. *China's Communist Party*. Berkeley: University of California Press.

———. 2013. *China Goes Global*. Oxford University Press.

Shirk, Susan. 2007. *China: Fragile Superpower*. Oxford: Oxford University Press.

———, ed. 2011. *Changing Media, Changing China*. Oxford: Oxford University Press.

Sun Yat-sen. 1924. "Sanminzhuyi" (Three Principles of the People). In *Sun Zhongshan quanji* (Complete works of Sun Yat-sen). Vol. 5, 185–96. Beijing: Zhonghua shuju.

Sturgeon, Janet. 2012. "The Cultural Politics of Ethnic Identity in Xishuangbanna, China." *Journal of Current Chinese Affairs* 41 (4): 109–31.

Tang Wenfang and He Gaochao. 2010. *Separate but Loyal*. Honolulu: East-West Center.

Terrill, Ross. 2003. *The New Chinese Empire*. Sydney: University of New South Wales Press.

Tsung, Linda. 2014. "Trilingual Education and School Practice in Xinjiang." In *Minority Education in China*, edited by James Leibold and Chen Yangbin, 161–86. Hong Kong: Hong Kong University Press.

Wang Lixiong. 2008. "A True 'Middle Way' Solution to Tibetan Unrest." *WSI China Security* 4 (2): 27–37.

Wang Shaoguang. 2002. "Zhongguo caizheng zhuanyi zhifu de zhengzhi luoji" (The political logic of fiscal transfers in China). *Zhanlüe yu guanli* 3:47–54.

Wang, Wendy. 2012. "The Rise of Intermarriage." *Pew Research Center*, Feb. 16. www .pewsocialtrends.org/2012/02/16/the-rise-of-intermarriage.

Wei Xing. 2007. "Prevalence of Ethnic Intermarriage in Kunming." *Asian Ethnicity* 8 (2): 165–79.

Woeser, Tsering. 2012. "The Moat and Apartheid." International Campaign for Tibet, July 26. www.savetibet.org/the-moat-and-apartheid/.

Wong, Gillian. 2013. "As Tibet Burns, China Makes Arrests, Seizes TVs." Associated Press, Jan. 18. http://news.yahoo.com/tibet-burns-china-makes-arrests-seizes -tvs-074227574.html.

Wu Yang. 2012. "'Sanhua' guanli rang liudong renkou zhaodao jia de ganjue" (The 'three transformation' management system makes migrant communities feel like a family). *Wulumuqi wangbao*, Sept. 20. http://news.xinhuanet.com/ city/2012-09/20/c_123738959.htm.

Xiang Ping. 2012. Zhongguo da luji: Mei you gongchandang, wei shenme bu xing? (The great logic of china: Why we cannot do without the CCP). Beijing: Taihai chubanshe.

Xinhua. 2014a. "Rural Poor Population in Ethnic Minority Areas Falls." *Global Times*, April 21. www.globaltimes.cn/content/855887.shtml.

———. 2014b. "Tibet's Second Railway Line Opens." Xinhuanet, Aug. 15. http://news .xinhuanet.com/english/china/2014-08/15/c_133558915.htm.

*Xinjiang Daily*. 2014. "Zhang Chunxian tongzhi dui geji ganbu shenru jiceng 'fang minqing hui minsheng ju minxin' huodong tichu mingque yaoqiu" (Comrade

Zhang Chunxian puts forward explicit requirement for cadres at every level entering the grassroots as a part of the "Explore the People's Conditions, Benefit the People's Livelihood, and Fuse the People's Sentiments" campaign). *Xinjiang ribao wang*, March 5. www.xjdaily.com.cn/special/2014/06/1027136 .shtml.

Yang Kunfei. 2012. "Minzu quntixing shijian de leixing yanhua yu chongtu ganyu yanjiu" (On the type, evolution, and conflict prevention of ethnic group mass incidents). *Guangxi minzu yanjiu* 3:21–26.

Yao Lu. 2013. "China's Provincial GDP Figures in 2012." *China Briefing*, May 16. www.china-briefing.com/news/2013/05/16/chinas-provincial-gdp-figures -in-2012.html.

Yee, Herbert S. 2005. "Ethnic Consciousness and Identity." *Asian Ethnicity* 6 (1): 35–50.

Zang Xiaowei. 2011. "Uyghur-Han Earning Differentials in Urumchi." *China Journal* 65:141–55.

Zheng Yongnian. 2008. "Nationalism: Dynamics of Domestic Transformation and International Relations in China." In *China and the New International Order*, edited by Qang Gunwu and Zheng Yongnian, 32–52. London: Routledge.

Zhou Minglang. 2010. "The Fate of the Soviet Model of Multinational State-Building in China." In *China Learns from the Soviet Union, 1949–Present*, edited by Tom Bernstein and Hua-yu Li, 477–503. Lanham, MD: Rowman and Littlefield.

Zhu Weiqun. 2012. "Dui dangqian minzu lingyu wenti de jidian sikao" (Some thoughts on issues related to current ethnic problems). *Xuexi shibao*, Feb. 13.

# Contributors

**THOMAS CLIFF** is an ARC Laureate Postdoctoral Fellow in the School of Culture, History, and Language at the Australian National University. He is one of a small team of researchers looking into "Informal Life Politics"—how people organize themselves to protect their health and livelihood from threats that may emanate from state action or the lack of state action—in Northeast Asia. Environmental threats in China and eastern Russia are the focus of Tom's part of the project. He has conducted long-term fieldwork in Xinjiang and has written on the aesthetics, histories, and social and political roles of the Xinjiang Production and Construction Corps and the China National Petroleum Corporation. He is currently finishing a book on experiences of being Han in twenty-first-century Xinjiang.

**TYLER HARLAN** is a PhD candidate in the Department of Geography, University of California, Los Angeles. His broad research interests pertain to uneven development and environmental governance in China and how these issues influence China's role as a provider of international development aid and expertise. His research in this volume was conducted as part of a larger masters' project on development and ethnic relations in western China. His doctoral work focuses on the "export" of Chinese investment and foreign aid via large-scale rural land transfers and extractive projects in Southeast Asia.

**CLÉMENCE HENRY** is a graduate student at INALCO (National Institute of Oriental Languages and Civilizations, Paris), Department of "History, Societies and Territories," specializing in Tibetan language and civilization. Based on fieldwork, her research focuses on the Chinese educational system in Tibetan areas.

**BEN HILLMAN** teaches comparative politics and government at the Australian National University. His research focuses on ethnic politics in Asia. He has published widely on ethnic politics in China and Indonesia. He is currently engaged in a three-year Australian government-funded research project investigating the recent wave of conflict in China's Tibetan areas.

**JAMES LEIBOLD** is a senior lecturer in politics and Asian studies at La Trobe University in Melbourne, Australia. He is the author of *Reconfiguring Chinese Nationalism: How the Qing Frontier and Its Indigenes Became Chinese* (Palgrave Macmillan, 2007); and coeditor (with Thomas Mullaney, Stéphane Gros, and Eric Vanden Bussche) of *Critical Han Studies: The History, Representation, and Identity of China's Majority* (University of California Press, 2012); and (with Chen Yangbin) *Minority Education in China: Balancing Unity and Diversity in an Era of Critical Pluralism* (Hong Kong University Press, forthcoming). His research on race, ethnicity, and nationalism in modern China has appeared in the *Journal of Asian Studies*, *China Quarterly*, *China Journal*, *Modern China*, and other publications.

**ERIC D. MORTENSEN** is an associate professor of religious studies and chair of the Department of Religious Studies at Guilford College, where he teaches courses on Tibetan and Himalayan religions and comparative religious theory. His current research and writing projects involve topics in the religion and folklore of Gyalthang, including raven augury, the relation of oral tradition to Naxi pictographic texts and ritual performances, and invisible villages in stories about *nags myi rgod* (wild people) in the region of Geza. For many of the past twenty years he has lived, taught, and conducted research in Northwest Yunnan.

**YONTEN NYIMA** conducts research in pastoral areas of Tibet and China. His main research interests are pastoralism, rangeland and natural resource management and access, development and environmental policies, indigenous knowledge and climate change, and cultural politics and resistance. Having earned degrees in human geography (PhD, University of Colorado, Boulder), international affairs with a concentration in economic and political development (MA, Columbia University), and meteorology (BS, Nanjing Institute of Meteorology), Dr. Yonten Nyima draws from political ecology and political economy in examining rationales for, implementation of, and socioeconomic, cultural, political, and environmental effects of China's ongoing development and environmental policies in pastoral areas.

**FRANÇOISE ROBIN** is head of the Tibetan Studies section at Inalco, Paris (France), where she teaches Tibetan language and literature. She is also the director of the Institut d'études tibétaines at Collège de France, Paris. Her research focuses on the contents, dynamics, and social implications of contemporary literature in Tibetan language in the People's Republic of China, and she has recently turned her attention to women's writings, as well as to the emerging Tibetan cinema. Besides scholarly articles on these topics and editing of issues in specialized journals, she has also published many French translations of contemporary Tibetan literature.

**ANTONIO TERRONE** received his PhD in Asian Religions from Leiden University in the Netherlands and is now a lecturer for the Department of Religious Studies at Northwestern University in Evanston, Illinois. He specializes in South and East Asian religions and cultures. His research interests focus on contemporary Buddhist practice in Tibet and in the Himalayas, and religious and ethnopolitics in the People's Republic of China. His publications include (coedited) *Buddhism Beyond the Monastery: Tantric Practices and Their Performers in Tibet and the Himalayas* (Brill, 2009); and "Messengers from Tibet's Past: The Role of Buddhist Charismatic Leaders in the Spread of Tibetan Buddhism in Contemporary China" (*Asiatica Ambrosiana*, 2012). He is currently investigating the nature of the religious revival and the intersection of religion and ethnopolitics among Tibetans and Uyghurs in the People's Republic of China.

**GRAY TUTTLE** is the Leila Hadley Luce Associate Professor of Modern Tibetan Studies, Department of East Asian Languages and Cultures, Columbia University. His current research project, for a book tentatively entitled

"Amdo (Qinghai/Gansu): Middle Ground Between Lhasa and Beijing," focuses on Tibetan Buddhist institutional growth from the seventeenth century to the twentieth and how economic growth in the Sino-Tibetan borderlands fueled expansion and renewal of these institutions into the contemporary period. Other long-term writing projects include coediting *Sources of Tibetan Tradition* for the series Introduction to Asian Civilizations; and *The Tibetan History Reader* (both with Columbia University Press, forthcoming).

**EMILY T. YEH** is an associate professor of geography at the University of Colorado, Boulder. She conducts research on nature-society relations, primarily in Tibetan parts of the PRC, including projects on conflicts over access to natural resources, the relationship between ideologies of nature and nation, the political ecology of pastoral environment and development policies, vulnerability of Tibetan herders to climate change, and emerging environmental subjectivities. Her most recent book, *Taming Tibet: Landscape Transformation and the Gift of Chinese Development* (Cornell University Press, 2013), explores the intersection of political economy and cultural politics of development as a project of state territorialization.

# Index

# Studies of the Weatherhead East Asian Institute, Columbia University

## Selected titles

(Complete list at: http://www.columbia.edu/cu/weai/weatherhead-studies.html)

*Chinese Law in Imperial Eyes: Sovereignty, Justice, and Transcultural Politics,* by Li Chen. Columbia University Press, 2016.

*The Age of Irreverence: A New History of Laughter in China,* by Christopher Rea. University of California Press, 2015.

*The Nature of Knowledge and the Knowledge of Nature in Early Modern Japan,* by Federico Marcon. University of Chicago Press, 2015.

*The Fascist Effect: Japan and Italy, 1915-1952,* by Reto Hoffman. Cornell University Press, 2015.

*The International Minimum: Creativity and Contradiction in Japan's Global Engagement, 1933-1964,* by Jessamyn R. Abel. University of Hawai'i Press, 2015.

*Empires of Coal: Fueling China's Entry Into the Modern World Order, 1860-1920,* by Shellen Xiao Wu. Stanford University Press, 2015.

*Casualties of History: Wounded Japanese Servicemen and the Second World War,* by Lee K. Pennington. Cornell University Press, 2015.

*City of Virtues: Nanjing in an Age of Utopian Visions,* by Chuck Wooldridge. University of Washington Press, 2015.

*The Proletarian Wave: Literature and Leftist Culture in Colonial Korea, 1910-1945,* by Sunyoung Park. Harvard University Asia Center, 2015.

*Neither Donkey Nor Horse: Medicine in the Struggle Over China's Modernity,* by Sean Hsiang-lin Lei. University of Chicago Press, 2014.

*When the Future Disappears: The Modernist Imagination in Late Colonial Korea,* by Janet Poole. Columbia University Press, 2014.

*Bad Water: Nature, Pollution, and Politics in Japan, 1870-1950,* by Robert Stolz. Duke University Press, 2014.

*Rise of a Japanese Chinatown: Yokohama, 1894-1972,* by Eric C. Han. Harvard University Asia Center, 2014.

*Beyond the Metropolis: Second Cities and Modern Life in Interwar Japan,* by Louise Young. University of California Press, 2013.

*From Cultures of War to Cultures of Peace: War and Peace Museums in Japan, China, and South Korea,* by Takashi Yoshida. Merwin Asia, 2013.

*Imperial Eclipse: Japan's Strategic Thinking About Continental Asia Before August 1945,* by Yukiko Koshiro. Cornell University Press, 2013.

*The Nature of the Beasts: Empire and Exhibition at the Tokyo Imperial Zoo,*
by Ian J. Miller. University of California Press, 2013.

*Public Properties: Museums in Imperial Japan,* by Noriko Aso. Duke University
Press, 2013.

*Reconstructing Bodies: Biomedicine, Health, and Nation-Building in South Korea Since
1945,* by John P. DiMoia. Stanford University Press, 2013.

*Taming Tibet: Landscape Transformation and the Gift of Chinese Development,*
by Emily T. Yeh. Cornell University Press, 2013.

*Tyranny of the Weak: North Korea and the World, 1950–1992,* by Charles K.
Armstrong. Cornell University Press, 2013.

*The Art of Censorship in Postwar Japan,* by Kirsten Cather. University of Hawai'i
Press, 2012.

*Asia for the Asians: China in the Lives of Five Meiji Japanese,* by Paula Harrell.
Merwin Asia, 2012.

*Lin Shu, Inc.: Translation and the Making of Modern Chinese Culture,*
by Michael Gibbs Hill. Oxford University Press, 2012.

*Occupying Power: Sex Workers and Servicemen in Postwar Japan,* by Sarah Kovner.
Stanford University Press, 2012.

*Redacted: The Archives of Censorship in Postwar Japan,* by Jonathan E. Abel.
University of California Press, 2012.

*Empire of Dogs: Canines, Japan, and the Making of the Modern Imperial World,*
by Aaron Herald Skabelund. Cornell University Press, 2011.

*Planning for Empire: Reform Bureaucrats and the Japanese Wartime State,* by Janis
Mimura. Cornell University Press, 2011.

*Realms of Literacy: Early Japan and the History of Writing,* by David Lurie. Harvard
University Asia Center, 2011.

*Russo-Japanese Relations, 1905–17: From Enemies to Allies,* by Peter Berton.
Routledge, 2011.

*Behind the Gate: Inventing Students in Beijing,* by Fabio Lanza. Columbia University
Press, 2010.

*Imperial Japan at Its Zenith: The Wartime Celebration of the Empire's 2,600th
Anniversary,* by Kenneth J. Ruoff. Cornell University Press, 2010.

CPSIA information can be obtained
at www.ICGtesting.com
Printed in the USA
LVHW032112310120
645499LV00002B/3